CAMPUS 1980

The Shape of the Future
in American Higher Education

CAMPUS
1980

The Shape of the Future in American Higher Education

EDITED BY

Alvin C. Eurich

AND THE STAFF OF

The Academy for Educational Development

DELACORTE PRESS / NEW YORK

ACKNOWLEDGMENTS

The essay by John W. Gardner was originally delivered
as a speech to the Fourth Annual California Conference
on Higher Education in May 1965, and later reprinted
in *Journal of Higher Education*, XXXVI: 7 (October,
1965). Reprinted by permission of the author and the
Journal.

The essay by Christopher Jencks and David Riesman
appears in slightly different form in their book *The
Academic Revolution* (N. Y.: Doubleday, 1968).
Copyright © 1968 by Christopher Jencks and David
Riesman.

The essay by William Arrowsmith was originally
delivered as a speech to the annual meeting of the
American Council on Education in New Orleans, October
1966, and later reprinted in the volume *Improving
College Teaching*, edited by Calvin T. Lee, published
by the Council.

The essay by Clark Kerr is reprinted by permission
of the publishers from *The Uses of the University*,
Cambridge, Mass.: Harvard University Press, Copyright,
1963, by the President and Fellows of Harvard College.

The essay by Allan M. Cartter has been adapted from
a chapter contributed to *Graduate Education Today*
(American Council on Education, 1965).

Contents

Introduction
by ALVIN C. EURICH   vii

Agenda for the Colleges and Universities
by HONORABLE JOHN W. GARDNER   1

The Magnitude of American Higher Education in 1980
by SIDNEY G. TICKTON   9

Higher Education and the National Interest
by LOGAN WILSON   23

Cities and Universities: Collision of Crises
by WILLIAM BIRENBAUM   43

The University and the World
by WILLIAM W. MARVEL   64

The Triumph of Academic Man
by CHRISTOPHER JENCKS *and* DAVID RIESMAN   92

The Future of Teaching
by WILLIAM ARROWSMITH   116

The Community College in 1980
by JOSEPH COSAND   134

Learning Never Ends: A Plan for Continuing Education
by A. A. LIVERIGHT   149

The College Student of 1980
   by NEVITT SANFORD   176

The Future Undergraduate Curriculum
   by LEWIS B. MAYHEW   200

Organizing for Better Instruction
   by ELIZABETH PASCHAL   220

Toward a Developed Technology of Instruction—1980
   by C. R. CARPENTER   236

Graduate Education and Research in the Decades Ahead
   by ALLAN CARTTER   254

The American Campus—1980
   by HAROLD B. GORES   279

Conservatism, Dynamism, and the Changing University
   by CLARK KERR   299

   Notes on the Contributors   323

Introduction

"We cannot, any more than past generations, see the face of the future," Ralph McGill has written. "But we know that written across it is the word Education." The basic premise of this book is that across the American future is written "Higher Education."

The campus will shape and be shaped by our nation's future. To the campus we will look increasingly for leadership in solving our manifold public problems, for new knowledge and the understanding to put it to good use, for the training our young people need to live useful and rewarding lives, and for the constant, independent criticism which alone keeps a democratic society vital. To envisage Campus 1980, then, is to consider what our society will or should soon become.

Nineteen eighty is imminent if one thinks in terms of the lead-time which large social organisms like universities need to adapt themselves to changes in the environment. One might think that the future shape of higher education would be quite clear by now. And indeed some things are clear—there are curves that can be projected to yield quite reliable ideas of the future. But the challenges facing the colleges and universities are so formidable that the next decade may well demand radical changes. So while some prospects for American higher education in the year 1980 are almost inevitable, others are shrouded in uncertainty.

For example, the students who will enter college in 1980 are already in school—we can count them and we can predict with fair assurance how many of them will apply for admission to college. The catch is that the whole process of "going to college" may be obsolete or changed beyond recognition by the time these youngsters are eighteen years old.

Contrasting future possibilities abound elsewhere in higher education—certainty seems to jostle uneasily with large question marks at every critical point. Professors who will teach the students of 1980 are already in graduate school—but by then the ways we organize collegiate instruction may have changed radically. Buildings that will grace or disgrace the campus in 1980 are being built now—but the needs of a college may change drastically in the next decade. Courses and programs for the years from now to 1980 and beyond are being discussed in faculty meetings and academic senates this year—but by the time these plans are fully operational, half the knowledge considered essential today may be outmoded, and there will be vast aggregations of new knowledge.

In short, Campus 1980 is here already, in a sense: it is being shaped today by our decisions, our projections, our dreams. The nagging question is: How closely will the results correspond to the real needs and demands of the campus and the nation? To bring present plans and future probabilities closer together is the purpose of this book.

The first order of business is to make an agenda: to propose, debate, and clarify some priorities among the myriad tasks which crowd in on the campus or spring up within the academic community itself.

Some urgent matters compel attention. Undergraduate life lacks focus and meaning; whether the response is riots or the formation of student-run "experimental colleges," the matter clearly commands attention and action. The curriculum needs reform, and methods of instruction must be adjusted for a new breed of students and a new kind of subject matter.

Again, the role of the campus in the community requires strengthening. Since the urbanization of the American population made the old agricultural extension service obsolete, we have fumbled around for a new philosophy and procedure for relating the university to its new environment: the city with its manifold problems. In the next decade, as universities emerge clearly as the brainpower centers of the "knowledge society," new arrangements for public service must and will be hammered out.

John Gardner, former Secretary of Health, Education and Welfare, puts these and other matters in perspective in his suggested "Agenda for the Colleges and Universities," a basic document for gaining an overall view of the challenges facing American higher education.

But the problems identified by former Secretary Gardner must be considered within certain constraints imposed by the environment: the large number of students who must be dealt with, the limited number of teachers available to instruct them, and the amount of money which can be raised to pay for the whole enterprise. The size as well as the shape of higher learning will have changed significantly by 1980. The explosion in the student population will have resulted in a vastly enlarged number of undergraduates and graduate students, and a continuing shortage of faculty. Moreover, the center of gravity will have shifted even further away from the private to the public sector as the public colleges and universities, especially the burgeoning community colleges and technical institutes, attract an ever larger proportion of students. Sidney Tickton, the vice-president of the Academy for Educational Development, documents these and corollary trends in his bracing dose of statistics.

Another set of constraints within which higher education must solve its problems comes from the nation as a whole, as embodied by the federal government. The "politicalization of higher learning" is one of the great themes of this educational era, as the schools and colleges are increasingly harnessed to national goals. Don K. Price succinctly satirized the basic relationship between the universities and government by quoting this limerick:

> There was a young lady from Kent
> Who said that she knew what it meant
> When men took her to dine
> Gave her cocktails and wine,
> She knew what it meant—but she went.

Logan Wilson, the president of the American Council on Education, gives a balanced projection of the future of this relationship, explaining why it will likely stimulate needed innovation on the campus and push colleges away from the present individualistic nonsystem with its costly duplication and waste of effort, and toward fruitful interdependence.

The external pressures on the universities come not only from the federal level; the anguish of our cities also demands university attention. William Birenbaum is currently working on experimental approaches to higher education in the ghetto, as president of the Education Affiliate of the Bedford-Stuyvesant D and S Corporation in New York City. He foresees a thorough revision of our conceptions of what a city is and what a university in a city should be. In fact, the two coalesce in his vision: the campus *is* the city. Gone are the hierarchical structure of academic life, the permanent buildings, the vast empty spaces. For Birenbaum, a campus for the city must embody the values of the city—openness, flexibility, mobility.

Still another set of responsibilities looms in the area of international studies and activity. As America becomes more and more a nation deeply involved in the world's problems, this dimension of higher education will perforce expand. William Marvel, the president of Education and World Affairs, looks ahead to 1980 with "uncertainty mingled with hope"—hope that an international outlook and style will come to pervade the entire campus instead of being confined to clearly visible and separate "institutes" and "centers."

Taken together, the new demands on colleges and universities —the exploding demand to go to college, the nation's need for training and research, the urban crisis, and America's international commitments—all combine to make the campus virtually the brain of society. Industry looks to the universities for trained personnel, government for future leaders, parents for their youngsters' education, the professions not only for future practitioners but for the new knowledge which keeps medicine, the law, and the sciences vital. But what does this "academic victory" mean for higher education itself? Are there costs and dangers as well as subsidies and prestige involved in this new role for academics? Will the colleges survive success?

One primary danger is that *all* institutions will be tempted to squeeze into the dominant pattern, so enticing are the rewards in terms of money and power. This tendency is dealt with by Christopher Jencks, fellow of the Institute for Policy Studies, and David Riesman, Professor of Social Relations at Harvard. They reveal how a few vastly influential institutions—the major universities with their graduate and professional schools, and the prestige colleges which feed graduates into them—exert a stranglehold influence on the rest of American higher learning. What these institutions are now, they argue, is the "model toward which almost all the 1,900 colleges are moving as fast as they conveniently can."

Another aspect of what might be termed, to paraphrase Julien Benda, "the treason of the universities" is the undermining of teaching as faculty members pursue research with increasing monomania. As John Gardner points out in his opening essay, our colleges and universities may, as they move toward the center of power and wealth, become mere "busy and populous frauds." This theme is picked up *fortissimo* by William Arrowsmith, University Professor in Arts and Letters at the University of Texas. Originally delivered as a keynote speech which rocked the 1966 annual meeting of the American Council on Education, "The Future of Teaching" proclaims that our university scholars are "unprecedentedly powerful . . . but their power is professional and technocratic; as educators they have been eagerly disqualifying themselves for more than a century, and their disqualification is now nearly total." In demanding a return to the "ancient, crucial, high art of teaching," Arrowsmith argues that there is no necessary link between scholarship and education, nor between research and culture. "It is men we need, not programs," he concludes—men who embody in themselves the values of the humanities which they are endeavoring to instill in their students. Yet the processes described by Riesman and Jencks, among others, have in Arrowsmith's view resulted in the bankruptcy of liberal education in this country: "By imitating the universities, the colleges have everything to lose and nothing to gain." Arrowsmith's specific proposal—a bold and dramatically simple one—is perhaps less significant than his general demand that we squarely face the crisis of values in American higher learning. Not all our reorganization and curriculum revisions will make education relevant on the campus of 1980 unless we can make it a congenial habitat for personal values and humane ideals.

Fortunately, new kinds of institutions are coming to the fore which aim specifically at meeting the students' real needs. The community college is the outstanding example. It is designed to offer an extremely diverse set of programs making it possible for virtually every high-school graduate to pursue some form of higher education leading to a worthwhile and rewarding place in society. Joseph Cosand, long a leader in this field and currently the president of the St. Louis Junior College District, envisions an ever-expanding role for these institutions in the years ahead—taking over the first two years of college work and leaving the four-year colleges and universities confined primarily to upper division and graduate work.

Another new institution keyed not to scholarship or research, but basically to the practical needs of students, is the college of continuing education for adults. As our society recognizes the necessity for lifelong learning, such institutions will move from blueprint to reality, taking on the responsibility for offering opportunities for all citizens to constantly enlarge their minds, update their vocational and professional skills, and find rewarding companionship through the learning process. A. A. Liveright, the director of the Center for the Study of Liberal Education for Adults at Boston University, portrays a college of this kind, constructed wholly of components already successfully demonstrated today, as it might look in 1980.

What will it be like to *be* on the campus in 1980? Will a distinctly new student character dominate the new generation? Will the ways in which students learn and professors teach have changed radically under the impact of social forces and an emerging technology of instruction? Will different courses of study be predominant—in response to the influx of students with a wider range of abilities and interests? What about the physical setting and facilities: will they have changed dramatically from the ivy-covered walls which still prevail today?

There is every reason to believe that remarkable changes in these and every other area of campus life will occur, and fast. Consider the character of student life, for example. The young demonstrators of today will, many of them, be the assistant and associate professors of tomorrow. From that vantage point they will probably support and arouse the students who follow them, and thus even further involve American students in their own governance and in the major issues of their society. Far from being a mere cyclical phenomenon, then, the present activism of college students is possibly the beginning of a continuing development. Nevitt Sanford, the editor of the monumental study *The American College* and the director of the Institute for the Study of Human Problems at Stanford University, foresees an increase in diversity and activism as the predominant trends in student life in the 1980s. The college generation of the 1950s was the last "quiet" one we will see in a long time.

To match these varied and more socially committed students, the undergraduate instructional program will have to become more relevant, flexible, and enterprising. Lewis B. Mayhew of Stanford University vividly sketches the typical academic career of tomorrow's student. His experiences will range from independent study of religion to Peace Corps work in a South American village, from work-study activity as an electronics technician to anthropological fieldwork, from a seminar in philosophy to a semester's immersion in Indian culture. In the course of his undergraduate work this typical student may drop out for a year, come back to the campus, get married, undertake independent work—all without in any way damaging his scholastic record.

Moreover, the time spent on the campus will be differently organized for more effective learning. No longer will students merely pile up credit hours through fragmented specialized courses. Rather, as sketched by Elizabeth Paschal, an independent educational consultant and formerly the secretary-treasurer of the Fund for the Advancement of Education, each student and his teachers will define the specific goals to be achieved, and then the means to those goals will be devised to meet the student's particular needs. He may attend class regularly or learn by reading in the library; he may master his field by watching televised lectures or by apprenticing himself to a recognized scholar. Only the end results—the criteria the student must satisfy to earn his degree—will be fixed (and with more precision and meaningfulness, one might remark, than nowadays).

Another major change in the quality of instruction will be brought about by the development of a full-fledged technology of teaching. The bold and sophisticated use of new media of communication and of computer technology, far from threatening to dehumanize students, provides perhaps the only avenue to keeping education humane as campuses get bigger and bigger. For instructional technology, properly conceived and used, aims to encourage what C. R. Carpenter, Research Professor of Psychology and Anthropology at The Pennsylvania State University, calls "the autonomous learner." Professor Carpenter sees the period from late secondary school through the early college years as one in which students can be weaned from dependence on personal teaching of all materials, and set on a more independent course toward deft use of a wide range of learning resources. "The general idea for the student," writes Professor Carpenter, "is the same as it is for the teacher: to master and control the technology and use it for his own purposes."

With more and more students avidly seeking advanced training, the nation's graduate schools will soon feel the same pressures for admission that today afflict the undergraduate college. How will the inevitable demands for expansion affect the quality of graduate study? Will the current "imbalance" in favor of research in the sciences be rectified, to bring the social sciences and humanities abreast? And what about nagging questions like: How good are the graduate schools and who should pay for them? Some answers are assayed by Allan Cartter, Chancellor of New

York University and a longtime analyst of trends in American higher learning.

Even the physical aspect of the campus will change drastically by 1980. "The physical campus will become mostly library and living room," writes Harold Gores, the president of Educational Facilities Laboratories. "The library (and its tentacles) will house the facts—and fancies. The living rooms, née classrooms, will provide the arena where the student, fortified with relevant information, and in company of his fellows and faculty, hammers out the values, the meaning of it all."

Perhaps the most perplexing question raised by all these projections of the future is whether American higher education can change enough to meet new challenges and new demands. Can colleges and universities apply to themselves the bold, innovating approach they have taught society? Clark Kerr, formerly the president of the University of California and currently the director of the Carnegie Corporation's study of American higher education, concludes the book by considering the dynamics of change on the campus. He sees universities as currently undergoing an extraordinary transformation as they move rapidly toward further changes of enormous consequence. The three areas of present "adjustment" are, in his view: swelling enrollment, changing academic emphasis, and involvement in the life of society. The new challenges he discerns, which will increasingly claim the attention of educators, are: the improvement of undergraduate instruction, the creation of a more unified intellectual world, more direct relationship of administration to individual faculty members and students, and the preservation of a "margin for excellence" in a populist society. If new and imaginative solutions are devised, Kerr concludes:

> they are most likely to come on the campuses of those old, private universities which have prided themselves on control of their own destiny, and on the totally new campuses of the state universities in America and the new public universities in Britain. The university for the twenty-first century is more likely to emerge from

these environments than from any others. Out of the pride of the old and the vacuum of the new may come the means to make undergraduate life more exciting, intellectual discourse more meaningful, administration more human. And perhaps there will arise a more dynamic demonstration of how excellence makes democracy more vital and its survival more assured. Then the universities may rise to "the heights of the times" and overcome "their inspirational poverty."

A word about the scope and thrust of the essays which compose this book. Each of the contributors has concerned himself professionally with higher education as a whole, and not merely with one particular aspect. Each of them has, therefore, approached his particular subject—whether it is the undergraduate curriculum, technology in teaching, or the architecture of the campus—from the broadest possible angle.

Thus there is inevitable overlapping as the different contributors consider how such basic factors as enrollment, say, affect their particular area of interest. Students, for example—the subject of Nevitt Sanford's essay—naturally crop up in nearly everyone else's. Again, Elizabeth Paschal in her discussion of how to improve instruction, Lewis Mayhew in his consideration of the undergraduate curriculum, and William Arrowsmith on the future of teaching all consider how college teaching is conducted and how students really learn.

Even more conspicuously, the contributors differ in the degree to which they stick to or depart from the probable. Some make sober extrapolations of present trends, on the assumptions that change in higher education comes perhaps surely, but certainly slowly. Others give fuller vent to their imaginations, stressing way-out possibilities which many readers might consider impossibilities. Still other contributors posit both the probable and the possible, analyzing the obstacles to the most hopeful trends.

The contributors produced their essays as individual efforts (a few have been chosen from previously published books). They come not only from colleges and universities, public and private, but from foundations, government, and voluntary organizations. Perhaps even more important, their styles of thought and expression cover a wide range, from demographic statistics to sociological analysis to neoclassical diatribe.

These varied voices accurately reflect, in my view, the pluralistic universe of discourse in which the future of higher learning must and will be determined. All these perspectives are relevant and compelling. To reconcile them sufficiently to hammer out major policy directions is the continuing and probably unending mandate of those devoted to nurturing our colleges and universities.

This book has been designed to open rather than close questions, to pose challenges rather than provide definitive solutions. By bringing together a composite vision of what Campus 1980 should and might be, the intention is to speed changes toward a better future. As Yeats wrote: "In dreams begins responsibility."

It is hoped that these essays will help educators see more clearly the problems, the options, and the prospects before them, that they may more vividly appreciate their immense responsibilities. For in the end the challenges set forth in the pages which follow will fall on the shoulders of individual educational leaders in colleges and universities throughout the nation. Under our decentralized system of higher learning, no single authority can hand down the answers to the hard questions ahead. Each college and university trustee, each administrator, each faculty member, each alumnus and each student must grapple with these as his problems.

ALVIN C. EURICH

February 1968

CAMPUS
1980

The Shape of the Future
in American Higher Education

◄ HONORABLE JOHN W. GARDNER

Agenda for the Colleges and Universities

Higher Education in the Innovative Society

THE COLLEGES and universities of the nation are facing what I believe will prove to be the most exciting and trying period in their history. They are enjoying extraordinary success today. What David Riesman calls the "Academic Victory" is virtually complete. But it will be possible for the colleges and universities to be busy and populous and yet fail in their essential jobs— which is to say that they could be busy and populous frauds. In short, the stakes are high.

There is no doubt that the colleges and universities would like to do what the times demand of them. But what do the times demand of them? I propose to list what I consider to be the major problems and challenges facing the colleges and universities, not in the order of importance but beginning with teaching, which is certainly central to any discussion of higher education today.

First, we must restore the status of teaching. Our institutions of higher education have three great traditional functions: research, teaching, and service to the community. The particular function emphasized depends on the institution. The two-year college and the four-year liberal-arts college are concerned chiefly with teaching; the graduate school is more heavily concerned with research; the land-grant university has traditionally placed great emphasis on service to the community. None of these func-

1

tions should be slighted. One of them *is* being slighted today, namely, the teaching function, particularly the teaching of undergraduates.

The reinstatement of teaching as an important function of the undergraduate college may be hastened by the current wave of student discontent. But the decisions that move us in that direction must be faculty decisions. The faculty should give serious attention to students' views, but the balance between teaching and scholarship, the qualifications for tenure, and similar issues must not be settled under pressure or adjudicated in an atmosphere of controversy.

Second, the colleges and universities are going to have to undertake a thoroughgoing reform of the undergraduate curriculum. We have now had a decade of lively reform in the high-school curriculum. A comparable movement for reform at the college level is already under way, and we shall be hearing a great deal more about it in the years ahead. It is certain to transform instruction in all major fields of knowledge. It will require searching reappraisal of the aims of education in each field. It will require thorough exploration of the possibilities of new teaching aids and methods. It will involve a more widespread and ingenious use of independent study. And it must involve a continuing effort to do justice to interdisciplinary approaches. Curriculum reform will be incomplete if its only consequence is that each specific subject is better taught; it must also reintroduce into the undergraduate program the breadth so essential for young people who will reach the peak of their careers in the twenty-first century.

Third, we must greatly improve our procedures for institutional planning. Up to this point we have been discussing changes that must be brought about by the faculty. Now we are discussing something that must be accomplished by administrators. I have noticed in the recent campus troubles that "administrator" has become something of a dirty word—the only one not spelled with four letters. And the only dirty word that no one has risen to defend.

In the interest of common justice, let me say a word in behalf of administrators. Many of the students engaging in demonstrations today would not have had a college to go to if a lot of hard-pressed administrators of the late 1950s had not seen them coming along and planned the expansion of our colleges and universities.

The problem of numbers has struck us full force, and we feel that we are swamped—but we haven't seen anything yet. We do not need to speculate about the college students of the 1970s: they are riding around on their bikes and skateboards today— and there are a lot of them. To make adequate preparation for them is going to require better planning within institutions, far better planning on a statewide level, and an attentiveness to the economics of education greater than any we have exhibited in the past. We are going to have to learn some hard lessons about planned diversity among institutions and about cooperation among institutions.

Fourth, every institution that has not already done so will have to reexamine the college calendar and the traditional four-year pattern for the A.B. degree. Virtually every institution is going to have to go into year-round operation through adoption of the quarter system, the trimester system, or some comparable arrangement. Less than 20 percent of our colleges and universities have faced up to that reform. Furthermore, every institution must introduce the flexibility into its four-year program that will permit the various kinds of acceleration bright students now demand. The advanced-placement program has been immensely successful. A number of universities now offer a four-year A.B.-M.A. program. Some leading universities offer the A.B. and Ph.D. in a total of six years.

But the aim of flexibility is not solely to speed things up. It must also serve, where necessary, to slow things down. We are ready to dispense with the tradition of a four-year, uninterrupted college education. We now know that many students benefit greatly by a break in the four years—for a year abroad, or a year at work, or a year traveling, or just a year to figure out what it is they want to be or do.

Fifth, we are going to have to find a way to bring the small independent liberal-arts college back into the mainstream of higher education. There are hundreds of these colleges that can no longer compete with the universities in attracting able and highly motivated faculty members or students. The reason they cannot compete is that they are too small to offer the richness and variety of resources and opportunities that so many of today's faculty and students expect. Because of this, the tide is going against them; and if it does not change, they will become a weak and deteriorated part of our higher-educational system. That would be a regrettable end for a great American institution.

The best chance of salvaging the small liberal-arts college lies in devising new means of cooperation among institutions. In some parts of the country these small colleges have banded together to cooperate among themselves. In other places they cooperate with nearby universities. In some places they do both. In all cases, the need is for the small college to relate itself to some larger system in such a way that it can retain its autonomy but still enjoy access to the richness and diversity of resource that professors and students demand.

Sixth, colleges and universities must give more thought to continuing education and off-campus instruction. We have abandoned the idea that education is something which takes place in a block of time between six and eighteen (or twenty-two) years of age. It is lifelong. We have abandoned the idea that education is something that can occur only in a classroom. A system of education suited to modern needs and aspirations could not come into being until these two notions were finally done away with.

The continuing-education movement does not need any special encouragement. It will develop at a rapid pace regardless of what the colleges and universities do. But I believe that the colleges and universities should provide intellectual leadership with respect to such education, and that depends on their own creative activity in this field. If they ignore it, the movement will pass them by and leadership will go out of their hands. If that happens, I think they will have reason to regret it.

Seventh, American colleges and universities pride themselves on their service to the larger community, and this service is posing some immensely significant challenges. I shall not discuss the relationship of universities to the government or the vitally important role that the universities have in every phase of international affairs. But I want to say a word about the relationship of the colleges and universities to another part of the larger community —the city. The city is the heart and brain of an industrial society. But our cities today are plagued with every conceivable ill: apathy, crime, poverty, racial conflict, slum housing, air and water pollution, inadequate schools and hospitals, and a breakdown in transportation. Coping with those problems is going to be very near the top of the national agenda for the next decade. There are no institutions better equipped to serve as a base for that struggle than the colleges and universities, but they have played a negligible role thus far. The strategic role played by the land-grant universities in developing American agriculture and the rural areas has no parallel in the cities.

And that brings me to my final point. We are going to have to give some thought to the internal health of our colleges and universities as functioning communities. One problem is that of size, and institutions throughout the country are experimenting with ways of solving it. The cluster concept is the most widely advertised solution, but there are many other approaches.

The large institution has been much maligned of late. I have been surprised by the censorious tone with which some critics now refer to large institutions, almost as though in growing to their present size these institutions had deliberately chosen to do an evil thing. This is ridiculous. The critics may, if they wish, attack the American people for being so numerous and so fertile. They may, if they wish, attack the society generally for holding such a liberal view concerning who should go to college. But they should not attack institutions that are simply trying to accomplish a well-nigh impossible task the society has handed them. The institutions being scolded for largeness today are the ones that have been most responsive to the American eagerness to broaden educational opportunities. We should have the grace to live with the consequences of our choices.

If we address ourselves to the problem of the college or university as a functioning community, we face at once the matter of student unrest. The student demonstration is a very imprecise instrument that turns up false issues as readily as real issues, but the question remains why this generation of students provides especially fertile soil for such demonstrations.

This generation of students has its exhibitionists and fools, just as our generation did. But over the nation as a whole, today's students are more aware of what is going on in the world, more serious about their own relationship to it, than any generation we have known. Out of this awareness and seriousness has come a whole array of constructive activities, such as tutoring disadvantaged youngsters, working for civil rights, and staffing the Peace Corps.

If one reviews the various incidents involving students on campuses around the country and attempts to sift the real issues from the extraordinary clutter of emotion and recrimination, it becomes clear that nationwide the students have hit upon at least one or two issues that go to the heart of the problem of the modern university. The question of whether undergraduate teaching is being neglected is a real one, and I am bound to say that in many colleges and universities the students have a real grievance. The question of anonymity and impersonality of student life is a real issue in many institutions—a problem worthy of all our wisdom and inventiveness.

We need new patterns for the organization of student life. There must be orderly channels for the expression of student grievances. There must be opportunities for students to work off their idealistic urges in constructive projects—preferably projects of their own devising and under their own management. There must be opportunities for them to exercise emerging capacities for leadership and decision.

The problem of the student's place on the campus might be simpler if the college or university community were a coherent whole. But on many, perhaps most, campuses there is a breakdown of communication among various elements of the university community: trustees, administration, faculty, and students. The resulting cleavages trouble me, because I believe that most academic institutions are going to have some difficulty in surviving as coherent and significant communities. The difficulty will be magnified if they are expending their best energies in civil war.

The traditional academic institution *was* a community. Those who spent time there knew they were members of a community. It had a "personality" that could be described and loved—or laughed at. Undergraduates were often marked for life by its style and spirit. And the community was to a very considerable degree what its members wanted it to be. In short, it was autonomous.

Such institutions still exist. But on every college or university campus in the nation, the sense of community is diminishing. Why? First of all, because of the spectacular rise of the academic professions. This is the era of the professional, and faculty men are like all other professionals in having a strong guild loyalty. The community of the physicist or the economist is his professional brethren scattered over the nation or the world. His ties to any local community are correspondingly weak. Second, the cohesiveness of the local community is diminished by the very strong ties that its constitutent parts have with elements external to the academic world, particularly with government. And perhaps one should add as a third point that it is in the nature of a highly organized modern society to be destructive of local communities.

Let us be clear concerning what is at stake. Even if the campus loses every trace of community, it can still be an orderly, busy, productive, important place, in the sense that a city block in the heart of one of our great metropolises is an orderly, busy, productive, important place. A group of activities do not necessarily diminish in significance because they are not welded into a community.

But it is hard to view that prospect with enthusiasm. The young people who pass through colleges and universities can profit immensely from membership in a local community that has its proud traditions and standards and *esprit*. Later they may shift their loyalty to nationwide or worldwide professional communities; but for the education of youth, the face-to-face community has incomparable advantages.

Equally important, the community that enjoys internal coherence and morale is in a position to defend and preserve its own autonomy and to shape its own future. The noncommunity will be shaped to a much greater degree by outside forces—by the federal government and other sources of funds, by political pressures, and by popular demands.

It is possible that in the years ahead, the college or university will become a less and less identifiable landmark on the national scene, as more and more institutions in the society encroach on its traditional activities. Research has long since ceased to be a university monopoly. As for instruction beyond the high school, everyone is in the act—industry, the military services, civil government, TV stations, publishing companies, and public-school districts.

If the college or university is to preserve its character as a community and forge for itself a distinctive identity and role in the vast clutter of scholarly, scientific, and instructional activities that will characterize our evolving technological society, it will have to have a considerable measure of internal coherence and morale. And that means that trustees, administration, faculty, and students are going to have to admit that they are all part of one community—distasteful as that may be to some of them—and they are going to have to ask what they can do individually or collaboratively to preserve the integrity and coherence of that community and to regain command of its future. I do not mean that they must subject themselves to some kind of unanimity or consensus. Every vital community has internal conflicts and tensions. But I do mean that there will have to be healthy forms of interaction and dialogue among them.

So much for the problems facing the colleges and universities. It is an overwhelming list. The objection may be made that I have proposed one or two unnecessary new tasks for institutions already dangerously overburdened. But I do not believe that the colleges and universities will go under because they are carrying heavy burdens. If they deteriorate, it will be because they lacked the morale, the internal coherence, and the adaptiveness to meet the requirements of the future; it will be because in the moment of their greatest success they could not pull themselves together to face new challenges.

◀ SIDNEY G. TICKTON

The Magnitude of American Higher Education in 1980

THE SHAPE of American higher education in 1980 will be determined in considerable measure by the sheer *size* of the enterprise. The purpose of this essay is to document certain basic demographic and financial factors which lead us to foresee, between now and 1980:

1. the crystallization of a national consensus that every high-school graduate who can profit from it should have at least two years of further education;

2. a very significant increase in the proportion of students enrolled in public junior or community colleges or other types of two-year public post-high-school educational institutions;

3. a sharp rise in the number of students enrolled in higher education—sharper than the estimates published by most government agencies concerned with the problem;

4. a considerable increase in the number of adults enrolled in higher education institutions;

5. a continuation of the historic shift of the center of gravity from the private to the public institutions, as the latter attract an ever-growing proportion of students;

6. the conversion of a number of private institutions to state-controlled or "state-related" status;

7. the development of strong statewide coordinating boards

9

or statewide systems of higher education in nearly every state, with influence extending over all areas of education beyond the high school, both public and private;

8. a continued upsurge in graduate education such that, during the 15 years ending in 1980–1981, the total number of doctorates earned will be no fewer than 375,000—one and one-half times the total number of doctorates earned in the entire earlier history of the nation;

9. a substantial increase in the number of faculty members and assistants—but not substantial enough to match the increase in enrollments (the gap will be filled by larger classes, use of technological aids to instruction, and reliance on more assistants in teaching);

10. greatly increased spending by institutions of higher learning to meet expanding needs for their services;

11. an expanding gross national product adequate to finance the needed expansion in higher education if the American people choose to allocate their public funds to that end.

A host of variations in future figures could be developed to take into account the many new developments in society which are influencing every level of educational activity—today, tomorrow, and in the generation ahead. This would result in virtually endless statistical labors, however, and would provide more data than anyone could possibly absorb. The projections that follow are limited, therefore, to a series of tables which provide key figures for 1965 and 1980 on the basis of the single set of broad assumptions as set forth in Table A.

TABLE A

Assumptions for Projections to 1980 for Higher Education

Item	Assumption
1. World situation	Will remain about the same as it was in 1967 until 1980; neither a major war nor widespread disarmament will occur.

TABLE A

Assumptions for Projections to 1980 for Higher Education

Item	Assumption
2. Gross national product	Will rise substantially along the lines of past trends; no severe economic depression will occur during the period.
3. Price level for goods and services	Will average out to levels existing in the fall of 1967.
4. National attitude toward higher education	Will develop to a point where at least two years of appropriate public post-high-school educational opportunity will be made available to all who seek it and can profit from it.
5. Number of students enrolled in higher education	Will rise sharply until 1980 and will continue upward thereafter but at a slower rate.
6. Enrollment at private institutions of higher education	Will rise more slowly than at public institutions. The rate of increase will be held down in part by the conversion of a number of private institutions to state control or to a "state-related" situation, and in part by a financial inability to expand.
7. Educational offerings beyond the high school	Will expand to meet a wide variety of academic, professional, cultural, technical, and social needs. There will be a large number of new types of jobs developing during the period for which unique educational programs at both the undergraduate and graduate levels will be developed.
8. Continuing education for adults	Will expand substantially and will include extensive training or retraining of persons beyond college age to meet expanding professional and technical demands of business and industry. In many fields there will be a large increase in educational offerings "not for credit," including subcollege courses designed to bring the capacities of minority and other groups up to college level.

TABLE A

Assumptions for Projections to 1980 for Higher Education

Item	Assumption
9. Training activities and educational programs of industry	Will be shifted in part to colleges and universities, particularly in the larger cities.
10. Salaries and benefits of higher-education faculty members	Will rise substantially over the years in order to attract a sufficient number of highly capable people into teaching, administration, and research.
11. Federal government aid to colleges and universities, public and private	Will increase substantially during the period with most of the federal grants focused on programs that are important to the nation as a whole (for example, research, student aid, the development of professional personnel needed by the economy, and the construction of specialized facilities).
12. State aid to private colleges and universities	Will expand substantially in most states, where necessary new forms of aid will be established.
13. Private gifts as a source of financing colleges and universities	Will increase in dollar amount over the period but will decline as a percentage of the total higher-education budget. Foundation grants to higher education will grow at a relatively slow rate.
14. Tuition gap between private and public institutions	Will widen during the period. Fund raising and government aid will not be great enough to hold down tuition increases at private colleges and universities.
15. Structure of higher education	Will include strong statewide coordinating boards or statewide systems in nearly every state. Their influence will extend to all areas of education beyond the high school, both public and private.

Against the background of these assumptions, an examination of materials on population, economic outlook, and the educational situation from the Census Bureau, the Office of Education, the Bureau of Labor Statistics, the Department of Commerce, and

from other public and private agencies leads to the conclusions
and projections set forth in the next seven tables.

The first of these, Table B, shows the college-age and the school-
age population in 1965 and in 1980 and the change during the
period.

TABLE B

Estimated College-Age and School-Age Population 1965 and 1980

Category	1965 December 31	1980 July 1	Fifteen-Year Increase (approximate)	Percentage Change
College-age population:				
18 years old *	3,736,000	4,244,000	508,000	+14%
19–21 years old	8,612,000	12,824,000	4,212,000	+49%
22–24 years old	8,396,000	12,100,000	3,704,000	+44%
Total, 18–24 years old	20,744,000	29,168,000	8,424,000	+41%
School-age population:				
5–13 years old	36,115,000	41,483,000	5,368,000	+15%
14–17 years old	14,289,000	16,051,000	1,762,000	+12%
18 years old *	3,736,000	4,244,000	508,000	+14%
Total, 5–18 years old	54,140,000	61,778,000	7,638,000	+14%

* Some young people in this age bracket are in college and some are in high
school. We show the figures in both sections of this table for a clearer indication of the totals that are relevant for projections.

As shown at the top of Table B, the college-age population is
expected to grow from 20,744,000 in 1965 to 29,168,000 in 1980, a
41 percent increase in 15 years. This compares with an increase of
only 14 percent for school-age children, as shown at the bottom of
Table B.

Obviously all persons 18 to 24 years old are not potential college or university students. On the other hand, the Census Bureau

estimates that in 1966 nearly one million persons older than 24 years were enrolled as students in colleges and universities, full time or part time. The number is expected to grow substantially in the future.

For a number of years, there has been an increasing trend toward going to college among the 18-to-24-year-olds. Allowing for a continued increase in the trend, and for more college-going among adults beyond college age as well, a reasonable projection for the total higher education enrollment in 1980 is shown in Table C.

TABLE C

*Total * Enrollment in Colleges and Universities
Fall 1965 and 1980*

Classification	Fall 1965 Actual	Fall 1980 Estimated	Fifteen-Year Increase	Percentage Change
Number of students:				
Public institutions	3,969,000	9,250,000	5,281,000	+133%
Private institutions	1,951,000	2,750,000	799,000	+ 41%
Total	5,920,000	12,000,000	6,080,000	+103%
Percentage distribution of students:				
Public institutions	67%	77%		
Private institutions	33%	23%		
Total	100%	100%		

* This table includes both full-time and part-time students. It also includes "noncredit" students—that is, those students who are enrolled in higher-education courses or programs but are not studying for a degree (a group usually excluded from the statistical tables published by the Office of Education and other government agencies).

In the aggregate, total enrollment in higher education at the beginning of the 1965 school year was 5,920,000 including both full-time and part-time students, and both credit and noncredit students. By 1980 enrollment can be expected to be approximately 12 million persons, an increase of 103 percent.

These enrollment projections are larger than those published by a number of federal government agencies because they allow for a substantially greater part-time enrollment in higher-education programs by people holding full-time jobs in business, industry, and government. By 1980 this may well become the national pattern for millions of people whose skills and backgrounds (business, professional, and technical) constantly will be updated and expanded.

Table C shows that the 15-year growth in enrollment by types of institutions can be expected to be uneven—up 133 percent at public institutions but up only 41 percent at privately supported institutions. The result will be a change in the proportions of students at public and private institutions as shown in the bottom section of the table. Public-supported and public-related colleges and universities enrolled 67 percent of the students in the fall of 1965. By 1980 they can be expected to enroll no less than 77 percent of the total (and, parenthetically, some 80 percent of the total by 1985).

The trend toward a greater proportion of enrollment in public colleges and universities has been continuing for 50 years and can be expected to continue for another generation. There are a number of reasons:

(a) the expansion of existing public campuses,

(b) the creation of new public campuses,

(c) the establishment of new public institutions (especially public junior colleges), and

(d) the conversion of private colleges and universities into state-supported or state-related institutions.

The wave of conversion from private to public status or to state-related status started in 1961. All the changes were for fiscal reasons. Included, for example, were the Universities of Buffalo, Pittsburgh, Houston, Youngstown, and Kansas City (Missouri); Temple University in Philadelphia, Fenn College in Cleveland, and Sinclair College in Dayton. Additions to this list can be expected over the years.

Among public institutions, there has been a shift in recent years from municipal to state control of "city" universities providing four-year programs and graduate work. This may be expected to continue and should be largely completed long before 1980. Wayne State University and the Universities of Wichita, Akron, Toledo, and Omaha have already converted into state institutions. The University of Cincinnati became state-affiliated in September 1967; the University of Louisville is seeking increased state support and the possibility of becoming a member of the state system of higher education in Kentucky. The motivating factor has been financial—in these cases the city tax base, largely the property tax, has been just too limited to handle adequately the rapidly growing needs of higher education in large urban areas.

The shifting trends in higher education are shown further in Table D, which analyzes the enrollment by type of institution and by level of instruction.

As shown at the top of Table D, more students proportionally are expected to be enrolled in public junior or community colleges or other types of two-year public post-high-school educational institutions by 1980—21 percent of total enrollment in 1980 compared with 13 percent now. Two trends are already under way:

1. Increased size. Many present junior or community colleges expect to grow substantially in size, particularly those in or near the major cities. For example, Cuyahoga Community College, which opened in some abandoned buildings in Cleveland in 1964, expects to enroll 20,000 students by the early 1970s.

2. New institutions. Many new junior colleges or other types of public post-high-school educational institutions (for example, technical institutes) are likely to be established. A 1967 tabulation showed that 110 junior or community colleges had opened recently or were in the process of development.

As shown at the bottom of Table D, by 1980 there are expected to be a great many more graduate and professional students than at the present time. The estimated total of no less than 2.4 million students will be three times the present number. Many of these students are likely to be in five-year and six-year programs preparing for entrance into technical, professional, teaching, social-

TABLE D

Percentage Distribution of University and College Enrollment
Fall 1965 and 1980

Classification	Fall 1965		Fall 1980	
	Actual Enrollment	*Percent of Total*	*Estimated Enrollment*	*Percent of Total*
By type of institution and control:				
Two-year institutions:				
Public colleges	789,000	13%	2,500,000	21%
Private colleges	111,000	2%	120,000	1%
Four-year institutions:				
Public universities and colleges	3,095,000	52%	6,750,000	56%
Private universities and colleges	1,925,000	33%	2,630,000	22%
Total	5,920,000	100%	12,000,000	100%
By level of instruction:				
Undergraduate students	5,160,000	87%	9,600,000	80%
Graduate and professional students (including medicine, dentistry, law, and other students studying for their first professional degree)	760,000	13%	2,400,000	20%
Total	5,920,000	100%	12,000,000	100%

welfare, and health careers. At the doctoral level, the demand for persons with doctoral degrees is high and can be expected to remain at high levels throughout the 15-year period.

What does this mean with respect to the number of college and university graduates? Some estimated figures are shown in Table E.

Table E shows that a big increase can be expected at all levels

TABLE E

Number of College and University Graduates Classified by Degree and Field 1965–1966 and 1980–1981

Category	1965–1966 Actual	1980–1981 Estimated	Fifteen-Year Increase	Per-centage Change
Bachelor's and first professional degrees:				
Natural sciences and related professions	136,600	255,225	118,625	+ 87%
Social sciences, humanities, and related professions	403,400	769,775	366,375	+ 91%
Total	540,000	1,025,000	485,000	+ 90%
Master's degrees (excluding first professional):				
Natural sciences and related professions	34,850	102,873	68,023	+195%
Social sciences, humanities, and related professions	91,350	172,927	81,577	+ 89%
Total	126,200	275,800	149,600	+119%
Doctoral degrees (excluding first professional):				
Natural sciences and related professions	8,890	25,290	16,400	+184%
Social sciences, humanities, and related professions	8,610	19,710	11,100	+129%
Total	17,500	45,000	27,500	+157%

and in all fields. However, the breakdowns by major fields are tied
to historical trends and therefore may be subject to a somewhat
greater margin of error than the totals.

Two comparisons of the figures are of particular interest:

1. The number of college and university degrees doubled
at all levels between 1953 and 1965. By 1980–1981 the number
of degrees earned is expected nearly to double again at the
bachelor's degree level and will more than double at the master's and doctoral degree levels.

2. No fewer than 375,000 doctorates are expected to be
earned during the 15 years ending in 1980–1981. This will be
one and one-half times the total number of doctorates earned
in the entire earlier history of the country.

How many teachers and faculty members will it take to handle
the enrollment projected for the school year starting in 1980? A
conservative estimate is in Table F.

TABLE F

Number of College and University Faculty Members
1965–1966 and 1980–1981

Classification	1965–1966 Actual	1980–1981 Estimated	Fifteen-Year Increase	Per-centage Change
Instructor or above:				
Full-time faculty	245,000	420,000	175,000	+ 71%
Part-time faculty	90,000	180,000	90,000	+100%
Assistant instructor, teaching fellows, and teaching assistants	65,000	145,000	80,000	+123%
Total number of faculty members	400,000	745,000	345,000	+ 86%

The 86 percent increase in the number of faculty members and
assistants between 1965 and 1980, as shown in Table F, is ex-

pected to be somewhat lower than the 103 percent increase in the number of students shown previously, in Table C. A number of leading institutions already believe that larger classes, made possible by the use of technological aids and a greater number of faculty assistants, are a practical method of providing high-quality education while meeting a portion of the student-growth problem. A broader use of the technique can be expected by 1980.

An increase of 345,000 in college and university faculty members and their assistants in 15 years is a pretty substantial increase. How well will they be prepared? How many will have the doctorate? How will they be distributed among the fields needed, by types of institutions, and geographically? These are unanswered questions to which only a limited amount of attention has been given.

Each of the factors noted above—more teachers, more students, more competition for highly trained educators, and a greater range and variety of educational services—may be expected to push educational costs (both operating and capital) upward between 1965 and 1980. What are the total expenditures likely to be? The projections are in Table G.

A rough estimate—and only rough estimates can be made no matter how carefully the underlying statistics are processed—is that expenditures by all colleges and universities can be expected to amount to $32.5 billion in 1980–1981, an increase of 114 per cent from the $15.2 billion of expenditures and capital outlay in 1965–1966. Inflation is excluded from these estimates and they must be regarded, therefore, as minimum figures.

The classification of expenditures between those made by public institutions and those by private institutions assumes the distribution for students and faculties indicated in previous tables and a somewhat better utilization of facilities in 1980 than in 1965. State-related institutions (for example, Temple University) are included in the projections for public institutions. Although the projections obviously are subject to a margin of error, they are close enough to indicate broadly the magnitudes that can be expected.

Can we afford it? Can we as a nation look forward with assur-

TABLE G

Expenditures by Colleges and Universities
1965–1966 and 1980–1981
(DOLLARS ARE BILLIONS)

Classification	1965–1966 Actual	1980–1981 Estimated	Fifteen- Year Change	Per- centage Change
Operating expenditures:				
Public institutions	$ 6.5	$18.8	$12.3	+189%
Private institutions	4.9	9.7	4.8	+ 98%
Total operating expenditures	$11.4	$28.5	$ 17.1	+150%
Capital outlay:				
Public institutions	$ 2.5	$ 3.0	$+ .5	+ 20%
Private institutions	1.3	1.0	− .3	− 23%
Total capital outlay	$ 3.8	$ 4.0	$+ .2	+ 5%
Total expenditures	$15.2	$32.5	$ 17.3	+114%

ance and even complacency to such a rapidly increasing level of expenditures for higher education? Take a look at the comparisons in Table H.

By 1980 the American people can look forward to a gross national product of no less than $1,300 billion, a 91 percent greater income and production than in 1965 (with inflation excluded from the calculations). If we as a nation agree to increase expenditures for education as indicated in the tables, the proportion of the gross national product allocated to higher education still will be only slightly greater in 1980 than it is now.

Clearly then, the level of these expenditures is a matter of national policy, not of resources. National production and income (the gross national product) can be expected to grow during the 15 years from 1965 to 1980. The nation will be earning the annual income necessary to provide adequately for higher education. However, thousands of decisions at higher-education institutions and government agencies will be required in order to allocate the

TABLE H

Expenditures by Colleges and Universities
Compared with Gross National Product
1965–1966 and 1980–1981*
(DOLLARS ARE BILLIONS)

Category	1965–1966	1980–1981	Fifteen-Year Change	Percentage Change
Expenditures by colleges and universities	$ 15.2	$ 32.5	$ 17.3	+114%
Gross national product	$681.2	$1,300.0	$618.8	+ 91%
Expenditures by colleges and universities as a percentage of the gross national product	2.2%	2.5%	——	——

* At 1967 price levels.

increased funds. These decisions will be required at a time when there will be competing demands from schools, health and high-way activities, hospitals, military activities, space and other research programs, and many other public services and agencies. It will be up to the American people, separately and collectively, to make the necessary decisions. There is every reason to believe that they will make them clearly and dramatically in favor of higher education.

◄ LOGAN WILSON

Higher Education and the National Interest

ANYBODY WHO imagines that the campus of 1980 will look vastly different from the campus of today needs to remind himself that colleges and universities symbolize continuity as well as change. Some of today's students, for example, are housed and instructed in buildings that date back to Colonial times. Library shelves contain materials going back to antiquity as well as volumes just off the press. Preserving and transmitting man's cultural heritage, in other words, is still an important function of higher education. But contemporary colleges and universities are becoming more and more oriented toward the present and the future. Already the typically landscaped campuses are in many places disappearing as trees and grass give way to high-rise buildings and asphalt parking lots. The two-way traffic between the campus and the outside world increases almost daily in volume and speed.

In the past, campuses were often merely enclaves of the surrounding society. What happened in higher education was of no great import for most of the adult population, and comparatively few of their sons and daughters went to college. Various levels of government helped support academic institutions, but higher education itself was seldom a political issue. Even when publicly supported, most institutions were left relatively alone to determine their own role and scope. They changed slowly, grew mainly

23

by gradual accretion, and rarely gave much thought to long-range planning.

The persistence of Gothic or Georgian architecture on the campus, however, belies the fact that, underneath the brick and ivory surface, striking transformation has taken place in American higher education: virtually all colleges and universities are now caught up in the vital concerns of a rapidly changing society. Their former independence or autonomy is being displaced by interdependence with other institutions and agencies. In particular, there is a growing mutuality of relations between institutions of higher education and government, local, state, and federal.

The sheer size and complexity of American higher education suggests that its relations with other sectors of society can hardly be simple, for there are more than 2,200 colleges and universities in this country. Of these, 664 are junior colleges, 823 offer work through the bachelor's degree, 472 offer the master's degree, 227 offer the doctorate, and 21 are unclassified. There are 12 under federal control, 424 under state control, 354 under the control of local government units, 524 private and nondenominational, 484 Protestant, 381 Roman Catholic, and 28 affiliated with other religious denominations. For the year 1965–1966, the count was 787 public institutions and 1,420 private institutions. The junior or community colleges comprise the majority of those related formally to local government; other types of publicly supported institutions are connected with state government. But nearly all colleges and universities now have some federal connections.

No other nation approaches ours in the number and diversity of institutions of higher education. In further contrast to other advanced nations, the United States has no formal "system" or governmentally organized arrangement of all colleges and universities. It is no wonder that many Americans find it difficult to think of education in national terms and that even professional educators are prone to behave as if the urgent problems were confined to their particular specialties, campuses, or constituencies.

Nonetheless, this myopia is fast disappearing. Higher education has become too important to the welfare of the various states and regions and to the whole nation for its development to be left entirely in local or private hands. The pressures for expansion and improvement require huge sums of money. Many of the urgent issues and problems cannot be handled adequately in piecemeal ways. With the growing collectivism of modern life, more and more decisions and actions affecting the development of higher education are being transferred from the private to the public arena, and from the local to the state or national level.

Some of these transformations are already evidenced in the changed anatomy of American higher education. The proportion of students enrolled in private institutions, for instance, declined from 61 percent in 1900, to 51 per cent in 1930, to 41 percent in 1964, and is projected to drop to 25 percent in 1980. To cite another indication of these trends, privately financed new educational construction grew from only $123 million in 1946 to $711 million in 1964, whereas publicly financed construction jumped from $101 million in 1946 to $3,323 million in 1964. As someone has aptly noted, "Roughly every second student living on a campus now sleeps in a government-owned bed."

Of course, American higher education still contrasts markedly with the Russian system, where education is entirely state-supported and is directly used as an instrument of political policy. In France, too, there is much more governmental control of higher education, as is evidenced in the centralized direction of such matters as admissions policy, curricula, examinations, academic awards, staffing, and budgeting. Even in England, the stronghold of institutional autonomy, formerly privately financed universities now derive about three-fourths of their annual income from governmental funds, and national policies are beginning to influence many of their decisions.

In former eras, America permitted wide latitude in the establishment, support, and control of institutions of higher education. Local independence in decision making was the rule. The diversification, decentralization, and institutional autonomy achieved under these circumstances are widely held to be unique strengths of our system of higher education.

Recently we have become more aware of the weaknesses that exist alongside the strengths; unplanned diversification is being called into question as a model for further development. As institutions of higher learning become more complicated and expensive, pressures for expansion and improvement are often attended by demands for improved efficiency and effectiveness. Although we still pride ourselves on the cultural pluralism of our free society and on the autonomy of our intellectual institutions, the growing importance, expense, and interdependence of higher-education agencies are forces compelling change.

Many states now have—and others are developing—statewide boards, commissions, or councils designed to formulate policies for all public higher education. The effect of such bodies, of course, is to reduce the authority of particular institutional boards, administrators, and faculties. All of these statewide boards are political in origin and usually consist of lay members appointed by the governor, who have no direct institutional affiliations. These boards in turn name their own staffs. In California, Texas, and many other states, central agencies of this sort have considerable power in determining the role and scope of the colleges and universities under their jurisdiction. They often prescribe budgetary policies and practices. They exercise a strong influence with legislatures regarding the establishment of new institutions which are to be state-supported. In short, they are potent political mechanisms making for the *outer* direction of higher education, and they inevitably will tend to diminish the *inner* direction: that is, the control of the colleges and universities by professors, deans, presidents, and trustees.

Certain federal actions since 1963 have also tended to give to state governors and those appointed by them (and to some extent by legislators) greater influence in the allocation of funds for the development of higher education. The Higher Education Facilities Act of 1963, for example, required that state commissions be designated to develop and submit state plans for utilizing the facilities funds under Title I. The enactments of 1965 contain comparable stipulations. These measures reduce the possibility of federal interference, of course, but only at the cost of interposing another layer of state agencies between academic institutions, private as well as public, and their sources of support.

The Education Commission of the States (an interstate compact recently organized with foundation support by former Governor Terry Sanford of North Carolina), the use of anonymous task forces to formulate educational policies and programs in Washington, and other recent changes also increase the outer direction and diminish the inner direction of higher education. Pointing out that, historically, American colleges and universities have for the most part been free from domination by political and other external agencies, a number of university presidents have publicly stated their fears that these and other such moves may constitute threats to this freedom by accelerating an already notable trend toward the politicalization of higher education.

In addition, in recent years certain trends in higher education have been markedly influenced by actions of Congress—in particular, through its indirect support of advanced learning by contracts for goods and services, and through categorical rather than general aid. From some quarters the complaint has been heard that federal funds for research in the physical sciences and engineering have forced the humanities into the background. There is also the familiar criticism that the emphasis on research has resulted in a corresponding neglect of teaching, particularly in the major universities. The liberal arts colleges, in turn, are alleged to have become the neglected members of the whole academic community.

In short, colleges and universities are much more affected by outside social forces than they once were. To remain viable, they can hardly escape taking into account popular conceptions about what they ought to be. Their curricula are heavily influenced by changing social and vocational requirements; their structure, by the growth of collectivism and bureaucracy; their expansion, by population increases; and even their aims, by the requirements which the larger society imposes. And in a democracy, the larger society makes its basic needs and wishes felt through political mechanisms.

It is perhaps inevitable, then, that higher education should become more politicalized, and in many respects this may be desirable. Although academicians are not so conservative as physicians about the social organization of their enterprise, historians have demonstrated that few of the important innovations in colleges and universities have originated within professorial ranks. Moreover, if institutions were left entirely alone and merely given financial support with no strings attached, wasteful duplication of effort would soon become insupportable. The interrelations of campuses with one another and with other sectors of society, and the common problems of higher education which necessitate a united approach call for an emphasis on interdependence rather than independence.

But to expect that a united front can be achieved through existing governmental structures is an unwarranted assumption; before it can be accepted, some imperative questions must be answered. Although we appear to be moving toward a national society and a corresponding nationalization of public policy, the states still contribute more toward the support of basic higher education than does the federal government. They do this despite inherent limitations in their tax structures and despite the irrationality of using state boundary lines as bases of compartmentalization in developmental planning to meet the nation's future educational needs. Moreover, there is so much confusion about the respective spheres of the states and the federal government as to make still more dubious the use of present political approaches to solve nationwide educational problems.

Some of our states, for example, do not have the financial resources to support first-class systems of higher education. Others have thus far not stirred themselves enough to promote equality of educational opportunity for young people who may have the capability but lack the means to go beyond high school. A few states and regions have concentrations of distinguished colleges and universities, whereas other regions of the country are wholly lacking in any that rise much above mediocrity. Although this country has no national university, most of our leading colleges and universities are indeed national in the scope of their service. How can the sights of other institutions be raised without discouraging local initiative? How can a national effort be made to improve higher education in some states and regions without indirectly forcing others down to a common level? These are only some of the questions now up for discussion and action in the political arena.

Since the answers to them affect the lives of millions of Americans and bear directly on the future of the nation, it is inevitable that educational issues will become political issues. The politicalization of higher education is in effect a public tribute to its greatly enhanced importance. The challenge to all who really care about colleges and universities is not to try to turn back the clock of history but to make the most of the reality we now confront.

Sentiments favoring decentralization, the nature of federalism, and constitutional problems of separation of church and state— these and other factors have caused the historical pattern of federal involvement in higher education to be primarily indirect, project-oriented, diverse, and sometimes contradictory. Three kinds of federal involvement were established as early as 100 years ago: (*a*) direct establishment and operation of institutions; (*b*) direct endowments of land and funds to aid state or local establishments and operations; and (*c*) indirect support of the advancement of knowledge by contracts for goods and services. These historical approaches are being supplemented by loans and grant-in-aid programs for educational facilities and students. All of these approaches have been aimed primarily at meeting specific government needs; only indirectly or secondarily have they been intended to fulfill educational purposes. Thus, federal involvement in higher education is, at the same time, both productive and erosive; a more coherent approach is called for.

While the federal government has been as sensitive as the institutions themselves about centralized control and domination, a growing recognition that the output of higher education—manpower, goods, and services—is essential and integral to the social welfare of the people and the national interest has furthered federal involvement. Serious national concern about education was manifested in the past several decades by the Hoover National Advisory Committee on Education Report in 1931 and the Truman Commission Report in 1948; but the passage of the National Defense Education Act in 1958 finally gave legislative recognition to the nexus between the needs of the nation and higher learning. In addition, the use of government funds to procure services from institutions has taken on a new political interest not only because of its increase but also because of the direct relationship of these services to the needs of the government.

The complexity and indirectness of federal aid has created between government and higher education a relationship which defies simple categorization. It can be called a seller-buyer affiliation, in the sense that the university sells goods and services. It can be called a doctor-patient relationship, in the sense that the university diagnoses and treats the ills of society. It can be called a lawyer-client association when the university gives advice to various branches of government; and certainly it can be called a mortgagor-mortgagee relationship when the government assumes the role of banker in lending money to institutions for educational facilities. Because the relationships are so diverse and so encompassing, the output of the university so essential to the government, and the funds of the government so necessary if the purposes of education are to be fulfilled, the university has evolved into what might be called a quasi-governmental institution.

Although a basic mutuality of interest prevails, the form and manner in which federal funds flow into the educational sector often produce tensions. The policy of categorical grants and contracts, for instance, may distort institutional objectives and deplete institutional resources. The government requirement that institutions share the cost of research projects—some of which are not related to institutional purposes—may be disadvantageous to the institution, which must then spend its own funds on projects external to its basic interests. The fierce competition for federal funds which pits school against school, department against department, and scholar against scholar, results in disunity and a weakening of loyalty to the institution.

The machinery of "advice"—task forces and advisory panels to the federal government—has also become a subject of controversy. To the arguments of the "insiders" that laissez faire, based on the merit principle, is the best way to run science, the "outsiders" have responded that, under this system, much merit goes undetected and that in any case one government mission must be to build excellence wherever the potential exists. The government's reliance on the project system and its understandable concentration of research in institutions of demonstrated excellence (to the extent that 25 universities get 60 percent of the federal research grants) may perpetuate an imbalance in the quality of institutions.

While few would argue that project support should be reduced or that funds should be diverted from the great centers of learning, it is contended that ways must be found to produce a wider geographic spread of participation and to permit more institutional determination of what research and which researchers are to be supported. Recognizing these problems, a recent presidential statement on research contracts emphasized: *a*) that funds should be distributed so as to improve quality where it is not at present high, and *b*) that quality where it already exists must be supported. For these aims to be realized, of course, there must be sufficient funds for both.

Thus, indirect approaches of supporting higher education as a means of broad development are being questioned. Should cost-sharing in government-supported research continue to be the norm? Or should funds be provided over and above the full cost of such research as means of strengthening total institutional programs? Should all research-supporting agencies develop programs of institutional grants as supplements to project grants for the support of basic research? Can ways be found to involve more institutions in the government research effort without sacrificing quality and without weakening leading institutions?

Other indirect approaches for supporting higher education, such as tax laws and various federal policies which would encourage the states and private philanthropy to make more funds available for institutional budgets, are being explored. Directly and indirectly, the federal government is being asked to offset the increasing budget deficits and higher charges levied on students.

The cost of education is such today that a dualistic system, one which balances the public with the private sector, cannot be maintained without governmental aid to private education. Those who plan for higher education's future are confronted by such critical problems as how public funds can be acceptably channeled to support private institutions, which institutions should receive this assistance, and under what circumstances, and whether it is constitutional to underwrite church-affiliated colleges and universities.

Because of its expanded needs, the nation can make full use of the facilities afforded by virtually all private institutions. Economically, it makes no sense to establish new institutions while staff and space in existing colleges and universities go underutilized. More important, in the minds of many, is the desirability of maintaining a pluralistic system of higher education and avoiding a monolithic scheme of support and control. A strong independent sector, it is argued, not only has its intrinsic values in a democratic society, but also is a useful competitive element and counterbalance to the public sector. Forcing private institutions to become just like their public counterparts eligible for tax support would indeed diminish their values for preserving a dualistic system.

Although educators do not object to governmental regulation and surveillance in the transportation industry, in the food and drug industries, and in other areas, most of them are strongly opposed to similar controls over the quality and quantity of education. Taxpayers, on the other hand, are understandably reluctant to exempt institutions of higher education from accountability for the expenditure of public funds, and to leave the purposes of academic enterprise to institutional determination. The growing interrelations of government and higher education therefore give rise to new challenges in the present and future.

Some of the circumstances affecting the present and future of American higher education are matters of fact rather than of opinion or preference. Population growth and increased student demand, a complex economy's needs for more highly trained manpower, a push for equality of advanced-educational opportunity, spectacular and unanticipated gains in knowledge—these and other circumstances are not debatable. But about the kind of educational system our society ought to have in response to changing needs, there are diverse opinions and preferences. And there is also a growing recognition that today's basic policy decisions *shape* as well as *anticipate* tomorrow's world.

In a rapidly changing society, tradition as a guideline for long-range development is necessarily weakened. Old ways of thinking and doing in higher education lose their viability. Moreover, the pressures to expand and improve the educational system cannot be met by gradual, unplanned growth. The establishment of a new medical school, for example, requires years of planning and the advance commitment of at least 30 or 40 million dollars. The output of scientists and engineers, unlike the output of automobiles, cannot be stepped up overnight simply by overtime on assembly lines already in existence. The growing sentiment to universalize 14 rather than 12 years of formal education and the need to revolutionize technical education pose public policy questions which call for decision and action now.

One set of issues centers on the broad question: Who should go to college? Even though some institutions are becoming more selective, the system as a whole is becoming less so, as is evidenced in the constantly increasing proportion of the college-age group enrolled in college. In plans for the future, places will have to be provided somewhere for all high-school graduates who wish to continue their formal education. This implies, of course, that in the future educational purposes and standards will be even more diverse than they have been in the past. It also implies that the public must assume more responsibility for financing both institutions and individuals.

The public junior or community college is one answer to the problem of providing relatively low-cost higher education on a massive scale. These institutions already represent a fast-growing sector in American higher education, and their proponents champion them as the best way of handling the problem of sheer numbers. Others, however, believe that the junior college is in actuality little more than a two-year extension of high school, lacking in many of the opportunities to be found in senior colleges and universities. They argue that comparable educational programs are no less costly in one type of institution than in another.

For the young person of considerable talent and affluence,

whether he will go to college is seldom a real question, and where he will go is largely a matter of personal choice. But for the individual of average ability and very limited financial means, whether he will go to college and where depends largely on the opportunities that society provides for him. Mass education, in contrast to elite education, is therefore intricately bound up with issues of public policy. The state of California provides an interesting illustration of a publicly determined approach to the "institutional mix" of educational opportunities. At present, California maintains 74 (a total of more than 100 is projected by 1980) publicly supported junior colleges which admit all high-school graduates, 18 state colleges which have four-year curricula (and some graduate offerings) for students who finish in the top third of their high-school graduating classes, and the University of California, with its nine campuses, which are open only to those high-school graduates who finish in the top eighth of their classes. The California system thus represents not only a carefully planned and controlled division of labor among institutions, but also a deliberate stratification of educational opportunity.

The state of New York, where private higher education has historically been the dominant pattern, has approached the "who shall go to college and where" question differently: its system of state scholarships gives the holders more individual choice and in effect has subsidized persons rather than institutions. It should be noted, of course, that New York is beginning an intensive development of public institutions and that—by way of low student charges in public institutions—California has indirectly subsidized individuals as well as the colleges and universities under state control.

Issues having to do with expanding and improving educational opportunity must be looked at in relation to issues of support and control. Some states are already committed to providing further opportunity for all high-school graduates who want it; but others have made no public decisions so far about how far down the talent ladder the "equal access" principle is to extend. In some states, public assistance goes only to public institutions and to the students enrolled in them; in others, state assistance is provided to private institutions as well as to individuals, who may attend any accredited college or university where they can gain admission.

A current difficulty in choosing sensibly among the alternatives available for the expansion and improvement of educational opportunity is our lack of objective knowledge about the possible consequences of such alternatives as public assistance to institutions (including private) *vs.* public assistance to students; massive scholarship *vs.* massive student loan programs; the most appropriate governmental level—local, state, federal—for determining various needs and priorities.

As has been noted, the federal government has in recent years concerned itself increasingly with all of these public-policy questions. In the past, our long-established tradition of decentralization and federalism in matters of education has tended to restrict Washington to giving grants-in-aid to states and to other agencies of education. But of late the federal government has become bolder. The heavy commitment of local and state revenues to established programs and the availability of more discretionary funds on the federal level have, of course, made Washington's innovative role more feasible.

In any event, it is clear that vastly more financial support will be required to underwrite the necessary changes in American higher education. This enlarged investment is likely to be accompanied by alterations in traditional forms of support and control. What should they be? Can existing institutions be utilized more effectively and expansion accomplished more economically by increased public aid to private institutions? Is it fair to this generation of college students and to future generations to force them to carry a heavier part of the financial burden of higher education through soaring tuition charges and loan programs? Will increased federal support programs have the effect of reducing state, local, and private support? At what point should increased public support (as a percentage of the gross national product or of the total tax dollar) begin to level off? At what points and for whom does an increased investment in higher education cease to pay off? These are some of the unresolved issues which require greater understanding and consensus if we are to plan more intelligently our educational future.

To move ahead effectively, we also need to develop a more efficient organization of higher education, and this we are already beginning to do. Public or state-supported institutions are coming more and more under the jurisdiction of coordinating councils or commissions. Both public and private colleges and universities are evolving consortia. Nationwide associations and the federal government, in the effort to develop solutions to nationwide problems, exert influences which emphasize the interdependence and coordination of educational activity. In short, social mechanisms for interinstitutional decision making are being developed.

Meantime, it is obvious that uncertainty and confusion still exist about which sorts of decisions are best made by centralized authority and which by localized authority. There is no consensus about how much voice the federal government should have in the planning, direction, and conduct of the total enterprise, or about whether the wide diffusion of authority in Washington itself is advantageous or disadvantageous from the point of view of higher education. Nobody has as yet made an objective assessment of the uses and abuses of statewide governing or coordinating bodies, even though they continue to increase in number. In many states, the question of the role of private colleges and universities is either bypassed or dealt with ambiguously in the development of statewide policies and plans. Whether the regional compacts will increase or decrease in importance, and what effects the Education Commission of the States will have upon state and federal legislation are not yet clear.

Aside from the issues and problems relating to interinstitutional organization and decision making, there are many concerns having to do with the patterning of individual institutions. Of vital concern to the public at large is the development of suitable numbers and types of post-secondary institutions to accommodate the expanded college population between now and 1980. What is the most economical and effective division of labor among different kinds of institutions for handling students of different ability levels, for emphasizing varied programs, for providing general and special, professional and graduate education? Does the present tendency of too many institutions to imitate indiscriminately the largest and most complex institutions dilute quality and undermine diversity? How much uniformity is desirable from one state or region to another? Should lay boards and commissions be empowered to establish those patterns? Who should decide the relative emphases on teaching, research, and public service for a particular institution?

Our resolution of these public-policy issues will be heavily influenced, of course, by the relative values we attach to freedom and order, to equality and excellence, to the particular and the general, to present satisfaction and future benefit. To make the Great Society a reality, it is manifest that wise discernment and resolute action are called for if higher education is to be a main instrument for its achievement.

Whether by drift or by direction, public-policy issues do get resolved. In a rational society the resolutions of issues are responses not only to existing pressures but also to anticipated problems and to mental images of future states of affairs considered to be desirable. More governmental involvement in the outcomes of higher education therefore implies more governmental involvement in planning, and in a period of rapid growth present decisions and actions necessarily must be oriented toward the future. Through their elected or appointed representatives in government, citizens are in a position to choose those alternatives which appear to offer the greatest gains and fewest losses. But in realistic planning, as contrasted to utopianism, feasibility no less than desirability must be taken into account. Governmental or any other kind of planning is thus an idle enterprise without the means of realization; however, a special advantage of governmental planning is that the body politic can command greater resources than any other agency.

Moreover, political decision making is an effort to shape the future and can become a basis for prediction in human affairs. To be sure, no present decision is likely to have much effect on the size of the college-age population in 1980, for it has already been born. No legislative or other current deliberations can do much to alter the forecast that an increasingly complex society will have a greater need for highly trained individuals. Some things are already known about the needs to be met between now and 1980— the responses we make to these and other circumstances through planning will constitute an effort to "invent the future" of higher education.

Even though nobody can predict today precisely what the pattern of higher education will be more than a decade hence, we need to take into consideration now as many important elements as possible and proceed with implementation. It can be anticipated, for example, that more adults as well as young persons will have to be accommodated by colleges and universities. Proportionately more of them will live in highly urbanized environments —a locale where 40 percent of the college-age group already goes beyond the secondary-school level, as contrasted to 14 percent in 1938. If we are not to retrogress educationally, our nation has no option but to enlarge vastly the scale of operations in higher education. Even without drastic alterations in the character of education per se, this change in scale means that a wider diffusion in the process itself is of considerable significance.

It is likely that the public sector of our economy will continue to expand at the expense of the private sector. Some economists assert that, whereas governments in advanced, non-communist nations now distribute about 30 percent of the national income, this proportion will go to anywhere between 40 and 50 percent. This general trend in turn will influence the movement in higher education toward increased public support and control.

During recent years many individual campuses have engaged in planning, but equally notable has been the rise of governmental planning for whole systems of higher education. Some states have already devised master plans for long-range development, and others are doing so, recognizing that vast expansions and improvements proceed more sensibly through coordinated design than through piecemeal reactions to problems after they have become critical. The more unimaginative planning exercises, of course, tend merely to project enrollments, plant and staff expansion, and project the future largely in terms of the past and present. The limited techniques used often fail to provide educational leaders and their constituencies with effective, meaningful alternatives and may even freeze debate and stall decision making. Sometimes there is a gap between relevant research knowledge and what the practitioners of planning could well use, and in other instances there is a general lack of understanding of the dynamics of educational change. Within government there are bureaucratic and other impediments to planned change, and on many sides there is a reluctance to take bold risks which might yield new dividends.

To plan more intelligently we need to know more about educational inputs and outputs of existing programs and institutions. What are the determinants of demand for higher education for a given institution, for a state or region, for the nation? Is a national testing program desirable or inevitable? Do we take into account sufficiently the changing and improving technology of education? Will collective bargaining become a more prevalent mode of behavior in the academic profession? Should the changing attitudes of students be given more prominence in educational planning? To what extent can colleges and universities assume further obligations of general social reform and uplift without weakening their capacity to conserve, diffuse, and advance what is traditionally known as higher learning?

Although it would be helpful to know in advance the answers to these and other questions, planning cannot be delayed until all relevant data are in hand. The exercise of planning, moreover, is useful as a means for reaching a consensus about goals and how to arrive at them. As contrasted with "muddling through," planning is more likely to identify basic problems, anticipate changes affecting higher education, and appraise the predictable consequences of alternate modes of action. Through planning, appropriate strategies can be devised to achieve some outcomes and forestall others.

In a democratic society where higher education is heavily supported by government and where progressively more people want to be heard about educational issues, it is to be expected that government itself should become a planning mechanism. As has been observed, this is already happening on state levels, where commissions and coordinating boards project the lines of development for statewide systems of higher education. Although nothing resembling a master plan for American education has as yet emerged in the nation's capital, past and present actions of the federal government have markedly influenced the direction of many institutions and of the entire system.

By granting or withholding funds, the federal government makes its influence felt. Contracts and grants-in-aid have accelerated scientific research, added momentum to campus building programs, fostered graduate study, encouraged student borrowing, and in many other ways expressed political determinations of priorities for present and future development.

It would be an error to conclude, however, that federal support for higher education has been guided by a coherent set of principles. Federal funds have been used and doubtless will continue to be used to underwrite both expansion and improvement, the status quo and innovation, uniformity as well as diversity, and to supplement as well as complement moneys from local, state, and private sources. In no instance has federal involvement supplanted local or other control. The strength of public sentiment favoring diversity in the development of higher-education is likely to continue in the foreseeable future; hence, it is improbable that a master plan emanating from Washington would gain much acceptance.

Out of deference to such sentiments, federal officials are careful to refer to central government as the "junior" or "silent" partner in the enterprise of higher education. Federal underwriting of the cost of higher education has already grown to an estimated one-fourth of the total outlay, nonetheless, and the proportion is likely to increase in the future. Under such circumstances, how long is the silent-partner role likely to last?

With the general movement toward managerial forms of government and the spending of larger and larger sums of public funds, it is perhaps unrealistic not to anticipate more governmental voice in setting educational standards. A national testing program is already in the formative stage for lower levels of education, and the same arguments can be made for a similar program on higher levels. Those persons who are held accountable for the expenditures of public funds are likely also to insist upon cost-effectiveness and cost-benefit analyses in an effort to further more rationality about spending procedures.

Aside from the prospects of more governmental involvement in the assessment of existing educational programs utilizing public funds, there is a growing interest on the part of politically elected representatives in shaping the future of American higher education. The President and many members of Congress, for example, are committed to the promotion of more equality of educational opportunity. The U. S. Office of Education uses federal funds to implement civil-rights legislation in such matters as the admission of students and the employment of faculty and staff. The virtually oligarchical control which scientists and other professionals formerly exercised through panels and other mechanisms over the expenditure of research funds for selected institutions is likely to be lessened by political pressures for a wider geographic and institutional spread of support.

As our nation moves toward universal higher education, with the vast sums of money required for expansion, it is probable that the federal government will assume even broader responsibilities of support and influence. But it is most unlikely that its support and control will ever become total, or even predominant. This means that the federal involvement will continue to be selective.

To maintain the assets of a pluralistic system of higher education and to avoid the liabilities of a monolithic scheme, the federal involvement should remain limited. Governmental planning for the future of education should stem from all levels of government and not just one. The private sector needs to be maintained and strengthened, not submerged. On all levels and in both sectors there must be more joint thinking about the future, but no single agency can possibly have a monopoly of vision about what that future will or ought to be.

Meantime, we should continuously remind ourselves that diversity of support and control are main strengths of the American system of higher education. They permit flexibility and experimentation. They foster a healthful competition among individuals and institutions. They forestall an irretrievable commitment to a single course of action which might in the long run be disastrous for all. Colleges ãnd universities, to be sure, share heavily in a common obligation to create a greater society and a better world, but to do so they must be reasonably free to shape as well as serve, to criticize as well as innovate. To be of maximum value, they cannot become government agencies; rather, they must be upheld and improved as intellectual institutions.

◄ WILLIAM BIRENBAUM

Cities and Universities:
Collision of Crises

I. FUTURE-THINK AND PLANNING

THE TROUBLE WITH future-think is that it seldom shakes free
from the gravity of the meanings and values we attach to what
is known—our prejudices about the way things are and seem to
be going. Present-bound, thought about the future never quite
reaches another planet—which is our world beyond today.

Recently a planning group took a look at the shape of the New
York metropolitan region, 1985. Among the things it saw was an
additional half million to 600,000 students demanding college admission in those areas of New York, Connecticut and New Jersey
within a 50-mile radius of Times Square. This conclusion was
based on a population projection and the usual assumptions such
projection involves. But the planning recommendations pursuant
to this future-guess also involved a number of conclusions about
what our colleges and universities are, should be, and will be like.
And these throw light on the planners' conception of city people
and how they are destined to live. From the prescription for handling the new collegiate population—where and how—emerged a
picture of Future-city, 1985.

Today colleges and universities are located on campuses. The
inevitability of the idea of "campus" was assumed. The foremost
current example of a system of planned campuses is the one in
California. Years ago those responsible for that system decided
that the most desirable campus population was 25,000 students.

43

Simple division—that magic California number into 500,000 to 600,000—shows the need for 20 to 24 new campuses to accommodate college enrollments in the fall of 1985 in the New York metropolitan region.

Where?

The flight to suburbia since World War II was studied. Multicolored maps portrayed the flow of people (white) to the bedrooms of Connecticut, New Jersey, Westchester, and Long Island. Spokes shooting out of the hub city marked the archaic transportation systems connecting the bedrooms to what is left in the center. Irregular rectangles along the spokes showed the places to which industry had dispersed in its escape from the cost of labor in the city and the antique tax, zoning, and other codes governing the game of urban commerce and manufacturing. A rash of "X's" appeared on the map marking the giant new drive-in shopping centers serving the people in the territories to which they had fled—at least for a part of their daily lives.

Now, there are alternative ways of dealing with this existing mess and about the way things will or should be. "Flight" and "dispersal," "city," "suburbia" or "exurbia" can be converted into a more wholesome 1985 language: "City-and-Satellites of the Future" —dense populations mapped so that people presumably can work, shop, be amused, edified, and recreated within walking distance of home. The dispersed industry, the industrial and commercial "parks" laid out along the transportation spokes, become the "bones" and the "sinews" of future "city-and-satellites." And the heart and the soul? Twenty to 24 new red dots strategically spotted on the 1985 map—the new campuses which will not only receive and process the hundreds of thousands of new freshmen, but will also provide the cultural life, the *élan* and *esprit* of "city."

The current bulletins of America's colleges and universities encourage such expectations about future academic capacities. They all say essentially the same things about the three grand reasons for their *present* being:

1. *Excellence in Teaching:* Each one advertises the most superior presentation of all that's gone before.

2. *High Adventure on the New Frontiers of Learning:* A real university is research-oriented—right out there on the cutting edges.

3. *Community Service:* The public-spirited outreach by the hand of Gown to the mind of Town offering the gems of Excellence and the fruits of High Adventure to the people living there.

Much of what passes for future-think is an imagination of what the present would be like if it "worked right." It's an imagination that counts heavily on technological solutions to basic current problems and assumes that an intelligent application of the present technology would make things work right and keep the future under control. It's an imagination which avoids confronting the political causes of the present gaps between our technological capacities and their application, and steers clear of the ideological implications of the technology itself. It is an imagination dominated by *now*, which aims to imprint the "best" of now upon the future. The trouble is that the "best" of now, with regard to City and University, is not very satisfactory. Our ideas about a university are not too friendly to the idea of what a city is or should be. The situation may be even more complicated: what a city *must* be may not be compatible with ideas Americans seem to be accepting about how they want to live. And our universities are essentially servants of the status quo—which also means: The great ones are tied to the future of our cities.

II. URBICULTURE AND THE UNIVERSITY

The modern city is a testament to the condition of human thought.

Ancient cities arose to protect people. They were places for barter and trade. Modern cities are marketplaces for values and ideas, though during wartime they may be death-traps. Industrialization, the handmaiden of the global growth of population, is an urban phenomenon. Economic and cultural progress will accelerate the rate of city growth—at least to the point where population density frustrates all progress.[1] American cities are the test tubes in which we are shaping the destiny of our national experiment. People in other lands who aspire to achieve the best in an advanced American society may be overcome, if they succeed, by what is the worst in our cities.

Much of the criticism of the contemporary American urban scene is colored by a nostalgia and mythology springing from the agricultural origins of the Republic. We tend to forget that life in the legendary log cabin, in the covered wagon or in the New England village was often hostile to popular modern conceptions of democracy, equality, cultural maturity, physical and mental health, and ease. The nostalgia and myth represent a longing for simplicity. The urban environment is a direct consequence of human complexity. Complexity in environment stimulates and agitates those qualities in a species most critical to its survival. In the human species the mind is tested.

The natural thrust of the human mind is the introduction of order into environment. Order need not be equated with simplicity nor is chaos necessarily a characteristic of complexity. Urban order, reflecting as it does thought and planning, is bound to be complex.

Thought and its relationship to action are what a university is supposed to be all about. A university is not just a library or a faculty or a large student body or bright new buildings financed through persuasion of public bodies or private money-givers. It is a combination of these elements mobilized to make people aware of and determined to overcome the ignorance and disorder in their lives. Thought, its relationship to action, and the indispensability of this relationship to survival in the new environment are the imperative bonds between the modern city and the contemporary university.

Great cities will naturally inspire great universities, and it will

[1] Earth's population reached 250,000 two thousand years ago. It passed its first half-billion at the time of the Pilgrims' landing on Plymouth Rock in 1620. The second half-billion took another two hundred years. Earth's population is now in excess of three billion, and the last half-billion grew in 11 years. Earth's population was about 1.5 billion when I was born, in 1923. It is expected to be six billion by the time I reach seventy, doubling twice within my lifetime.

become increasingly difficult for institutions of higher education to be great apart from the urban environment. Most of the country's outstanding universities are urban-based. Those which aren't are reaching out for the nearest city as rapidly as they can: Illinois at Urbana for Chicago; Michigan at Ann Arbor for Detroit; Wisconsin at Madison for Milwaukee; Missouri at Columbus for St. Louis and Kansas City; etc. The conditions which allowed a Cornell to become great no longer exist.

The flavor and style of national life, as well as its salient issues, are urban. Three out of four Americans now live and work in metropolitan settings. Less than nine percent earn their livelihood in agricultural pursuits. Along the intricate web of expressways and airlines, through the instantaneous flash of the television screen or explosion of radio sound, an urban culture ties distant cities together and permeates the remotest hamlet. The universities cannot afford to be detached from the sources of that urbiculture, from where the action is.

While impersonality of human relationships, detachment from nature, and the frenetic tempo of daily routine may be inevitable consequences of urban life, they are also the inevitable bench marks of the new national life—of which the university is a part.

It is doubtful that a major scientific breakthrough will save the urban day. The deep crises of urban living will not be solved merely by the application of medicine through public health; or of engineering to sewage disposal; or of advanced concepts of public administration to the government of metropolitan regions. Improved health, a more equitable distribution of goods, the expansion of physical comfort, and efficient government are quite naturally the common aspirations of Americans, Russians, Africans, and Chinese. They are also the minimal promises held out by *present* technology.

There is the allure of simplicity in an administrative and technological approach to the huge, often vague, and always complicated issues of urban life. The sheer growth and new complexity of our academic organizations have evoked what are essentially administrative and technical responses. The leaders of the modern American university have reacted to their problems in the same manner as the political leaders of our cities have to theirs. But their reactions have not bridged the growing schism between academic administrators and teachers or stemmed the tide of student unrest. The assault on the problems of health, slums, congestion and corruption requires the most effective mobilization of technology and administrative innovation. But monumental convention arenas and amalgamations of governmental agencies do not make a city any more than the data-processing of admission papers and the mere manipulation of credit systems make a university.

III. CITIES, NON-CITIES, AND ANTI-CITIES

Urban renewal and the use of land, housing, traffic, police, air and water pollution, food and shelter for the poor, and provisions for public education—these are the problems that obsess the day-to-day operations of governments, capture headlines, and imprint what "city" is all about upon the popular understanding.

These problems suggests what a city is, how it may be defined. The basic terms of reference are physical and economic:

1. land occupied and the uses made thereof;
2. the size and density of population;
3. the number and character of enclosed spaces and the pattern of their arrangement relative to pedestrian and vehicular thoroughfares;
4. and other service and economic aspects of group life, especially those subject to statistical analysis and quantification.

Still, these elements do not by themselves account for differences in the quality and tone of public and private life in various large, densely populated areas—areas which, because of the population concentration, exhibit all of the problems listed above. Des Moines, Denver, Kansas City, Dallas, and Los Angeles have tempos and personalities distinctly different from those of San Francisco, New York, Atlanta, Chicago, and Boston.

Suburban rings around Los Angeles, Chicago, and New York contain populations almost as large as the cities they encircle, and within those rings there are pockets of density as great or greater than the averages for the cities to which they relate. Yet those rings are clearly not citified territories.

Detroit with its two million people, plus two million more in its metropolitan region, is an especially interesting place about which to ask: Is this a City?

Detroit occupies a large land area even relative to its large population. The majority of its people live in single-family dwellings. Green grass and trees are plentiful within the city; high-rise residential developments are not. One can ride for miles through the city into suburbia without noting any significant change in the land- or cityscape. The central commercial section of the city is as desolate and deserted after dark as a suburban residential street. Commerce and retail business have been divided into thirds: the older downtown center and two vast shopping plazas imposed on the borderlines of the suburbs at the outer extremities of the city. There are few good restaurants, and these are dispersed. In fact, there are few places in the city which invite public discourse, leisure, or conversation. There is a civic center and a cultural center, and within each there are superb facilities often used by first-rate organizations. Detroit has an art museum and a symphony orchestra worthy of any great city. But the neighborhoods containing the excellent galleries and halls which accommodate these institutions are relatively empty of inviting places to go to or to walk in, before and after events.

Perhaps the most striking feature of Detroit is the powerful monoliths which hold it together as an entity. It is a city of powerful units—almost of monopolies. One bank is many times larger than all the rest. One department store virtually dominates that category. There is one art museum, one orchestra of repute, one industry to which almost all others relate, and one labor union, which is organized around that industry. There is one large public university and one large Catholic university. In this setting the utility monopolies—gas, electric, and telephone—are at home. Indeed, it can almost be said that decisions on any subject vital to the welfare of Detroit—the development of the port, cultural life, or the economy—can be made at a conference attended by a top officer from one or two of the automobile companies, an executive of the UAW, one officer each from the big department store, the big bank, and one or two of the big utilities, one university president, and a few well-known patrons of civic causes (who most likely will be connected to the other categories represented at the conference).

It is not the mere presence or absence of slums, pollution, and corruption which distinguishes a city from a non-city. The expanse of land occupied and the density of population are relevant but not conclusive "city" indices. What counts are *other* conditions, which produce certain attitudes and styles among the leaders and the led, conditions which establish the parameters for decision making.

Foremost among these conditions is the opportunity for mobility, not just of persons and things, but in status (social, cultural, and economic) and in the possession and use of power—all kinds of power including political. Mobility in status presumes the possibility of going down as well as up. The generator of mobility is the presence of a large number of alternatives—the ever-present imperative to choose. "City," as a way of life, implies the potentiality and the necessity for recurrent choice in almost everything—jobs, housing, amusements and leisure pursuits, modes of dress. Only a wide variety of alternatives gives meaning to the act of choosing—variety in architecture, the marketplace, the economy, the arts, in politics and in associates and friends.

Different people naturally chose different things. Choice from among a wide variety of alternatives in any category produces differences of opinion and a constant contention for power. Conflict and controversy are implicit in "city." City people have a special receptivity for and outlook toward conflict; they develop a special threshold of tolerance for it. Politicians in every country in the world must take this fact into account as they bargain for urban, as distinguished from rural, support.

The ultimate point of a real participation in the contention for power is to redistribute it. Only through participation in citified contention and controversy is mobility accelerated, variety enhanced, and tentative reorderings accomplished. The nature of these reorderings is crucial. Either they favor the further dispersal of power—a more equitable redistribution of it—or they don't. Either they serve as catalysts for future mobility, the mutiplication of alternatives, and the participation of the people in the process, or they don't. Understanding this process, it is clear why most suburbs and many places we identify as cities through the criteria of size and population are in fact non-cities.

. The urban ghetto is anti-city. The ghetto is a static island in the sea of urban change. Segregation by race and economic status precludes variety, a plenitude of alternatives, effective choice. There is no place to go within the ghetto, and the chances for getting out are slim. There is no mobility. While there is growing conflict between the ghetto as an entity and the rest of the city, it is an unequal contest. The inequality of the contest subverts the quality and meaning of controversy *within* the ghetto. The ghetto's internal conflicts almost always fall short of the achievement of an effective reordering. They are contentions among an inadequate and meaningless supply of alternatives and proceed from a premise of immobility. They are factional feuds. They have the effect of perpetuating the inequality of the contest between the ghetto and the rest of the city. More often than not, they terminate in the disengagement of the ghetto people—a popular disinclination to participate—or in street violence, crime, and riot, which may be viewed as the only alternatives available to express the longing for mobility and the chance for change, a redistribution of power.

American universities are more than places for classroom teaching and laboratory research. They pretend and advertise themselves to be, and in fact they generally are, going communities. Often they are consummate welfare-state communities, feeding and housing the student-citizens (and often the faculties, too), regulating their political relationships, providing medicare programs of their own, and maintaining, in addition to the parking lots and athletic stadia, systems for influencing and shaping the cultural and social lives of their inhabitants.

The more detached and isolated a university campus is from the city, the greater is its need to construct and maintain the total paraphernalia of a going community. But even in the great cities the concept of "campus," as a separate, self-contained operational community, persists.

Within these communities, rank and status are fixed. Basically, the citizenry is divided for the purposes of governance into four categories—students, faculty, administration, and "others." Within these categories, the students are pegged by year of entry, faculties are ranked and tenured, and political power is apportioned among administrators in accordance with rigid bureaucratic hierarchies. Salary rewards and tuition assessments are related directly to the status structure. Curricula are measured and paced in keeping with the credit-hour degree system. And the entire campus is wrapped in the principle of separateness and detachment—a principle designed to impress upon its members an appreciation for their differentness, and upon the public beyond a respect for the alleged objectivity, neutrality, and elite quality of the academic "community."

Within the urban campus, what meaningful alternatives do the university's citizens enjoy? To what extent are they encouraged to participate in choice that counts? Of what does mobility consist? What is the campus threshold of tolerance for controversy and conflict? How may teachers and students achieve the reordering of their own affairs in pursuit of their own best interests?

To the extent that our urban campuses are or are becoming ghettoized, they may be or become anti-city.

IV. THE PERSUASION POSTS

There are relatively few places to which Americans in the cities turn at the critical moments in their lives when questions of life or death, health or illness, or the protection of treasure and wealth arise.

The key urban persuasion posts are occupied by lawyers, doctors, psychologists, psychiatrists, undertakers, accountants, clergymen, investment counselors, some bankers, some social workers, and those responsible for television programming and the composition and production of daily newspapers. (In the last two cases the confrontation is through the media rather than face to face.)[2]

These professional experts have been produced by the universities. The occasion for consulting them usually is a need to solve a technical or specialized problem. But the solution of these problems almost always depends upon related matters falling outside the expertise of the consultant. In other words, the key experts in our urban society—through the exercise of their expertise—enter a realm of generalization for which they have not been particularly well-prepared by either undergraduate or professional education in the university.

A lawyer asked to draw a will or confronted by a client seeking to initiate a divorce action or to adopt a child is immediately plunged into giving advice and counsel which goes far beyond the intricacies of probate or family law. It is in the nature of the crisis-laden confrontation that expert knowledge is the *last* rather than the first to be applied in the course of resolving the crisis.

The persuasion posts represent a concentration of advice-giving power in American life and illustrate the gap between the functions performed by the key counselors in urban society and their preparation to perform these functions through formal education.

At a more general level, it can be said that the hard problems of urban life (and therefore of this society) do not conform to the ways universities are organized. In general, universities are organized according to the academic disciplines. The hard problems of urban life disregard these classifications. They transcend them. These problems no longer revolve simply around training men to earn livelihoods (universities have mastered this kind of production problem pretty well) or even around updating professionals once exposed to higher education (a responsibility in which the universities still have a long way to go). The hard problems arise in the areas of public philosophy, government policy, cultural quality, and men's relationships to the state and, beyond buying and selling, to each other.

[2] A strong case can be made for adding managerial scientists and militarists, and the growing army of poverty-program community counselors to this list. A less strong case may be offered in behalf of politicians (at the precinct and ward levels).

A list of the key problems must include the mass media, the aged, juvenile delinquency, the popularization of the arts, the condition of the American Negro, the conduct of our nation on the international front, peace. Each of these issues comes to focus in urban arenas, for no one of them can be approached without the mobilization of the talents and power uniquely present in the cities.

Almost always the most urgent and interesting urban issues are controversial, and the really significant ones are those which draw men out of their occupational slots into the public forums, where their conduct will be governed by knowledge and experience mainly unrelated to the know-how they possess as wage earners.

As it confronts the turmoil and variety of the city, the university (as an institution) is often inept and ill-equipped. Too frequently the assumption is made that the university can simultaneously be neutral, catalytic, and intellectual—that water, fire, and oil can mix. A catalyst is by its nature not neutral. It is a force which releases energy in a particular direction. The leaders of an urban university, which by its location if nothing else has a vested interest in the life of the city, possess the power to affect the public destiny. A university in the city, just by being there, affects that destiny. The University of Illinois persuades the public power to dislocate a slum on the West Side of Chicago and to finance the new Circle Campus. Columbia, unable to pack up and move operations to the safety of Westchester or Long Island, acquires more properties in and around Harlem. Clark Kerr and Ronald Reagan meet, and the consequences are something more than a friendly conversation about the weather.

In most societies universities are social institutions and forces. By the assertion of their ambitions, they declare a position and invite a popular inquiry into the tradition of neutrality, to which they would like to retreat when the going gets rough. The people uprooted on the West Side of Chicago claim a vested interest, and they want to know what the Circle Campus means *for them*. It will no longer do for the academic leaders and the research professors to respond with an assertion of noble objectivity.

Pushed hard on its pretensions as a center for research and alert to the controversial implications of its functions as a provider of technical services for the general community, the university may seek refuge in its traditional role as a teacher. But even as a service station for the conveyance of knowledge, the university's performance merits the closest reexamination. In a world where the "facts" are overwhelming in number and rapidly changing, "teaching the facts" depends upon prior decisions about what the facts are. The proliferation of knowledge explodes the very meaning of the concept of knowledge. A "hard" curriculum depends upon the delicate art of selection, and selection calls upon the powers of generalization. This is one of the realities of academic life from which no faculty committee or administrative council can long escape, though they certainly try to. Unless a university simply doesn't think about what it teaches (and many don't), then it must make choices, the consequences of which are not neutral.

The universities in the city are often not the best or the exclusive reservoirs of modern knowledge. In most cities, public libraries, for example, are more extensive and accessible compendiums of knowledge than the universities. Many urban art museums possess both scholars and treasures far superior to those possessed by the universities. Practicing politicians sometimes display far greater wisdom and teaching talent than practicing political scientists. Throughout American urban society, many institutions other than the universities provide laboratories and workshops for some of the nation's keenest minds. Beyond the universities, one need only look to the Pentagon, Solidarity House, the Rand Corporation and other "think tanks," the Committee on Economic Development, The Twentieth Century Fund, or the General Motors Technical Center to grasp what is essentially a point about the competition for talent.

This competitive point underscores the challenge to the university as a thriving and healthy center for thought, and it suggests strongly that our universities, often inefficiently organized bastions of conservatism, are not always the friendliest settings for thoughtful men. Indeed, throughout U.S. institutions of higher

education, the most critical and controversial men are critical first
of the academic institutions and are at war almost always with the
traditional aspects of the university organization itself.

V. THE SHAPE OF THE CONTENT
OF HIGHER EDUCATION

In American university life, as in the life of our cities, a mecha-
nistic and organizational approach to the problems seems to be
preferred. The inflated importance of the appearance of things is
a distressing symptom of a deep schizophrenia in our culture.
Questions about the content of urban life are too difficult and
therefore seem to practical men to be impractical. It's a time of
images—corporate, institutional, national, and individual—and
the image, being but an imitative reflection, is purposely designed
to conceal the reality.

Ben Shahn, the American painter, once gave a lecture at Harvard he called "The Shape of Content." He was dismayed by the
attempt to divorce the content of art from its form. "Content," he
said, "may be and often is trivial. . . . But it can be said with
certainty that the form which does emerge cannot be greater than
the content which went into it. Form is the visible manifestation,
. . . the shape of content."

Among a free and urban people there is an irrevocable bond
between the content of their freedom and the urban form their
life takes. The form of American life is the shape of its content.
The form of the American University is the shape of its content.

When the forms of our life come to dominate its content, the
disconnection between values and conduct can be dangerous. In
our civilization the ascendancy of the forms means that the machine and the organization dictate to the man. Not only the machine but the man as well becomes automated. The man, not only
the organization, becomes bureaucratized.

The formalities of academia threaten to overwhelm the content
of higher education. We educators have become the merchants of
packages which bear the labels of the degrees. We pack the har-
vests of centuries into neat plastic containers which are four,

three, or two years big, and the ultimate reward we give to our students is not for what they understand but for their capacity to conform to the system. The academic calendar relentlessly establishes the boundaries of the courses, which are the basic receptacles into which the academic institution stuffs the bits and pieces of civilization. The credit system arbitrarily evaluates the past as we contemporaneously see its relevance to the present and the future.

The politics of this approach is based upon the laws of scarcity and monopoly. There simply are not enough receptacles to accommodate the productivity of the human enterprise. The courses become crowded tenements, the curriculum, a confused and noisy slum. The premium is placed upon knowing a lot about a little, and the successful scholar becomes in effect a monopolistic slum-lord—keeper, inviolate, of a vertical shaft of knowledge, uninterested in and ill-informed about the other tenements on the curricular block.

The primacy of form over content in the American university has been encouraged in the context of a much larger system, one almost coextensive with the apparent demands of our urban society. As it has appeared that the health of that society is at the mercy of a frivolous technology, we have insisted that the universities accommodate that frivolity. As we have entered into a competitive era in the realms of power politics and science, we have insisted that the universities concentrate upon training people to compete within that framework—and like it.

The form of American life is urban and industrial. Technology is a part of the shape of our content. The content of American life is the guilt and the danger of acquiring and having in a world where most people cannot acquire and have. The content of American life is the sadness of beautiful things once grown from virgin soil now withering and dying on the asphalt. The form of American life is practicality and action. Optimism has been a part of this. The content of American life is a gnawing doubt of the old meanings and the absence of new ones. The content of American life is change and a search for the meaning of it.

Practicality and action, technology, industry and city life place under extraordinary stress the values by which we profess to live.

Those values emerged from a different time and setting. In the twilight of an agricultural age, a growing abyss separates the shape of our life from what we believe we ought to. In the morning of an urbicultural era, we sense the risks of being too venturesome and flirt with the danger of not being bold enough, soon enough.

VI. TENTS, AND THE CITY AS THE CAMPUS

A first small step toward boldness is no longer a matter of choice: it is a necessity compelled by a citified America. The impact of new knowledge upon the content of education forces a reconsideration and overhaul of the formalities and organizational structures of the learning enterprise. We are at a crossroads where the emphasis must be shifted from an educational system which merely serves the technology to a technology harnessed in the service of a new educational system. How may we preserve the great academic traditions of the past and preshape the university mechanism so that the inheritance may be projected effectively into the future?

Within the concept of the modern city, the idea of "campus" is archaic. The wide-open spaces, the monumental and inflexible architecture, and the insulation combine into an anti-urban phenomenon. The campus is more than a place; it is a system. It assumes turning the flow of human relationships inward. Its success depends upon imposing an isolated, contrived community upon the lives of its inhabitants. It is tenured, by the ranks, on a full-time basis in a world where there is no tenure, ranking is officially abhorred, and no man can or should be "full-time" at anything.

Neither the lives of the teachers and the students, nor the problems confronting them, nor the configuration of urban talent conform to the "campus" version of life. "Campus" organizes the university's outrageous presumption that it can and does monopolize the best talents in order to do what it claims to do. In great cities, this presumption is absurd. It leads to the unnatural barracks-like life of the dormitory, to the deadening overlay of welfare-state services undertaken in behalf of "Learning for Freedom." The result is not the life and learning of free men, but a phony world leading students, teachers, their parents and friends to feel that "going to college" is a interlude rather than a part of life.

For the city-based university, the circumstances of the urban environment and the rapidly changing nature of the content and methods of education raise the question: Why build forever? Instead of the conventional approach to building urban academic facilities for permanence and endurance, why not new standards to honor *impermanence* and to accommodate the reality of change? There is tremendous waste in the current processes used to plan and build academic facilities. Many of the new buildings, created to endure a half century or more, embody imperfect translations of what is needed to house the *present* educational operation. (Surprisingly few faculties and administrations can convey clearly to architects and engineers what they are doing *now*.) But there is an almost complete failure by those responsible for building the university to anticipate physical needs ten years ahead— let alone fifty.

Almost no collegiate facility should be financed or built to endure for more than a decade in its original form. The future educational enterprise should be housed in "tents"—the best tents an advanced technology can produce, tents which can quickly be put up or taken down, moved or altered to suit the consequences of the incredible knowledge growth we already confront. Monumentality contradicts the terms of contemporary learning. It is an academic luxury. If it is desired and can be afforded, fine. But the concept of the tent carries with it novel planning and aesthetic possibilities of its own. And it corresponds more accurately to what is in fact going on within the realms of knowledge and the urban territory.

In many ways, the lower schools are the real front lines for the confrontation of the significant urban issues. It has been in the elementary and secondary public schools that the problems of racial integration have hit first and hardest. It has been in these schools that there has been an honest search for new teaching methods, new ways to handle subject matter and to use technology.

Our children in the elementary schools are being taught a

different content at a different pace than we were taught. Current innovations are rapidly changing conceptions of what a high school is. A new understanding of the mission of the secondary school necessarily alters views of what the elementary school is and of what the college and university should be. Future high schools—well before 1980—will do with people aged fifteen and sixteen all or most of what colleges now do with people eighteen and nineteen years old. In consequence, the university arrives at the threshold of profound transformation. Undergraduate education—especially the first year or two of it—is even now unprepared to receive and accommodate the students whom secondary schools are capable of sending them. Teacher education, as it is now practiced in most colleges and universities, *is* embarrassingly irrelevant to the requirements and aspirations of the lower schools in the city.

At the other end of the spectrum—post-degree and adult education—the universities have been equally nonchalant or detached or both. University adult education in the United States is an especially sensitive reflector of the fear of adventure and the dominance of *form* in the academic establishment. For the most part, university adult education has taken the form of a simple translation of the assumptions, pretensions, and contorted content of the undergraduate and graduate curricula. Beyond the assertion of the right of adults to have access to these programs designed for youth, higher adult education in America has had little to say.

Adult education is essentially a renegade aspect of the main theme. It is not pro-credit—it is usually noncredit. If the undergraduate degree programs at night were not inferior to the ones convened during the day, how could the universities justify the main sources of their income or the main objects of their expenditures? A successful adult education program is a serious challenge to the pretensions of the rest of the university. For the highest rewards the university can convey (credits, grades, degrees) are not predicated on the assumption that learning is a lifelong process. Quite the opposite: the traditional university puts a period (the degree) at the end of its sentence, while adult education insists realistically upon a comma.

Too often this dimension of university activity is regarded as a way to accommodate the bothersome cultural lust of an increasingly sophisticated adult urban public, or as a worthwhile therapy for bored middle-class women in search of new status-laden diversions, or as a kind of intellectual garage in which people repair the dents in their educational histories and the damage caused by the impact of a changing technology upon the job market or by the growing American status demand for at least an undergraduate degree.

Except for the limited public to whom the principle of the second chance can legitimately be applied, it is doubtful that undergraduate programs designed for eighteen-year-olds can ever successfully be translated into adult education. Most undergraduate education in our country today is not directed toward the totality of being an adult, but only toward that part of being adult with which a graduate education or the job market is concerned.

At most universities, the graduate faculties have very little to do directly with adult education, except for the people in the colleges of education who service the public-school teachers returning to classes at night in pursuit of promotion and salary increments. Almost every recent study of graduate education in the United States has commented on the conservatism of graduate faculties, the dampening effect of the tenure system upon young talent, the restrictive influence imposed by the rigor of the study of modern science, the dubious impact of empiricism upon the study of the social sciences and the humanities, and the continued unfriendliness of academia to the creative arts. The truth is that the graduate model of higher education is inappropriate for most adult-education programs because it is too narrow or too special, too timid or too easy, too late or too irrelevant.

Most universities, trapped by their own images, see no alternatives for their present adult programs except the models of milder versions of the traditional undergraduate or graduate degree programs or courses. Still, thousands of adults have returned to the great centers of thought with the certain and often desperate conviction that the universities ought to have something to say to them. The educated American adult knows that he lives in a new society, and it is reasonable for him to expect that the great centers of thought respond to the urbicultural content of that society with a relevant, if not a fresh, statement.

The style of city life—the problems of urban people and the patterns of their lives—and the changing content of knowledge combine to suggest the imperative of a continuum in the educational process. The insulation of "campus"—the place and the social system—will no longer do in the city setting. The exclusiveness and separateness of "university" are no longer acceptable, given the educational objectives we have established in this country. A new unity in educational activities at all levels is required.

To achieve this new unity, our universities must rely upon a much broader range of talents than they now employ. Many of the people upon whom the academic institution will have to rely should not and will not devote their full time to the university. Tomorrow's universities will have to be innovators in the mobilization of the best of the total community talents in order to teach, do research, and serve society. The part-time academic connection undoubtedly will become more prevalent than the full-time affiliation, especially in the city where the competition for brain power is bound to intensify.

The future university—reliant upon a wide variety of industrial, governmental, and artistic resources and talents, but unable in view of the competition to *monopolize* the best of these talents available—will be compelled to redefine its concept of "campus." Necessity will lead to an extension of its day-to-day operations beyond the pieces of real estate upon which its special buildings stand. The function of the university will inevitably reach into the theaters, museums, industrial laboratories, libraries, and centers of financial, social and political research housed in other urban institutions.

The future "campus," therefore, will be coincident with the pattern of location of central urban resources and will reach out to where those resources actually are. Great museums may become the future "departments of art." Symphonic and musical organizations may become the future "departments of music." Research centers in banking and finance may become the foundations of future "departments of finance and economics." Hospital research centers may become the future "departments of life sciences." Government commissions and research staffs may become the backbones of future "departments of political science."

Finally, the city itself may become the new campus, and learning—which is in fact coincident with living—intricately interwoven with the day-to-day activities of the city people.

◀ WILLIAM W. MARVEL

The University and the World

THE RETURNED Peace Corps Volunteer has become a familiar phenomenon on American campuses. Recently, one of these bright young men, just back from a two-year stint in a Latin-American country, found himself in a social gathering at the university where he had enrolled in graduate school. During the disjointed conversations that make up such occasions, he was approached by a faculty wife who wanted to know what he felt had been the chief significance of his Peace Corps experience.

His answer showed real penetration. "As I look back on it," he replied frankly, "I am not at all sure that we had much of an impact on the community where we were working. I am afraid our group may not really have been able to leave much there. The big thing was what it all did to us, or at least to me." He went on to explain how those two years had given him a profound respect for the difficulty of bringing about social change, of launching and sustaining programs that move less developed communities even a few inches forward. He would always be much more skeptical, he said, about the charges of inefficiency and "boondoggle" often made against technical-assistance efforts.

"But the really surprising thing," he continued, "was how much my understanding of my own country matured as I saw it and thought about it from that remote spot. All through college I had been told about this, how one could truly know his own country only if he had seen it with the perspective gained by looking at it from afar." But during college this had been only so many words,

64

only an abstract concept. The meaning had not really come through then, but during his two years in Latin America it did.

"The race riots in Harlem and in the Watts section of Los Angeles took place while I was overseas," he said. "I didn't know the details or the immediate causes of those outbursts. But I had a context of grinding poverty and frustration and misery to see them in, because that was what I had all around me. I really doubt that for most comfortably fixed middle-class Americans the words 'poverty' and 'social discrimination' are much more than abstract concepts. For me they have become a living reality."

KNOWLEDGE AND RESPONSIBILITY

This returned Peace Corps volunteer was not deliberately addressing himself to the meaning of international education. He did not intend to discuss the relationship of American universities to the outside world. But unwittingly he had perceived one of the fundamental purposes of this whole area of endeavor by United States higher education. If our schools and junior colleges, our four-year colleges and universities, and our graduate and professional schools could all succeed in implanting in the minds and hearts of Americans a few simple understandings of this kind, one of the chief goals of international education would be within reach. That goal—simple to state but hard to achieve—is to provide *all Americans* with the knowledge, habits of thought, and sense of curiosity such as to enable them over a full lifetime—at least as concerned citizens, perhaps as active participants—to confront and deal with the complexities of this imperfect world. Thus, our interest as a nation is both intellectual and instrumental: we want to understand the great forces that are acting on the different countries of the world, including our own, and that are influencing the relations among them; but also, from a position of informed understanding, we want to help shape and guide those forces toward the major goals we believe all men share. *All* Americans must be included in this definition of national purpose, because under our political system every American is assumed to bear responsibility as an informed citizen. Otherwise, where could we draw the line to demarcate those citizens for whom knowledge of world affairs was deemed irrelevant?

Finally, such a formulation of this national objective includes our many efforts to assist people of other countries—through education and other means—and to learn from them in the process. But to succeed in those efforts, we Americans must first be educated. We must be knowledgeable of and sensitive to the cultures and ways and aspirations of others. Thus, we come quickly back to our universities and colleges, for on them rests the heavy burden of leadership and performance in this formidable task of educating ourselves.

Our hope in this essay is to look ahead and perceive what the forces of interaction between the universities and the world at large will produce by 1980. What changes will a dozen years bring? What new problems will emerge? What old problems will deepen? What current issues may hopefully be resolved?

The most useful framework in which to consider this matter, it seems to me, is the several levels of responsibility that confront American education as a consequence of our position of both leadership and interdependence in the world. These are familiar, but they are worth restating because they provide the ultimate rationale of all the effort and resources we put into international education:

1. There is first the *overall responsibility of the United States as a nation* to contribute to a peaceful and progressive world order, a responsibility growing out of the prosperity this country enjoys and the appalling power that it commands, a responsibility that can be met only if the world of higher learning accepts a primary role.

2. There is then, the *responsibility of education generally*— from kindergarten through the Ph.D.—to prepare young Americans as educated citizens ready to handle their part of this imperative. There is, more specifically, the responsibility of teachers and institutions, at each educational level, to interpret and implement their own distinctive roles in the large pattern.

The elementary and secondary schools, the technical institutes, the junior colleges, the extension systems and continuing-education programs—what standards must they measure up to in world-affairs education?

3. And at the apex of our system, there is the *special—and formidable—responsibility* that rests on the universities and colleges.

We Americans expect a great deal of our institutions of higher learning: to teach students and the teachers of students; through research, to add to the pool of knowledge and understanding in all fields—liberal, scientific, professional and technical; to stimulate educational progress and reform in the schools; to contribute manpower and skills to the solution of almost any social problem; to assist the people, the school systems, and the universities of other countries—in a word, to provide leadership not only for education and the so-called knowledge industries, but for society at large.

Is this too big an order? Have the colleges and universities already exceeded reasonable limits in accepting more responsibility than they can effectively manage? Many intelligent observers believe they have; and this issue—"galloping multiversity-itis" *versus* "cultivator of the minds of men"—will be vigorously debated for years to come.

The question that interests us here—the impact of world affairs on the U.S. university, and the university's impact on the world— is wrapped in this theme of multiple levels of responsibility. However an individual institution reacts, whatever the response of American universities collectively, the forces and the challenges of international affairs will exercise a powerful influence on every campus. This is the case today. It will even more emphatically be the case by 1980. Trends just now discernible will accelerate. Things now experimental will be generalized. And, if we are lucky, a few bright new ideas will be churned up to help resolve our multiplying dilemmas. Perhaps our greatest hope for these next 12 years should be that the ability of the universities to interpret and define their responsibilities more knowledgeably than before, set their priorities more skillfully, and cope more effectively with the demands made on them by developments in every corner of the world.

LOOKING BACK TO SEE AHEAD

Most of the current trends and directions on the international side of higher education have emerged during the living memory of those who now labor in this vineyard. But to many of us, the pace seems painfully slow. The road is winding and full of ruts. Our patience wears thin. There is no easier exercise than to describe the shortfall as American education has sought to come of age in international affairs.

But have we truly moved only at a snail's pace these last two decades? If our object here is to make some educated guesses as to how this aspect of higher education will develop by 1980, we must first be clear as to where we stood 15 or 20 years *ago;* 1946 is a good bench mark. It was midway in a decade dominated by depression and war, a period of little ferment in the universities and colleges of the land. In fact, there was relatively little development in the world-affairs aspects of higher education during the entire 30 years down to 1950. So to take a rough measure of how far we had come by 1966, we could go back to 1946, or 1936, or indeed to 1926. True, there would be decade variations, but over all, it was, in the matters that concern us here, a remarkably "stable" period.

Let us, therefore, fix on a bright young student who, as a freshman in 1936, was highly motivated for the study of international relations. He entered a major Eastern university, one of the very few institutions in the country with any kind of reputation for prestige work in international studies. In the curriculum, he found that most of the work which interested him was confined to a set pattern of courses: European diplomatic history (those tedious meanderings through the chanceries of Vienna, Berlin, Paris, and London); international economics and finance (a highly traditional laissez-faire approach to the theory of international trade and monetary transactions); and international politics, law, and organization (where some time was spent analyzing and much time lamenting the ineffectiveness of the League of Nations and the paralysis that afflicted the Anglo-Franco-American world as the storm clouds of a new war gathered).

Among his teachers, he was unlikely to encounter any sociologist, psychologist, demographer, or perhaps even anthropologist who had intimate firsthand knowledge of any other part of the world than Europe. "Overseas research" was a phrase that had not yet entered the educational lexicon; it was apparently an activity engaged in by archeologists in the Near East, with pick and shovel, or by classical scholars at the American Academy in Rome, or by historians in the Paris archives and the London Museum. Teachers of French language and literature went to Provence during vacations and professors of international organization summered in Geneva. But the foreign experience of faculty people rarely extended beyond these conventionalized patterns.

The young man's career opportunities probably appeared to him as a crossroads at which he stood looking down two straight highways that moved into the future at sharply angled directions. He could take the Foreign Service exams and become, if he passed, a Class 8 vice-consul in the Latin-American tropics, inching his way upward through the diplomatic service over the next 40 years. Or he might go on to graduate school and become a teacher of the subject, or to law school and hope to find his way into the esoteric world of international law. There was neither AID, USIA, or Peace Corps; nor were there opportunities abroad with the Ford or Rockefeller Foundations; and almost none of the present complement of private agencies that send young Americans to study and work in foreign countries had been developed. In fact, during his undergraduate and graduate years and chances of his having an overseas experience were close to zero. There was no Fulbright program, no Social Science Research Council Training Fellowships, no Ford Foundation Foreign Area Fellowships. Rare indeed was the university that had money of its own to permit students at any level to work or study in a foreign country.

The educational possibilities in world affairs open to our student of the 1930s mirrored the actual role of the United States in the world. The content was parochial, underdeveloped and Europe-focused; the approach tended to be traditional and moralistic (recall how the nation was then defining its national interest through endless debates over the finer points of the Neutrality Act!); and his teachers knew little of the vast world of Russia, the Near East, Asia, Africa, and Latin America that lies out beyond the familiar capitals of London, Paris, Rome, and Vienna.

It is worth remembering, finally, that we set the stage for this vignette of the 1930s in terms of one of the large Eastern institutions that could, in that day, claim leadership in the study of international affairs. We were not reviewing an "average" situation. This suggests how bleak the general landscape was for university-level work in world affairs.

The sharp contrasts awaiting the son of our student from the 1930s as he enters college in 1968 are too apparent to belabor: they are implicit in every characterization of that earlier period. Opportunities abound for young men and women today to build their higher education around the subject matter of international relations and the study of other cultures, or at least to learn something about this field along the way as they pursue their degrees in other professional, scientific, or disciplinary areas. The world has surely come to the doorstep of the American campus. And the student quite literally does make the world his campus.

TWO KINDS OF FORECASTS FOR 1980

There is little in the present picture to portend a reversal of this trend. On the contrary, many forces are at work to sustain it and to accelerate it. We may confidently look forward to the further unfolding of rich experience-opportunities by the time the entering freshmen of 1980 arrive on campus. Inexorably, the United States will move closer to its goal in international education, giving an appropriate degree of familiarity with—of basic "literacy" in—world affairs to every young American.

In attempting to visualize the American campus of 1980 in its world affairs relationships, we must take account of two kinds of forecasts. One kind is easy, as it concerns changes that seem so probable as to be almost inevitable. Here are included the ideas, programs, courses, and approaches which are now so well "seeded" through American academia that we can anticipate their "sprouting" on the average campus at least by 1980.

The other kind of forecast, however, is fraught with doubts and uncertainties. There are several complex but compelling problems that block the way to the full flowering of international educational activity. These issues require the most rigorous grappling with basic knowledge and fundamental administrative arrangements, and demand heavily concerted efforts for their solution. But since, as of 1968, they are not receiving anything approaching the attention they deserve, it is exceedingly risky to predict how and when and if these problems will be solved. They are, in my view, the major challenges we should keep in the forefront of our thinking as we head up the road toward 1980. Holding these refractory problems aside for the moment, however, let us first consider the more easily definable trends, the developments that are likely to move along steadily with the momentum already generated.

THE UPWARD TREND CURVES

The first and most obvious forecast for 1980 is that there will be, as it were, more of everything. The visual evidence of international activity on the American campus will continue to mount. All trend curves will be up. More foreign students will come to our shores, although a growing proportion of them will be at the graduate level. With respect to undergraduates from abroad, we will begin to show increased sophistication in the way they are screened and selected for admission to American institutions. We will make some progress in fitting foreign students—graduate and undergraduate—more imaginatively into our educational framework. We shall get around at last to making adaptations and special arrangements on our campuses so that their training here will be more relevant to the needs and opportunities of their own countries in Africa, Asia, and Latin America.

Again, although the numbers will probably grow, there will be a slowing down of the proliferation rate of American undergraduate programs abroad. It requires a high degree of optimism to believe that we shall have brought greater ordering and higher quality into the present array of such programs; but inasmuch as we are finally becoming aware of the serious problems American undergraduate programs are creating for foreign universities, there are grounds for cautious hope that we shall see some progress.

The exchange of professors and scholars will increase numerically, although new frameworks will emerge and many of our present programs will have been reviewed and revised before 1980. We will almost certainly have reached a new and higher plane of understanding concerning the international mobility and migration of high-level manpower, especially intellectual and scientific manpower. We will no longer be discussing these problems under the essentially perjorative rubric of "brain drain." Twelve years hence we shall have come to understand how to reduce those aspects of the migration which seriously impinge on the underdeveloped countries, and on the other hand, how to accommodate to those flows of academic people which are inevitable and which strengthen and enrich human society generally.

One will, of course, find important indices of growth in the university and college curriculum itself. There will continue to be readaptation, refinement and spread of various approaches so far begun experimentally or developed in the limited setting of one or a few institutions. We are now farther advanced in offering suitable programs for students who wish to specialize in the international field than we are in assuring through the curriculum that the great body of American students gains some familiarity with world affairs. So by 1980 we may expect to see considerably more experimentation and development in the infusion of existing "high traffic" courses with an international dimension, further refinement of non-Western studies in liberal education, the strengthening of area-studies programs, and more general international-affairs courses covering a spectrum of disciplines. All of this will tend to diminish the chances for even the unsuspecting college student of the 1980s to move through his undergraduate years without rubbing up against courses and professors that will leave him with some sense of world affairs.

Even if the drives within the world of education itself were not moving matters in this direction, developments bringing on the era of mass jet-speed travel and instant global communications would be doing so. Beyond all the changes that will come as the result of the conventional thought and work of educators, the 1980 atmosphere will be literally full of the means of rapid travel and fast communications (two-hour plane trips to Europe and prospects beyond Telstar for mass intercontinental communication). The impact of all this on the American campus will produce a quantum jump in the sense of proximity which students in 1980 will have to the larger outer world.

FLEXIBILITY IN TIME AND SPACE

The world affairs content of education will be much affected by this upward movement in the numerical indices. But there will be another kind of outcome of at least equal significance for the students of 1980: a new flexibility and adjustability in the flow and sequence of the educational process. As a nation and as a complex of two thousand or more campuses, we will move ever farther away from the traditional concept of a "college education" as a four-year block of time spent on a campus with one's agemates. Instead, "higher education" is being transformed into a series of experiences of different types, interspersed through much of one's lifetime after the adolescent years. This is by no means a phenomenon exclusively of the international dimension in higher education, but it is influencing, and being influenced, by the world-affairs relationships of America's campuses.

Already the four-three sequence (four undergraduate years immediately followed by three graduate or professional school years) is breaking up. Significant educational experiences are intervening—within each level and between college and graduate school. The Peace Corps overseas and the various domestic service corps at home represent perhaps the major new factor tending to press the sequence into a four-two-three chain. Internships in the U.S. or abroad, in government and in business, are further complicating the old, straight progression. At the college level such innovations as Princeton's critical-languages program are fostering a new degree of intercollegiate mobility for students during the four undergraduate years, in this case for those who decide to embark early on the mastery of one of the difficult and "exotic" foreign languages. (The revolutionary implications of international education are infinite: the critical-languages program, under which students from other institutions spend one year at Princeton, has brought the first breach in Princeton's 220-year tradition as an all-male college!)

The idea of midcareer training, or carefully designed "career development" in which the individual alternates between periods on the job and refresher work on the campus, is an increasingly familiar phenomenon. And it seems likely that the universities and colleges will in general assume a larger responsibility for adult education in all its forms, including the continuing education of mature citizens in subjects relating to world affairs.

As the old pattern—four years in college and then out to a job —breaks down, there will be important results for the international dimension of liberal learning in America. Back-and-forth movement between work and education, at whatever level, is obviously in better tune with the dynamism and rapid change of the present world, and the consequent need for retraining and catching up on new developments, than is the conventional static concept of having an education for all time once it is obtained. Furthermore, there is created an enriching flow of knowledge and experience from the campus to real world situations and back again. And finally, the more there is of this movement to and from the campuses, the more easily individuals can transfer between essentially educational settings and work settings, then the more likely it becomes that we will develop the kind of broadly qualified and experienced people we must have to tackle the immensely complicated jobs which face our country and every other country of the world.

DIFFUSION AMONG THE COLLEGES
AND UNIVERSITIES

The third change we must note is also easily predictable but it is of great importance for the nation as a whole. It is here that "the average American campus" begins to experience the impact of world affairs. By 1980 we will be far along in the diffusion across the face of American higher education of courses and programs concerned with the peoples and cultures of other countries and their political and economic development—the world-affairs content of education now confined to a minority of institutions. What was limited for our entering freshman in 1936 to a very few campuses, has been extended in reasonable measure to 250 or 300 higher institutions by 1968. By 1980 it will have been felt at virtually every institution of higher learning in the United States. The so-called developing institutions will quicken the pace of their advance on this front during the next 15 years. Those junior colleges, four-year colleges, and even universities which are starting from lower baselines, will discover new ways to introduce the subject matter of international affairs into their curricula, to retain or extend the competence of college teachers, and to discover other means of giving their instructional programs and campus life a significant world-affairs content even though they cannot count on the high-priced faculty talent and research programs such as are available to the leading universities. The distance separating the front-rank institutions from those at the end of the file will narrow considerably—which is not the same thing as saying that the gap itself will be insignificant. It is simply that, beginning in the late 1960s, their rate of advance will be relatively faster than that of those universities and colleges which are already well out in front.

More federal money will become available for the colleges, for their student programs and faculty development. The advantages of multi-institution cooperative arrangements will be more widely recognized. Texts and other teaching materials to support college-level work in non-Western and international studies will be produced in greater quantity and improved quality. The large contingent of community and junior colleges will gradually enroll in the ranks of institutions giving their students a meaningful exposure to world affairs. This process of diffusion will be an outward extension of courses, programs, and study arrangements throughout the fabric of American education. Its result will be to reduce substantially the likelihood that any student who goes on to postsecondary schooling will emerge illiterate about the great forces at work in this fast-changing world.

ADMINISTRATION AND COORDINATION
ON THE CAMPUS

The activities of American universities and colleges in the area of international affairs—whether on the home campus or overseas —are only one of the sets of factors making them ever more complex institutions. Just as other developments related to their conventional domestic roles have pushed them toward more elaborate administrative structures, so this tendency has been reinforced by the requirements stemming from their new international responsibilities. Increasingly, the universities have recognized the need to define appropriate relationships among the foreign students on campus, overseas contracts and programs, non-Western and area studies, training programs for foreign service, and the variety of other activities which are a part of the institution's web of involvement with the outside world. A new pattern is therefore becoming common: the focusing of central institutional responsibility in a dean of international programs, chairman of an interdepartmental faculty committee on international studies, an assistant to the president, or in some cases even a vice-president or vice-chancellor.

The first explicit move of this kind was the establishment of the post of Dean of International Programs at Michigan State University in the mid-1950s. Less than ten years later some reasonable equivalent of this position had emerged on at least 75 other campuses. The rapid expansion of university international activities means that by 1980 we are likely to find that every university of any consequence will have responded to this need for coordinated central planning by creating this kind of new administrative post. Many colleges will also probably have moved in that direction, but here we can expect a more diverse pattern of separate institutional response because of the many different patterns of internationalization of curriculum and campus life which the hundreds of college-level institutions will adopt.

This trend is not to be deplored, it seems to me, as some kind of inexorable Parkinsonism in university administration. The mutual reinforcement among programs and activities and the maximum enrichment of institutional life, are not likely to be achieved unless concerted efforts to that end are made. The reasons for moving to this new administrative arrangement on the campus will vary—local institutional politics, prestige considerations, the more effective pursuit of outside funds, or the determination of president or trustees to prevent technical assistance and overseas activities from gaining ascendancy over the instructional program on the campuses. But in almost every case the decisive factor will be the need felt by the president, dean, faculty, or the students themselves for the university to make regular assessments of its total pattern and role in the area of world affairs. This need does not arise so long as the institution is confined to offering a few conventional courses in foreign languages, history, economics and politics, and to having a couple of dozen foreign students on the campus. As its involvement deepens, however, as it moves along the spectrum toward the Universities of Wisconsin, Stanford, Illinois, and Indiana, it will soon find that the relaxed individualism and unplanned laissez faire it had been enjoying will have to give way to concerted institutional policies and priorities.

FINANCE AND FEDERAL RELATIONS

One cannot long speculate on where higher education is headed in its international dimension without soon raising questions as to future financial support. Carrying our full complement of colleges and universities forward in the directions they will want to go is a costly proposition. Funds will have to be provided in an entirely new order of magnitude. To undergird the total effort we will be capable of sustaining by 1980, the federal government is almost certain to become the dominant source of funds, whereas in 1967 it was clearly the junior partner.

Recent developments provide some important clues to what the picture will look like 12 years hence. The International Education Act, passed during the closing hours of the Eighty-ninth Congress in 1966, is a landmark for the sector of American educational development we are concerned with here. It places international education firmly in the framework of American national interest; it authorizes sharp, progressive increases in funds to be made available for international studies at both the graduate and under-graduate levels; and it makes certain shifts and rearrangements in the pattern of federal support.

The Act enlarges considerably the authority and responsibility of the Department of Health, Education and Welfare in this field. It portends the movement of the center of gravity in international education away from the foreign-affairs agencies which have been dominant until the present time (the Department of State, the Agency for International Development, and the United States Information Agency), toward that department—HEW—which is charged with the chief responsibility for the health and progress of American education itself. It is reasonable to expect that, well before 1980, HEW and its newly created Center for Educational Cooperation will have begun to carry out the charge President Johnson has given them: to become the focal point of thought and leadership in the federal government for international education.

The delay that occurred during 1967 in Congressional funding of the International Education Act proved disappointing for all who had hoped for a rapid start-up of this new federal program. But a balanced view of the situation, based on recognition of the special problems obtaining in the 1967 session of Congress, supports the hope that we have witnessed a shift in the timetable of federal support rather than a basic change in our national commitment.

Another development of 1966 which portends new and more sophisticated federal-private relations by 1980 relates to government sponsorship and financing of social and behavioral research

overseas. Various episodes and events which came to the forefront
of national attention during 1965 and early 1966 revealed the extent to which certain elements of the scholarly community and a
few federal agencies had fallen into rather easy and casual practices.[1] Responsibility for the embarrassment occasioned by these
revelations and for the more general doubts and anxieties which
they generated, was fairly evenly divided between the private
scholars and the government agencies involved. Neither the Defense Department, the State Department or CIA on the one hand,
nor certain groups and individuals in the university community on
the other, had given serious attention to devising a code of ethics
or a statement of acceptable practices. And short of this, it is unlikely that the reputation of independence and objectivity of
American research can be sustained. That reputation was weakened especially in the eyes of the intellectual and scholarly communities of other countries.

There is now a reasonable hope that by 1980 (indeed, we must
reach this point much earlier) we shall have achieved a relationship of greater integrity and maturity between the sensitive
foreign-affairs agencies and the private scholars whose work is of
interest to them. In 1966 for the first time we witnessed a sober,
concerted confrontation of this problem. Professional groups, national scholarly and scientific bodies, a Senate subcommittee, certain universities and colleges, and a number of individual scholars
—all engaged in profound soul-searching and probing reexamination of the rights, the duties, and the stakes involved in sorting out
this tangled skein between the government and the private academic community. Not this year or next, but within four or five
years, there is a good prospect that we shall have pushed these
matters up on to a new plane of candor and openness.

If this hopeful forecast proves out, the result will be to reorder
and regularize the flow of money from the federal government

[1] This was written prior to the widely publicized disclosures of February
1967 concerning covert CIA support of certain U.S. voluntary organizations
in international affairs. Although the focus here is on federal government–
scholarly community relationships in overseas research, the basic principles
involved are similar to those the nation was vigorously debating during the
first half of 1967.

into the scholarly community for social and behavioral research, especially funds to conduct field studies in foreign countries. U.S. scholars could obviously use more funds for overseas social-science research than are now available. But it would be alarming rather than comforting if the amounts were to be increased before the crucial job of rethinking the ethics and propriety of the relationship had been accomplished. If the present momentum is maintained, however, the next several years should bring substantial progress toward honorable accommodation. This would be a development of critical significance not only in calming the fears and suspicions that are abroad in the U.S., but in reassuring the intellectual communities of Chile, Nigeria, India, the Philippines, and other countries where American researchers seek ready access and a friendly reception.

One further aspect of the financing of international education should be noted: the need to ensure full and constructive use, for education and related purposes, of the large sums of U.S. held foreign currencies. As a nation, we have been singularly unimaginative in putting these resources to work for the mutual benefit of the U.S. and the "host country." Such utilization as has occurred (the Fulbright program, other scattered exchange activities, and the local currency budgets of U.S. embassies and missions) has been woefully ineffective in preventing these reserves from growing, in some cases, into veritable Fort Knoxes of foreign-currency holdings. Finally, in 1966 we had a glimmer of the possibilities for the future: the proposal for a large binational foundation in India financed by U.S.-held Indian rupees. Here was the first substantial idea to release the enormous power for constructive action which is locked away in these foreign-currency holdings. If this proposal can be translated into action and other creative means found to deal with the problem of excess currencies, 1980 will see a vigorous flow of benefits to the campuses of America.

ULTIMATE INFUSION

There is one last angle from which the future impact of world affairs on the American university and college should be considered. In one sense, this is a summary and generalization of all the trends that have been projected in the preceding pages. What we are likely to produce in this country is an educational system almost every segment of which—every department, nearly every professional school, many courses, all sections of the multicampus universities—will have a significant international perspective woven into its own fabric. No discipline will be unaffected, no student will be untouched.

This means that by 1980 we will then have moved far across the spectrum from the usual situation 20 years ago, when almost everything having to do with foreign affairs was set apart in separate and highly visible institutes, centers, and formal programs. But by 1980, instead of being the preserve of a relatively small group of specialists, "international affairs" will be a widely distributed aspect of education and of life—something that most students and professors experience and work on through the course of their adult lifetimes. This imperceptible permeation of world affairs through higher education generally and through almost every campus will reflect the way the life of our national society is itself becoming increasingly "international"—in tone, in orientation, and in concern.

THE GROUNDS FOR OPTIMISM

Lest this effort to glimpse an important aspect of the American campus in 1980 seem excessively sanguine, we should be clear about the grounds we have for a reasonable degree of optimism. There is, of course, no implication that all of this will get done while we lie back and let "inexorable forces" already in motion guide us along. The sheer amount of work to be done, the new efforts to be mounted will be easily sufficient to challenge us all. The task can absorb every bit of energy and ingenuity we can summon.

The optimism which has pervaded the essay to this point springs from the conviction that the right combination of resources will be available over the next 12 years for us to show dramatic progress—if we are ready to work at it. We have a reasonably clear picture of our goals. There has already been considerable experimentation with methods and techniques, both curricular and cocurricular. There is bright prospect for funds, from both public and private sources, which will be adequate to support the extension of a world affairs dimension throughout the campuses of the land. Above all, there seems every reason to expect a sustained supply of the necessary "raw materials": the flow of bright young men and women interested in world affairs, as professionals or as citizens, shows no sign of tapering off.

There is one aspect of our situation which above all others justifies a certain modicum of optimism. No other country in the modern period has ever exhibited such massive, concerted, and organized intellectual curiosity about other peoples and other cultures. It may be only self-interest that drives us to learn about Indian religion and philosophy, Nigerian federation and tribalism, the relationships between Argentina and Chile, the dietary habits of the Tibetans, the mystical politics of Indonesia, and about hundreds of other questions generally in the area of world affairs. But if it is self-interest, it is an extraordinarily enlightened self-interest! It rarely damages those about whom we indulge our curiosity—indeed, the net effect on this nation may well be to make us more sophisticated and more compassionate in the way we wield our fearsome power.

To sharpen the contrast, what other great nation at the pinnacle of world power spent generously of public funds to encourage serious university study of the peoples, the civilizations, and the cultures of practically every part of the world? One case in point is the recent and rather late development of such studies at British universities. Despite centuries of British involvement in Latin America, for example, there has been little academic interest and next to nothing offered in the curriculum concerning that major group of countries. Other evidence comes easily, for the same general picture characterizes France, Germany, Italy, Belgium, and Scandinavia. Some will consider this a self-serving comparison and will say that we alone are prosperous enough to afford these expensive research and teaching efforts. Others will attribute everything to American leadership in the social sciences. But these answers are too pat. The better explanation is that there were men in this country during and after World War II who read correctly the auguries of the American future. They realized that great power and vast responsibility in the world were the United States' destiny but that such power and responsibility could not be wisely exercised without a formidable educational undergirding. So the issue was joined and by 1950 the building of those foundations got under way in earnest. Clearly the end is not in sight.

THE TEMPERING OF OPTIMISM:
SOBERING REFLECTIONS ON THE TASK AHEAD

To pursue this line of discourse further, however, is to risk being lifted off the ground into a state of complacency. As noted earlier, there is a second kind of forecast, must riskier than the first, that acts to curb easy optimism about present trends. So we must stop short and ask ourselves whether indeed our road into the future is such a wide, straight 80-mile-per-hour superhighway, clear of obstacles, ruts, and detours. May there not be some high hurdles to clear if the United States is to be as proud of its record in 1980 as perhaps it has the right to be in 1968?

There is, of course, no doubt that we face stern challenges. Every observer has his own preferred list. The three issues with which I will conclude this essay are those that seem to me most complex and most compelling. One has to do with the problems of the universities as complex institutions; another concerns the need for a new kind of professional person; and the last is the question whether we can mobilize the intellectual power necessary to solve one of the great riddles of national development in the less advanced countries.

These three problems are separated out from the trends and forecasts in the earlier part of the essay because here we have small cause to be sanguine. There is no hint that practical answers await us just around the corner. Little experimentation has occurred. We are still groping, extemporizing, often fumbling. But the stakes are high—for American education and for the progress and stability of the disadvantaged peoples of the world.

THE UNIVERSITY: WHOLE OR FRACTURED?

The first of these challenges is to bring a new unity and sense of concerted purpose into the university. We are all familiar with the landscape as it now is—with schools and departments resembling local field stations of their respective professional societies more than integral parts of a single institution; and with the lines of affiliation and respect running between schools and departments in the same field on different campuses rather than forming the cement within the institution itself. Can ways be found to restrain and then reserve this trend toward massive disunity and incoherence within the university? Can a more meaningful relationship be established among the parts? Can some measure of wholeness be restored to the academic institution?

The importance of this goal lies not in satisfying some formal sense of symmetry and compactness. Even less does it mean that the university can become fully unified and coherent in a world that shows the opposite characteristics. What it points to is an urgent need that we have as a people: that there be at least one kind of institution in our society that serves as a countervailing force against the driving power of high concentration and narrow specialization. Somewhere men must strive for the larger picture, the wider concepts and approaches capable of relating to a larger scheme the contributions of the deep-burrowing experts and the ingenious technicians. Where will this happen if it does not happen in the universities?

International programs and involvements obviously are not the only centrifugal influences at work on the university, but they help to dramatize the problem. They are part of the fracturing process. One major subdivision of the university, its social-science and humanities departments, encompasses the teaching of students in non-Western cultures and international studies. There is usually little relation, and almost no communication, between those departments and the overseas service and technical-assistance activities largely emanating from the professional schools on the campus.[2] And if the foreign-student adviser is closely in touch with either of these academic complexes, if he is striving to relate foreign students on campus to the larger teaching and service roles of the university, this is likely to be one of those fateful accidents, the great exception that proves the rule.

There is more than apocryphal legend in the oft-told tale of the engineering school which some years ago undertook an AID program in the Philippines. Several members of the engineering faculty had been at work in the field for some months before encountering several social-science scholars who turned out to be from the same home campus 10,000 miles away. Five minutes' conversation revealed that they were part of the parent university's area-studies program on Southeast Asia—which happened to emphasize the Philippines and happened to be situated on campus about 150 yards from the engineering building!

Among other purposes, it is to avoid such egregious noncommunication and mutual ignorance among the several parts of the campus that many large complex institutions are appointing university-wide deans, program directors, and coordinating-committee chairmen for international activities. In practical fact, however, these new academic administrators usually function within the perimeters of the liberal-arts sector of the university. Even when their responsibilities are defined more broadly, they tend to have little influence in the professional schools. But, in any event, we could not afford to rely on this kind of administrative and organizational answer to so profound a problem, one that goes to the very heart of the university's role, purposes, and functions in society. And clearly the question is not one that can be answered in terms of the international side of higher education alone. Nevertheless, any progress we can show toward cohesion

[2] Neither the on-campus teaching contingent nor the professionally based overseas group is, of course, a monolith. Each is likely to be riven through with disunities and fractures of its own. Neither social scientists nor humanists nor engineers nor agriculturalists nor any other disciplinary or professional group is, to say the least, uniformly dedicated to the importance of an international dimension in higher education.

and reintegration within the universities *generally* will also make them stronger and more effective institutions for their expanding role in world affairs.

THE NEW ACADEMIC PROFESSIONAL

On the human-resources front, American universities face a sharp test of their ability to gear up for the demands they and the nation will face in 1980. This is the question, whether they can define, train, and provide a hospitable setting for the new kind of academic professional man that the times call for. This man is the generalizer, the synthesizer, the one who can transfer ideas from one field to another, who acts as catalyst and can function as stimulator of constructive action. He may be a social architect or institution builder, an original-minded innovator or a skilled adaptor of the ideas of others.

This new professional man must be one who can function across disciplinary and professional lines. He may be an adviser to other countries on the development of their universities and on the planning of their educational systems. Or, on a very different front, his skill may be in sifting out the best and most relevant of university and college work in international studies in order to adapt it to the lower-school levels.

Obviously this is not *a* new man we have defined so much as a number of new kinds of men, all professionally trained academic generalists with different combinations of education, experience, and skills. But is it realistic to expect the universities to train such people? One's optimism on this question is quickly tempered by looking out over the academic landscape. High-quality interdisciplinary programs of the type needed to develop our new professional generalists are quite the exception. Confinement of education within the high walls of traditional departments and professional schools is still the rule.

In estimating the prospects for turning out these broad-gauged professionals in substantial numbers by 1980, we must never underestimate the power of academic conservatism. We must be reminded that the large majority of university faculty and research people, after all, work primarily in the circumscribed setting of a department or professional school. (Anyone who knows campus life, furthermore, realizes how often social life is concentrated within the same group setting!)

Few faculty people have occasion to stand off and think broadly about their university as an institution performing certain key functions in society. Rarely have they the opportunity to see it whole or to understand the problem of striking a balance among its diverse responsibilities for research, teaching, and service, both at home and in the outside world. Short of major shifts in orientation and attitudes, therefore, it is doubtful that the universities will succeed in evolving the academic programs necessary to produce the new professional types so urgently required for the tasks of international education.

Equally gloomy, it seems to me, is the outlook for the establishment by the universities of suitable long-term career patterns for the new academic professional type. There would have to be the kind of flexibility which permits—indeed, which encourages—a man to move in and out of an institution by design, to build a productive, respectable, and satisfying career while dividing his time between teaching and research at home, and service activities overseas. To attract and hold men of high ability in this professional generalist role, they must somehow be able to achieve a status of "full accreditation" in the intellectual life of the campus.

Unfortunately, all the canons and conventions by which the inner departmental heartland of American academia is governed militate against this result. The demands on the "proper professor" are unchanging over time—except in the direction of greater rigidity. He shall publish much, engage in controversy little, and make his absences from the campus brief and occasional! So we cannot conclude on a note of confidence. The prospects seem slim indeed for gearing fully into the university community this new corps of "irregulars," of scholar-practitioners, of men of both thought and action. Still, the job deserves working at; and perhaps somewhere this side of 1980 we will find the new leverage points by which the glacial inertia can be overcome.

THE CRUCIAL RIDDLE OF NATIONAL DEVELOPMENT

We have now asked whether 12 years hence American universities will have demonstrated their ability to handle the growing responsibilities being pressed on them in the realm of world affairs, first, by achieving greater cohesion and focus inside the institutions themselves, and second, by providing the kinds of education and training needed to produce a new kind of professional generalist. And, with respect to both questions, we have concluded that the jury is still out.

Finally, we turn to one of the most formidable and complex problems we could raise, one that literally poses the issue of life or death for most of the world's underdeveloped people. It can perhaps best be stated as the circular cause-and-effect relationship, the complex interaction, among three sets of phenomena: medical and public-health knowledge and techniques; population growth; and increase in the production of food.

In most underdeveloped countries, a tenuous balance prevails between population and food. Any intervention may upset the delicate relationship. Down through history, most such interventions were by the natural forces of flood, drought, and pestilence. When they occurred, they produced famine, starvation, epidemic illness, and widespread death. A new balance was then established between man and his means of subsistence, but at a lower population level.

In his present efforts to bring modernization to the less advanced countries, *man* intervenes in this causal cycle. He possesses the knowledge and techniques to act on several of the forces which affect the balance. Through medical science and public sanitation, health is improved and life prolonged. The population increases, not through any dramatic change in human fertility but because of a sharp decline in mortality: fewer people are dying younger, so to speak, all the way from infancy to senility. At the fertility end of the cycle, of course, man has the technical knowledge to restrain population growth through birth control.

And his new scientific knowledge and agricultural techniques can expand food production.

But—and it is a most formidable "but"—this process of human intervention upsets the balance by affecting unevenly the rates of change. Man's instruments are more powerful and more instantly effective in the medical and health fields (leading to relatively rapid increases in population) than in birth control and the increase of food production. In the very short run, the death rate can be cut precipitously because the introduction of health measures corresponds to one of mankind's basic elemental drives, that of being rid of disease and clinging to life. Even in the most primitive societies, there are few cultural resistances to potable water supplies, vaccines and injections, and maternal and child care.

But the expansion of food production is slow and tedious and often not very successful. Other forces in a modernizing society may, at least in the short run, tend to reduce agricultural production. Forced-draft industrialization draws men away from the land at the very stage of development when there is no food margin for survival. This tendency is reinforced by the strong magnetic power exerted by the cities, drawing people off the land by the thousands into the maelstrom of urban congestion and unemployment. With both the agricultural revolution necessary to keep food in balance with population and the newer approaches to family planning and population control, efforts on both of these fronts are likely to encounter powerful cultural, religious, and philosophical resistances.

But merely to restate this problem of the vicious public-health-population-food circle, especially in the simplified version presented here, does not advance matters greatly. It is already familiar, with all its cataclysmic overtones. Our purpose in reviewing it is to provide the background for this question: How can America weld its vast resources of scholarly knowledge and practical skills into a formidable weapon capable of piercing the tough hide of this problem? We have both the fundamental knowledge and the men who can apply it, the experts and technicians in each relevant field. But have we the intellectual capability to shape a strategy based on the *interaction* and the *time-space relationships* among these forces of social change?

Such a strategy must take account of the serious moral and ethical implications of the problem. The population surge stems directly from the fast-acting effects of simple health and sanitation programs, unrestrained by birth-control measures, which are slow in producing impact. But we are repelled by the mere thought of *not* intervening with medical and scientific measures, and of thereby allowing the Malthusian law to work its inexorable course. Our most profound instincts tell us that we cannot simply stand by in the presence of misery and suffering. We *cannot* do other than share our vast knowledge and techniques to alleviate mankind's burdens of malnutrition and disease. And so we move on, around and around the circle.

Perhaps to suggest a comprehensive strategy of social action in this situation is to call for an analysis of which we are not capable. Perhaps the tough hide of this problem *is* impenetrable. But as we contemplate this problem and realize its grave implications for at least one half of the world's people, we cannot deny it top priority on the advanced-nations' agenda of unfinished business. There could be no brighter star in the crown of American university achievement than a real breakthrough on this front, in both concept and practical application. To make such a breakthrough will require the collaborative efforts of men from various disciplines and professional fields. It will depend on having available some of the new academic men we have identified, the professional generalists. It will turn on our success in conception and analysis of a complex set of interrelationships, and then in building the bridges of application to massive human needs. If this cannot be done by the combined intellectual resources of the United States represented in the universities, it is not likely to be done at all.

The reader who has persisted down to this point will probably be tempted to say that we have not succeeded in sketching a very clear and distinct picture of "campus 1980" in its international ramifications. He is, of course, correct. The reason is partly the great diversity among American colleges and universities: "campus 1980" will have many forms. But it is mainly the supreme importance of questions that cannot now be answered. How will American universities and colleges respond to the challenges that so obviously confront them? Will there be enough of the precious qualities of innovation and resolute will? Can we count on the emergence of educational leaders who can compound all the ingredients into a formula of achievement? Again, we come back to questions rather than answers.

The note on which we conclude, therefore, is not unlike the reaction of the returned Peace Corps volunteer who doubted whether he had succeeded in helping the primitive people he worked with but was sure he understood himself and his own society better. These are, after all, the two great objectives of assuring a strong international dimension in higher education: to know ourselves more profoundly through knowing other cultures, and to be able to share our accomplishments with the less-advantaged peoples in order to assist their progress. In the pursuit of goals so noble and compelling, perhaps we should not expect to see the future in any terms clearer than uncertainty mingled with hope.

◀ CHRISTOPHER JENCKS AND
DAVID RIESMAN

The Triumph of Academic Man

IT WOULD TAKE a long book to describe the changes in American society which led to the establishment of national institutions and of what seems, at least in comparison to earlier times, to be a relatively homogenous upper-middle-class culture. The underlying factors were probably technological, but this should not be interpreted in a narrow sense. Industrial technology (e.g., the assembly line) played some part, forcing many enterprises to reorganize so as to achieve economies of scale. But this was by no means a uniform need or trend. Industrial technology in the narrow sense may have led to the creation of a Ford Motor Company, but it did not account for General Motors and still less for the Chase Manhattan Bank or General Dynamics. These were products of what Kenneth Boulding and others have called the organizational revolution, which enabled powerful individuals to exercise effective control over larger and larger numbers of people. This revolution depended on technology (the typewriter, the telephone, now the computer), but in a very different way than the industrial revolution of earlier vintage. There is no clear evidence that the large organizations created in this way were more efficient than the smaller enterprises they usually supplanted, or that they served the public better. All that can be said is that they were not conspicuously less efficient. Their spread must probably be explained in other ways. The agglomeration of power and accommodation of interests within the framework of a single institution inevitably appealed to those in a position to dominate that institution. If such organizations were not egregiously incompetent compared to smaller ones and if the ideological and legal checks on their growth were weak, they were bound to grow simply because their leaders had more power and resources available than anyone else. The ability of large businesses to retain income and thus free themselves from money-market control has facilitated their ability to grow by their own rather than Wall Street's devising.

There were, of course, many other factors involved in the establishment of overarching national institutions: the closing of the frontier and, later, the end of migration, the decline of sectarianism and religious fervor, the rise of a national market for both jobs and goods, the emergence of national magazines and, more recently, radio and television, the growth of the national government as a major force in people's lives, the unifying effect of foreign wars. These changes were accompanied and intensified by changes in the dominant political ideology of American society, in family structure and child rearing, in the character of relationships between individuals, and in individuals' self-perception. The cumulative effect of these changes appears to have been the destruction of the nineteenth-century Jacksonian world, in which every dissident could cut loose from his fellows and go into business for himself. The major conflicts and concords of twentieth-century America were shaped within a complex of large, firmly established, loosely interrelated institutions.

Or so it seems. Actually, it might be somewhat more accurate to say that the old Jacksonian world has been overshadowed rather than destroyed. There is, after all, still an enormous amount of small business in America, both in the narrow economic sense and in the larger social sense. The evidence is not clear, but it may actually be easier to start a small business today than it was a hundred years ago, and the prospects of success, while far from bright, may be no worse than they were a century ago. On the other hand, there can be no doubt that the overall economic picture has been radically altered by the fact that the bulk of the nation's business is now done by big corporations, and that most young people considering business careers now choose to work for these corporations rather than take the risk of striking out on their own. A similar line of argument could be developed in other areas. The dissident clergyman who wants to start his own denomination has clearly not disappeared from American life; on the contrary, the number of small fundamentalist sects seems continually to grow. What *has* happened is that the big, affluent, highly organized denominations play a much larger role than they did in the Jacksonian era. Analogous changes have taken place in other areas in American life. The net result is probably not an absolute decline in opportunities for independent entrepreneurship but only a relative decline, and a parallel rise in opportunities for advancement through established institutions.

The fact that so much of the old Jacksonian world has survived right down to the present time makes it extremely difficult to date with any accuracy the changes we are describing. Historians and people generally are always torn between looking for watersheds and looking for continuities. Laurence Veysey has argued to us that the coming of the railroad was the most important break between the earlier pluralist and loosely federated America and the later, more centralized, unified, and industrialized one. In some respects the Civil War served as a catalyst for changes that had begun earlier. It both symbolized and facilitated a shift of emphasis from the second to the first word in "United States." Yet even today this shift is incomplete, its resolution depending on the nature of the issue, the local as well as the national political climate, and the kinds of deterrents local, state, and federal institutions possess.

Whatever the causes or timing of the change, few would deny that established national institutions play a much larger role today than they did a century ago and that their dominance is likely to increase. The character of American life is in good part determined within such diverse and sporadically conflicting enterprises as the Chase Manhattan Bank and the Treasury Department, the Pentagon and General Dynamics, the Federal Courts and the National Council of Churches, CBS and *The New York Times*, the State Department and the Chamber of Commerce, the Ford Motor Company and the Ford Foundation, Standard Oil and Sun

Oil. It is not determined to anything like the same extent by small businessmen, independent professionals, or eccentric millionaires. This does not, of course, mean that farmers, doctors, or Texas oilmen are without influence. It does mean that they exercise influence through organizations like the Farm Bureau and the American Medical Association, and that they exercise influence mainly on other large institutions rather than directly on individuals. Institutions of this kind have in some cases crowded smaller and more marginal competitors entirely off the stage. This is the case, for example, with national news magazines and automobile manufacturers, to take two dissimilar cases. In other enterprises, such as local newspapers and home construction, small entrepreneurs can still break in. In yet others, such as intellectual quarterlies and fashion design, off-beat individuals can sometimes find a niche. Still, it seems fair to say that established national institutions set most of the ground rules for both stability and change in contemporary America.

The mere existence of well-established institutions does not, however, tell us anything about their management and control. The late C. Wright Mills used to argue that established institutions of this kind were controlled by a small group of men who had been to the same schools, shared the same values, and manipulated the rest of society to suit their own needs.[1] One of the authors of this essay earlier argued the contrary, suggesting that the activities of these institutions are subject to the veto of a wide variety of vested interests both within each institution and within the larger society.[2] Both of us still take this view. While initiative often comes from the top, this is by no means always the case—especially if the top is taken to mean boards of trustees and directors as against top administrators and professionals.

There are, of course, variations from one institution to another. In general, control over organized violence is in fewer hands than control over capital, and control over capital in fewer hands than

---

[1] See especially *The Power Elite* (New York: Oxford University Press, 1956).
[2] See David Riesman, with Reuel Denney and Nathan Glazer, *The Lonely Crowd* (New Haven: Yale University Press, 1950), Chapter XI. For further discussion of the difference between Mills and Riesman, see Riesman's preface to the Yale University Press paperback of *The Lonely Crowd*, 1961.

control over ideas. The Federal Bureau of Investigation is more centralized than the State Department, but both are more centralized than the Office of Economic Opportunity or the Department of Urban Affairs. There are similar variations in the private sector. Texas oil tycoons exercise more personal control over their empires than the Rockefellers over theirs. But almost any profit-making corporation is more completely managed from the top down than any church, university, or professional association.

Nonetheless, even the managers of the most centralized organizations, public and private, believe they have little room for maneuver. They feel hemmed in by rivals for power within their organization, by competitive organizations, by their prospective clients, by their lawyers and their boards of directors (or fellow directors), and even by their subordinates. The latter exercise their power in many ways which deserve more attention than they have gotten. Boards of directors sometimes go along with the company president because they have no ready replacement and because they fear he may take another job if he is not given his head. President Kennedy ordered resumption of nuclear testing in 1962 because, among other things, scientists threatened to leave the weapons laboratories if their hardware was not tried out. And, of course, as we shall see in more detail later, university trustees and administrators are constantly readjusting both the means and the ends of higher education so as to attract eminent scholars to their institutions.

We hope this view of America will be reflected in our rhetoric. We have chosen to speak of "established institutions," not of "the establishment." [3] We see established institutions as the framework and battleground within which most changes in the American system are now worked out, but we do not see America as ruled by an interlocking directorate or clique. Established institutions are a

[3] It is interesting to note that the term "establishment," carried to America from England, was originally used in the way we use the term "established institutions." It applied to the Church of England and was then extended to include the Civil Service. Only in recent years has it been aimed at individuals rather than institutions, becoming a synonym for something like Mills' "power elite." See Hugh Thomas, ed., *The Establishment* (London: Anthony Blond, 1959), especially the essay by Henry Fairlie.

mixed bag, and their ascendancy does not fully define either the character of modern American life or the expectations and aspirations of the young people who will live and work within them. Yet the hegemony of these institutions does exclude some possibilities and encourage others.

To begin with, the sources of differentiation in American life are changing. The old nineteenth-century divisions between Irish and Yankee, Baptist and Episcopalian, North and South, country and city seem to be losing their significance. Even the struggles between Negroes and whites and between Catholics and non-Catholics, while certainly far from settled, strike us as legacies of a vanishing past rather than as necessary features of the contemporary American system. This system is increasingly meritocratic, in Michael Young's sense of that term.[4] It tries to divide people according to competence, interests, and achievement rather than according to origin. (Background and competence are very much related, as the example of Negro failure to meet "objective" white standards indicates. But the correlation is far from perfect.) While there are still plenty of exceptions to the general meritocratic rule, and plenty of reasons for ambivalence about its increasing acceptance, it seems to us the wave of the future.

The rise of meritocracy brings with it what we will call the national upper-middle-class style: cosmopolitan, moderate, somewhat legalistic, concerned with equity and fair play, aspiring to neutrality between regions, religions, and ethnic groups. Not everyone who has money, power, or visibility in America subscribes to this set of ideals even in theory, much less in practice. There are many who take a narrower and more overtly self-interested view of the world, especially among those who have only recently climbed to within hailing distance of the top. Nor do these attitudes affect all aspects of life equally: men who think America has dealt unfairly with Negroes may, for example, see no comparable source of regret in America's treatment of the Vietnamese. None-

[4] See *The Rise of the Meritocracy, 1870–2033* (New York: Random House, 1959); and see discussion in Riesman, "Notes on Meritocracy," *Daedalus*, June 1967.

theless, we would argue that the ethic we are describing, like the institutions which encourage it, is growing stronger rather than weaker.

These changes in the character of American society were inevitably accompanied by changes in higher education. The most basic of these changes was the rise of the university. This had many consequences. College instructors became less and less preoccupied with educating young people, more and more preoccupied with educating one another by doing scholarly research which advanced their discipline. Undergraduate education became less and less a terminal enterprise, more and more a preparation for graduate school. The result was that higher education ceased to be a marginal, backward-looking enterprise shunned by the bulk of the citizenry. Today it is a major growth industry, consuming about two percent of the gross national product, directly touching the lives of perhaps four percent of the population, and exercising an indirect effect on the whole of society.

The rise of the university has, of course, been gradual rather than sudden. The Civil War can again be taken as the first watershed. The first PhD was awarded in 1861 by Yale. The year 1869 saw the inauguration of Charles Eliot as President of Harvard and the opening of Cornell under Andrew White. Yet it was not until the 1900s that anything like a modern university really took shape in America.[5] Perhaps the most important breakthroughs were the founding of Johns Hopkins and Clark as primarily graduate universities. Eliot's success in instituting the elective system at Harvard was also important, both in its own right and because it facilitated the assemblage of a more scholarly and specialized faculty. The 1890s saw further progress, with the founding of Chicago, the reform of Columbia, and the tentative acceptance of graduate work as an important activity in the leading state universities. This was also the period when national learned societies and journals were founded and when knowledge was broken up into its present departmental categories (physics, biology, history, philosophy, and

[5] For a brilliant, erudite, and comprehensive account of this development see Laurence Veysey, *The Emergence of the American University* (Chicago: University of Chicago Press, 1965).

so forth), with the department emerging as the basic unit of academic administration. Medicine and law also became serious studies of graduate study at this time, with Johns Hopkins leading the way in medicine and Harvard in law.

By World War I two to a dozen major universities had emerged and, while the number has grown slightly since then, the changes have been slow.[6] These universities have long been remarkably similar in what they encourage and value.[7] They turn out PhD's who, despite conspicuous exceptions, mostly have quite similar ideas about what their discipline covers, how it should be taught, and how its frontiers should be advanced. (This does not mean that there are *no* differences of opinion on these matters within the academic profession. It only means that, when contrasted with trustees, administrators, parents, students, or the present authors, the outlook of PhD's in a given discipline seems quite uniform. Not only were these men like-minded at the outset, but they have established machinery for remaining like-minded. National and regional meetings for each academic discipline and subdiscipline are now annual affairs, national journals publish work in every specialized subject, and an informal system of job placement and replacement has come into existence. The result is that large numbers of PhD's now regard themselves almost as independent professionals like doctors or lawyers, responsible primarily to themselves and their colleagues rather than their employers, and committed to the advancement of knowledge rather than to any particular institution.

[6] If we arbitrarily define a major university as one which turns out more than one percent of the nation's PhD's each year, we find that 22 universities met this test in the period 1926–1947. By 1962 the number had risen to 30. (The absolute number of PhD's needed to meet the criterion had quintupled.) Analyzing the problem another way, the dozen largest producers of PhD's accounted for 55 percent of all PhD's between 1926 and 1947, compared to 36 percent in 1962. See Allan M. Cartter, ed., *American Universities and Colleges* (Washington: American Council on Education, 1964), pp. 1263–5.

[7] For evidence on this point, see Allan M. Cartter, *An Assessment of Quality in Graduate Education* (Washington: American Council on Education, 1966). The extraordinarily high degree of consensus about the relative standing of departments in all academic fields suggests that the standards used to evaluate departments must be quite uniform. Rankings over time also show remarkable stability.

These attitudes were greatly strengthened by World War II and its aftermath. Not only in the Manhattan Project, but in other less glamorous ones, academic scientists helped contribute to the war effort, and, for this and other reasons, a dramatic increase in federal support for academic research ensued. This support soon became available not just in the physical sciences but in the biological and social sciences as well. In recent years Washington has even begun to put small sums into the humanities. Unlike previous support for universities, these federal grants and contracts are for all practical purposes given to individual scholars or groups of scholars rather than to the institution where they happen to work. More often than not, if a man moves to a new institution his federal grants are transferred, too. Not only that, but these federal grants are made largely on the basis of individual professional reputation and competence, with only minimal consideration of an institution's location, sectarian ties, racial composition, or whatever. The result has been to enhance further the status of the academician, who is now a prime fund-raiser for his institution. Since the amount of research support grew much faster than the number of competent researchers, talented men were soon in very short supply and commanded rapidly rising salaries. They were also increasingly free to set their own working conditions. The result has been a rapid decline in teaching loads for productive scholars, an increase in the ratio of graduate to undergraduate students at the institutions where scholars were concentrated, the gradual elimination of unscholarly undergraduates from these institutions, and the parallel elimination of unscholarly faculty.

The professionalization of university professors brought conflict on many fronts from the very start. Late nineteenth- and early twentieth-century academic history is replete with battles in which the basic question was whether the president and trustees or the faculty would determine the shape of the curriculum, the content of particular courses, or the use of particular books. The professors lost most of the battles but won the war. Today faculty control over these matters is rarely challenged, and conflict usually centers on other issues. The faculty, for example, have sought the right to choose their colleagues. While they have not usually won this right in the formal sense of actually making appointments themselves, their recommendations are sought at all reputable colleges and universities. Faculty committees are, it is true, sometimes overruled. Occasionally this is because the colleague group has rejected a notably popular teacher whose publications may not meet the standards of the guild as locally defined. Sometimes this is because a capable scholar has aroused the Philistines by, in one epoch, backing oleomargarine over butter, or today Ho Chi-minh over General Ky. Public universities are in this respect somewhat more vulnerable than private ones, holding quality constant, because of their dependence on the local legislature; but even elected state-university trustees are seldom eager to force issues of academic freedom into the open. As long as faculty members stick to problems defined by their disciplines, they are not apt to run into public controversy except in the most provincial milieus. And while administrators or trustees sometimes reject faculty recommendations, they almost never foist their own candidates on an unwilling faculty. The faculty has also sought to apply to the selection of undergraduates the same meritocratic standards that have long been used to select graduate students. Here again they have largely won the day, although marginal exceptions (geographic distribution, alumni sons, faculty sons, etc.) still stir sporadic controversy. The faculty has also sought some voice in choosing top administrators and in this, too, it has been increasingly successful. Once chosen, these administrators have broad powers to make policy (in the name and with the consent of the trustees). But even here a *unified* faculty has an informal veto at most universities and colleges.

It is important to know clearly what these victories mean. College professors have not for the most part won significant *formal* power, either individually or collectively, over the institutions which employ them. On paper the typical academic senate is still a largely advisory body whose legal jurisdiction is confined to setting the curriculum and awarding degrees. Departments, too, have little *formal* power, except sometimes over course offerings and requirements. Ultimate control mostly remains where it has always been—with the administration, the lay trustees, and in some cases the legislature (in some states the legislature's powers are being absorbed by the governor, by executive audits and the like, as well as by coordinating councils for higher education, though of course the legislature retains a veto power).

The trustees, however, are seldom what they once were. Most are more permissive than their nineteenth- or early twentieth-century predecessors. They are also more sensitive to individuals and groups unlike themselves. They share the general upper-middle-class allergy to "trouble," of whatever sort. If there is strong internal pressure for a given course of action, they are likely to go along. They are also more likely than they once were to delegate authority to the college administration, either *de jure* or *de facto*. In part it is because the complexity of the university has increased, so that lay trustees feel less competent to deal with its affairs on a one-day-a-month basis. In part it is because college presidents are today usually PhD's rather than clergymen and can therefore claim apparently relevant but esoteric expertise which other board members lack. This gives the president a certain authority *vis à vis* his board, which was less common before the professionalization of academic work. The tremendous competition among leading and aspiring institutions means that the decisions on recruitment and promotion of faculty must be made swiftly and would be too much delayed if subjected to detailed board review. (One reason boards spend so much time on buildings and grounds is that trustees feel at home in this area, presidents regard it as useful occupational therapy for them, and decisions can sometimes if not invariably wait.) To be sure, there are enormous differences in the degree of self-confidence of trustees. Some still "meddle" regularly in the affairs of "their" colleges and universities, settling issues the faculty considers its own prerogative. Those with access to public or private money also still throw their weight around at times. But the overall trend seems to us toward moderation and an increasingly ceremonial role for trustees.

The transfer of power from boards of directors to professional administrators has not, of course, been confined to higher education. The so-called managerial revolution, while not so widespread, complete, or progressive as some of its prophets have suggested, has taken place in many nonacademic enterprises. What is perhaps unusual about the academic world is the extent to which the top management, while nominally acting in the interests of the board, actually represents the interests of "middle management" (i.e., the faculty), both to the board and to the world. Despite some notable exceptions, today's college and university presidents usually start out as members of the academic profession. When they become administrators and have to deal more often with nonacademicians, they inevitably become somewhat deprofessionalized. Nonetheless, most university presidents still see their institution primarily as an assemblage of scholars and scientists, each doing his own work in his way.[8] At bottom, they are still engaged in "making the world safe for academicians," however much the academicians themselves resent the necessary (and unnecessary) compromises. Their greatest ambition for the future is usually to "strengthen" the college, and operationally this usually turns out to mean assembling scholars of even greater competence and reputation than are now present—though of course there are still administrators who suffer from the traditional edifice complex, and others who want innovative new programs that attract outside support even if no competent men can be found to run them.

In the course of institution building, administrators usually find it expedient to pretend that the interests of the university and of the larger society are identical. Many even come to believe it. At that point they may lose sight of some of the distinctive objectives and prejudices of their faculty. More often, however, they compromise in order to fight (or run away) again another day. This usually offends the faculty, which has the luxury of being able to go elsewhere if its insistence on its principles brings reprisal against its institution. In the course of trying to "strengthen" their faculty, administrators of upwardly mobile institutions also usually offend many of the "weak" faculty currently on the payroll.

[8] Even Clark Kerr's much maligned but marvelously perceptive study, *The Uses of the University* (Cambridge: Harvard University Press, 1964), takes this view.

And in the course of trying to keep the peace among warring departments and contending professors within departments, administrators inevitably offend most individual professors at one time or another.

Academicians are neither a tolerant nor an easygoing species, and their apparently congenital feeling of irritation and frustration requires scapegoats. Administrators serve this purpose, and they serve it best when their actions can be attributed to nonacademic considerations. So they are usually regarded as the enemy. Nonetheless, we would argue that administrators are today more concerned with keeping their faculty happy than with placating any other single group. They are also, in our experience, far more responsive to students and more concerned with the inadequacies and tragedies of student life than the majority of the faculty. We have also found that the administrative actions which offend academic liberals and elicit bitter talk about administrative tyranny are usually disapproved by only a minority of the faculty. This minority then finds it convenient to blame the administration instead of blaming its complacent colleagues for what is done with their tacit consent. Sometimes, indeed, the dissidents blame the administration for actions which the majority of their colleagues insisted on, forgetting that faculties are themselves diverse and assuming if their colleagues do not agree with them it must be because they were "pressured," "bought," or "manipulated." [9] While it would be an exaggeration to say, as noted earlier, that the faculty exercises an absolute veto over administrative action in a modern university, it is certainly fair to say, as noted earlier, that trustees and administrators only rarely override faculty opinion, and then seldom for long.

The redistribution of power in the universities has been accompanied—and to some extent caused—by a change in the relationship between the university and other established institutions.

[9] In a generally liberal academic setting, moreover, faculty members may overlook the significance of a small but vocal group of right-wing faculty who are not at all complacent but who tell their right-wing political and business cronies that the general run of professors (and students) is even more "subversive" and dangerous than outsiders realize. Much American anti-intellectualism depends on the pedantic documentation and conspiratorial interpretations supplied by intellectuals.

The universities, especially their graduate professional schools, have become pacesetters in the promotion of meritocratic values.[10] In Talcott Parsons' terms, they are "universalistic," ignoring "particularistic" and personal qualities in their students and professors. This means that they choose professors almost entirely on the basis of their "output" and professional reputation. Students in the graduate professional schools are selected by similar criteria: by their ability to write good examinations and do good academic work. The claims of localism, sectarianism, ethnic prejudice and preference, class background, age, sex, and even occupational plans are largely ignored.[11]

The graduate professional schools have in turn been leaders in imposing meritocratic values on the professions themselves. The leading law firms hire men who made the law review at the most competitive law schools, and the leading hospitals offer internships and residencies to doctors who did well in the most competitive medical schools. Most conspicuous of all, colleges and universities scramble for PhD's who have done well in the most competitive graduate departments. The result is that many traditional prejudices affecting recruitment have broken down: local boys today enjoy little advantage over outsiders, white Anglo-Saxon Protestants monopolize fewer and fewer occupational slots, and family connnections count for less than they used to. Even corporation managers with long traditions of self-interested exclusiveness have in recent years frequently yielded to a broader vision of their enterprise and of America. Big employers today re-

[10] Here as elsewhere we treat the graduate departments of humanities, social science, and natural sciences as professional schools no different from graduate schools of medicine, law, education, and the like. We use the phrase "graduate schools" to include all professional schools requiring a BA for admission, and the phrase "graduate professional schools" should be read in the same inclusive way.

[11] There are some exceptions. Law schools admit brilliant students who confess that they do not plan to practice law, but medical schools take a narrower view. Graduate departments in the arts and sciences will usually admit a good candidate even though they think he will "sell out" and become a scientist in industry, but they will usually reject even the most brilliant candidate if he does not plan to take a PhD. There is also a residual bias against girls in most graduate admissions committees, and in the past few years a bias in favor of Negroes. For historical reasons, some institutions show other idiosyncrasies, but these are of marginal importance.

cruit university graduates in an increasingly evenhanded way, paying ever less attention to "irrelevant" factors like class background, religion, and ethnicity. Partly this is because of competition for skilled specialists, partly because of the stirrings of conscience, partly because they fear adverse publicity. Companies have grown larger, have had to rationalize recruitment policy, and can therefore no longer conceal nonmeritocratic discrimination from themselves or (consequently) from the general public. Furthermore, with the growth of democratic ideology and the decline of old-fashioned social snobbery, even college fraternities have become less exclusive, as have leading prep schools. This brings a cumulative element in the growth of meritocracy, since even if an employer wanted to discriminate he would have a hard time finding channels that made this easy for him. Legacies of earlier discrimination obviously remain both in recruitment and training— and in the feeling of appropriateness of people for specific positions. A Negro is not likely soon to become president of General Motors nor a woman president of Harvard University, but both have been Cabinet members and either might become a vice-president of AT&T.

We do not want to exaggerate the tightness of the links between the modern occupational structure and higher education. The big Wall Street and Washington law firms may hire the top graduates of the top law schools, but there is another legal world where lawyers trained in night schools pick up not-so-good livings chasing ambulances, writing wills, settling insurance claims, and generally acting as brokers between the uninitiated and various bureaucracies. Similar chasms separate the top doctors who practice in teaching hospitals from those who have no hospital privileges anywhere. There are also colleges where, as Everett Hughes has put it, the faculty not only includes no scholars but includes nobody who has ever studied under a scholar. There are still many roads into these lower levels of professional practice, and on some of them academic competence counts for less than persistence and animal cunning. There are even more roads to the top in business: sales, accounting, engineering, law, and so forth. The Robert McNamaras who come up through the top graduate schools of business administration are still nothing like a majority.

Nonetheless, the role of graduate education in job distribution seems to be growing and should be stronger than ever by 1980. At the same time, and for related reasons, the values and methods promoted in the graduate professional schools seem to be increasingly accepted in the larger society. This does not mean that the outlook of professional-school faculty and the professions themselves are ever likely to be the same. On the contrary, there will always be tension between the "theorists" in the graduate schools and the "practitioners." By the time the AMA accepts compulsory health insurance, group practice, and other reforms long advocated by large numbers of medical professors, for example, the professors will have shifted their attention to new problems and will be attacking the conservatism of the practitioners on new grounds. The same is true in other areas. The striking thing, however, is how often the opinions and practices of the professional schools foreshadow those of the profession as a whole a generation later.

The rise of the university in the late nineteenth century did not at first have much effect on undergraduate education. The overwhelming majority of students continued to attend special-interest colleges, and even those who attended the undergraduate colleges of universities were for the most part terminal students. While a significant proportion eventually did some kind of work beyond the BA, very few graduate professional schools offering such work had highly competitive admissions. Similarly, while administrators at special-interest colleges were often impressed by the scholarly achievements of faculty at leading universities, and some made an active effort to acquire a similar faculty at their own institution, their success was at first limited by the shortage of PhD's, especially "productive" ones. As in the larger society, the groundwork for a system was being laid, and the giant enterprises which would dominate that system were being organized, but the bulk of the nation's business was still being done by independent enterprises of limited means and limited views.

The revolution accelerated somewhat after World War I, for the 1920s and 1930s were a period of unprecedented growth in enrollment. (It is always easier to redistribute resources and power in periods of growth, because the progressives can be given more without the stand-patters' appearing to get less.) By the outbreak of World War II, the majority of the nation's college students were attending institutions staffed by academic professionals—though there were still many enclaves of provincialism such as the teachers colleges, the Catholic colleges, and the Negro colleges. The professionalization of the faculty reduced the internal homogeneity of many special-purpose colleges. Upper-class colleges got literary critics with the wrong ancestors, Southern colleges hired more historians who had grown up in the wrong region or even the wrong country, women's colleges hired psychologists of the wrong sex, and Methodist colleges took on philosophers of the wrong faith or no faith at all. Such "mismatching" had, of course, sometimes taken place accidentally even in presumptively homogenous special-interest colleges, but professionalization made it far more common. It also put trustees and parents who opposed heterogeneity very much on the defensive. A New York millionaire might not have liked the idea of having his son study economics with some Jewish radical at Yale, but if the boy's teacher had been publicly defined as "one of the leading economists in the country," the millionaire's objections seemed bigoted and irrelevant. (Which did not, of course, always prevent them from carrying weight, in Montana if not at Yale.)

Until the 1950s, most undergraduates seem to have remained relatively unaffected by these changes. The proportion going on to graduate school in the arts and sciences had risen slowly, but the proportion going into law and medicine had fallen correspondingly. As a result, the overall proportion of BA's earning graduate degrees probably changed relatively little for some decades.[12]

[12] Statistical measures of this trend over long periods are hard to come by. Until very recently the U. S. Office of Education's statistics lumped graduate students in law, medicine, theology, and some other professions with undergraduates. Figures on graduate enrollment and degrees included only those taking degrees in fields which offered an undergraduate major—mainly the arts and sciences and education. The proportion of undergraduates going on in professional fields like law and medicine has declined steadily since 1900, but this does not show up in USOE's figures on graduate enrollment. En-

In the late 1950s, however, the effects of the academic revolution on undergraduate life began to multiply. Both the absolute number and the proportion of young people applying to college were rising steadily. This gave many colleges a choice between expansion and greater selectivity. The faculty preferred selectivity, and this preference proved influential in colleges of all sorts and decisive in private ones.[13] As a result, the leading undergraduate colleges, both public and private, began demanding higher academic aptitude and more proof of academic motivation from their entrants. These students, in turn, found the academic profession and ancillary activities increasingly glamorous, while mostly rejecting careers in business and other fields requiring only a BA.[14] The proportion of undergraduates who wanted to go on to graduate school therefore began to rise rapidly. The same pattern was repeated to a lesser extent at less selective colleges.[15]

---

rollment in the areas which USOE traditionally defined as graduate-level have, on the other hand, risen much faster than undergraduate enrollment. The result is that USOE data greatly exaggerated the actual change in the ratio of total graduate to total undergraduate enrollment.

The *1960 Census of Population, Volume I, Part 1*, Table 173, shows that, among those completing four years of college, the proportion going on to complete a fifth did not change significantly between 1910 and 1950. Among men who were born between 1885 and 1930, about 40 percent of those completing four years of higher education went on to complete a fifth. For individuals born after 1930, 1960 Census data are not very useful, since such individuals were still returning to graduate school in significant numbers in 1960. The 1960 Census therefore tells us relatively little about trends in graduate enrollment for men earning BA's after about 1950.

[13] No doubt in individual instances there are other reasons for selectivity, e.g., the failure of a capital bond issue or the lack of building sites for expansion. In some instances, inertia favors growth; in others, stability.

[14] Among the elite students in the elite universities there has been a general rejection of business careers, even those requiring advanced degrees, but a certain proportion of men with PhD's and LLB's will nonetheless end up in business, holding insurance against their employers by virtue of their professional training.

[15] Since the early 1950s the steady growth of graduate work in fields like education, business, engineering, and the arts and sciences has more than offset the continuing lag in first professional degrees like the LLB and MD. A 1963 National Science Foundation survey of 1958 BA's found that 58 percent had done some graduate work. (See Laura Sharpe, "Five Years After the College Degree, Part I, Graduate and Professional Education," Washington: Bureau of Social Science Research, 1965, mimeographed.) The NSF figures include some students who had not completed a full year of graduate work and who in theory would not be entitled to report "five or more" years

Many if not most undergraduates came to the old special-interest colleges in order to kill time, get away from home, make new friends, enjoy themselves, acquire saleable skills, and so forth. Undergraduates with such aims were not, by and large, very vulnerable to faculty pressures. Most, of course, wanted a diploma, and that meant they had to meet whatever formal requirements the faculty set. But these requirements served mainly to sift and intimidate the less competent students. The abler students could get C's without doing much work, and most capitalized on this opportunity. The spread of graduate study altered these attitudes appreciably. Today a substantial fraction of the undergraduate population wants not only a degree but an undergraduate transcript sufficiently distinguished to ensure entry into a competitive professional school of some sort. Unlike many employers, these schools are mostly reluctant to take undergraduates with poor grades. The faculty can use this fact as a weapon to make undergraduates do far more academic work than was common in the traditional terminal colleges. This external threat has been reenforced in recent years by changes in the mass media's portrait of established national institutions. These institutions are increasingly shown offering prize jobs to men who have intellectual skills.

---

of higher education to the 1970 Census. It is therefore likely that the increase in the proportion of BA's entering graduate school was less than the apparent contrast between NSF and earlier Census figures. But probably not much less.

More recent studies by Alexander Astin and his colleagues at the American Council on Education show that, since 1958, the proportion of entering freshmen who *plan* to do graduate work has continued to rise. In Astin's sample of 45 four-year colleges, the proportion of all freshmen planning to get some sort of graduate degree rose from 49 to 67 percent between 1961–65. This sample appears to be representative of other four-year colleges, though the percentages would be somewhat lower if junior-college entrants were included. A 1965 *followup* of the students entering 246 four-year colleges in 1961 showed that the proportion planning to do graduate work rose from 42 to 70 percent over the four years. These plans were admittedly unrealistic in many cases. (Only 60 percent of this same sample had even earned a BA at the time of the followup.) Many of the non-BA's were not even enrolled in college at the time they outlined their plans for graduate study. Nonetheless, it seems fairly clear that graduate plans and enrollment are today rising much faster than college entrance or graduation rates. Although women are generally less likely to go to graduate school than men, the recent increase has been about equal for the two sexes. This suggests that draft deferment is not the primary cause.

Students are therefore constantly searching themselves for signs of intellectual competence and worrying about signs of stupidity. Many cannot settle for C's, if the graduate schools would, for they cannot accept the idea that they are only "worth" a C.[16]

The fruition of this change was the birth of what Frank Bowles has called the "university college." In our usage, this is a college whose primary purpose is to prepare students for graduate work of some kind—primarily in the arts and sciences but also in professional subjects ranging from law and medicine to business and social work.[17] It may be part of a university with big graduate schools, as is the case with Yale or Michigan, or it may be administratively independent and geographically removed from any big university, as is the case with Amherst, Oberlin, or Vassar. But even if it is nominally independent, it is a *de facto* prep school for a small number of graduate professional schools, in much the same way that Groton, Andover, and Farmington are prep schools for Ivy League and Seven Sister colleges. Such a university college usually draws most of its students from the top tenth of the national ability distribution. It seldom loses more than a fifth of them during the undergraduate years. (More than a fifth may drop out, but many return and many others graduate from other colleges.) It usually sends nearly three-quarters of its men and a third to half of its women to graduate school. If such a university college is administratively part of a larger institution, it is likely to share its faculty with the graduate school of arts and sciences. But even if it is separate, it is almost certain to draw its faculty from the same manpower pool as the graduate schools of arts and sci-

[16] Indeed, the enormous expansion of institutions seeking to offer graduate instruction has made places available to many who do not have distinguished undergraduate records at distinguished places. Still, the more energetic and competent undergraduate teachers generally want their students to go on to "good" graduate schools and steer them away from the more anemic ones, including the home institution at times. An undergraduate education itself tends to expose its student devotees to the names of luminaries at leading graduate schools, even though many textbooks and readers are written by men at the less visible places.

[17] This term is used in an entirely different sense in Great Britain and parts of the Commonwealth, to indicate a budding university which has not yet achieved sufficient stability and reputation to deserve complete autonomy, and which awards degrees through another institution.

ences, seeking the same virtues and looking askance at the same presumed vices.

The university college is the fruition of the academic revolution at the undergraduate level. Out of more than 2,000 undergraduate colleges, probably no more than a hundred today really fit the above description. Yet these are the most prestigious colleges in the country, to which the ablest and most ambitious students usually gravitate. They also attract the ablest faculty and administrators and the most generous philanthropists. And they provide a model toward which almost all the other 1,900 colleges are moving as fast as they conveniently can.[18]

Virtually all terminal colleges want to hire faculty of the kind now hired by the university colleges. Whether or not these faculty come out of the subculture to which the college has traditionally been tied is secondary. In most cases the terminal colleges also want to recruit students entirely on the basis of academic ability. They would prefer to ignore traditional considerations like geography, religion, ethnicity, and class. Specialization by sex and occupational intention is also somewhat less common among undergraduate colleges than it once was. Even administrators and trustees seem to be chosen more often according to the criteria of achievement, competence, and judgment which prevail in established national institutions than according to the criteria of the special-interest group which initially founded the college.

That these developments make colleges more useful to other established national institutions can hardly be doubted. They make higher education look like a fairly effective instrument for meritocratic sorting and grading of the future employees. They probably also help promote and disseminate values and skills useful in the maintenance of established institutions. The university colleges and their emulators usually try, for example, to help their students transcend whatever subculture they are born and raised in, and move them out into a slightly more cosmopolitan world. In part this is a matter of exposing students to heterogenous class-

[18] For a brief description of this process of emulation see David Riesman, "The Academic Procession," in *Constraint and Variety in American Education* (Lincoln, Nebraska: University of Nebraska Press, 1956), paperback edition.

mates—heterogenous, that is, by traditional demographic criteria, even though often quite homogenous in terms of academic aptitudes. In part it is a matter of exposing them to professors who know something of a larger world than the students have encountered, and who may, if they are wise or charming, lure their students into it. In part it is a matter of giving the students books to read. In part it is simply a matter of giving young people with a yen for mobility the diplomatic passport they need to cross the borders of their sexual, racial, religious, economic, or generational parish.[19]

These efforts at emancipation are, it is true, necessarily limited in scope. Some colleges manage to bring together students and faculty of diverse class backgrounds, but this diversity almost never extends to class aspirations. Wherever they come from, college students by and large plan to end up in the upper-middle classes if they can, and they meet professors who have succeeded in doing just this.[20] Similarly, while some colleges bring together students from different regional backgrounds, few mix them with more than a handful of foreigners, and even fewer create an atmosphere which appreciably curtails nationalistic biases. Then too, while many colleges attract a substantial number of students older than the undergraduate norm and all employ professors who run the full age range, few are successful in establishing really close cross-generational contacts or in counteracting the mutual chauvinism of young and old *vis à vis* one another. Nor can any college do much about the parochialism which comes from having lived only in the twentieth century. The formal curriculum, of course, usually tries to overcome all these limitations, but the number of students who can significantly be affected by books has always been fairly small, especially when the message of the book

[19] In Greek the word "diploma" meant a doubled-over piece of paper and hence a letter of recommendation. A "diplomat" was one who carried a "diploma." Today it could be said that the "diplomats" who serve as go-betweens for America's many subcultures and who hold the country together are the "diploma-holders" from these subcultures.
[20] A small but interesting minority of students, often from the upper social strata, profess aspirations for downward mobility, often identifying with Negroes as the American equivalent of the proletariat and meeting on the way down Negroes and others on the way up.

is reenforced neither by human contact nor by daily experience.

These almost inescapable limitations are in most cases supplemented by self-imposed limitations, often inherited from the special-interest group which founded a particular college. Local colleges, for example, often deliberately exclude students from outside their state or even their city. While some Catholic colleges and universities seem to their traditional faculties almost to be prejudiced against Catholics in their efforts to become ecumenical, others still on occasion deliberately discourage non-Catholic applicants for teaching positions, and even occasionally screen reading lists with an eye to orthodoxy. Upper-middle-class colleges sometimes make no effort to provide scholarships for students from poorer families. White colleges often make life intolerable for black students, and Negro colleges often do likewise for white faculty. Professional schools frequently cling to a narrow view of their students' future responsibilities, and sometimes resist affiliation with a multipurpose university. Single-sex colleges, while sometimes attracted to coeducation, also sometimes cling to their exclusiveness with pride.

Just as some small businesses will probably continue to earn high returns in the interstices of a corporate economy, and local governments to take on new responsibilities despite the parallel increase in federal power, so too the old nineteenth-century system of special-purpose colleges will endure despite the rise of the national university system and the magnetic appeal of the university-college model. By the same token, local car dealers may survive and flourish, but the future of the automobile industry is determined in Detroit, New York, and Washington. In higher education, while the old special-interest colleges and the energies they embody may give the present much of its flavor, they do little to shape the future.

What is taking place in America is a transition characteristic of any really successful institional invention, of which colleges are certainly an example. Special-purpose colleges were established by laymen to serve a particular purpose and were initially very much committed to that purpose. The local college was local first and a college second; the Catholic college was Catholic first and a college second; the Negro college was Negro first and a college second; and so forth. But as time goes on, these disparate institutions take on lives and purposes of their own. The college begins to change its reference group. Undergraduates stop thinking of themselves primarily as girls or Baptists or future teachers and start thinking of themselves primarily as students, having a common interest with students in all sorts of other places called colleges rather than with girls, Baptists, or teachers who are not students. Similar changes are taking place at the faculty level. Even the college president begins to think of himself less as the president of a college in San Jose, of a college catering to the rich, or of a college for Irish Catholics, and more as the president of a first-rate, second-rate, or third-rate college. More and more, his reference group ceases to be the trustees or the traditional clientele and patrons of his institution, and becomes the presidents of other colleges, many of which have historically different origins and aims.

The result is a trend toward the triumph of meritocratic academic values and the acceptance of the university college as the only viable model for the future. This model is certainly better suited to the "impossible" requirements of 1980 than any traditional terminal college would be. Nonetheless, *some* form of terminal education will still be needed then, and even for those who plan on graduate school, a mini-PhD program will often be unnecessarily restrictive.

◄ WILLIAM ARROWSMITH

The Future of Teaching

LET ME SAY immediately that I am concerned here with only
one kind of teaching. I mean the ancient, crucial, high art of
teaching, the kind of teaching which alone can claim to be called
educational, an essential element in all noble human culture, and
hence a task of infinitely more importance than research scholarship. With the teacher as transmitter or conductor of knowledge,
as servant or partner of research, I have no concern. He is useful
and necessary and, because he does the bulk of university teaching, it is important that his job be effectively performed and intelligently evaluated. But as long as the teacher is viewed as merely
a diffuser of knowledge or a higher popularizer, his position will
necessarily be a modest and even menial one. And precisely this, I
think, is the prevalent view of the teacher's function, the view
overwhelmingly assumed even among those who want to redress
the balance in favor of the teacher. Is it any wonder, then, that
the teacher enjoys no honor? For if the teacher stands to the
scholar as the pianist to the composer, there can be no question of
parity; teaching of this kind is necessary but secondary. So, too, is
the comparatively subtler and more difficult kind of teaching that
is concerned with scholarly methodology and the crucial "skeletal"
skills of creative research. Only when large demands are made of
the teacher, when we ask him to assume a primary role as educator in his own right, will it be possible to restore dignity to teaching. Teaching, I repeat, is not honored among us either because

its function is grossly misconceived or its cultural value not understood. The reason is the overwhelming positivism of our technocratic society and the arrogance of scholarship. Behind the disregard for the teacher lies the transparent sickness of the humanities in the university and in American life generally. Indeed, nothing more vividly illustrates the myopia of academic humanism than its failure to realize that the fate of any true culture is revealed in the value it sets upon the teacher and the way it defines him. "*The advancement of learning at the expense of man,*" writes Nietzsche, "is the most pernicious thing in the world. The stunted man is a backward step for humanity; he casts his *shadow* over all time to come. It debases conviction, the natural purpose of the particular field of learning; learning itself is finally destroyed. It is advanced, true, but its effect on life is nil or immoral."

What matters, then, is the kind of context that we can create for teaching and the largeness of the demands made upon the teacher. Certainly he will have no function or honor worthy of the name until we are prepared to make the purpose of education what it always was—the molding of men rather than the production of knowledge. It is my hope that education in this sense will not be driven from the university by the knowledge technicians. But this higher form of teaching does not die merely because the university will not practice it. Its future is always assured, since human beings and human culture cannot do without it. And if the university does not educate, others will. Education will pass, as it is passing now, to the artist, to the intellectual, to the gurus of the mass media, the charismatic charlatans and sages, and the whole immense range of secular and religious street-corner fakes and saints. The context counts. Socrates took to the streets, but so does every demagogue or fraud. By virtue of its traditions and pretensions the university is, I believe, a not inappropriate place for education to occur. But we will not transform the university milieu or create teachers by the meretricious device of offering prizes or bribes or "teaching sabbaticals" or building a favorable "image." At present the universities are as uncongenial to teaching as the Mojave Desert to a clutch of Druid priests. If you want to restore a Druid priesthood, you cannot do it by offering prizes for Druid-of-the-year. If you want Druids, you must grow forests. There is no other way of setting about it.

THE DISQUALIFICATION OF THE SCHOLAR

I am suggesting what will doubtless seem paradox or treason—that there is no *necessary* link between scholarship and education, or between research and culture, and that in actual practice scholarship is no longer a significant educational force. Scholars, to be sure, are unprecedentedly powerful, but their power is professional and technocratic; as educators they have been eagerly disqualifying themselves for more than a century, and their disqualification is now nearly total. The scholar has disowned the student —that is, the student who is not a potential scholar—and the student has reasonably retaliated by abandoning the scholar. This, I believe, is the only natural reading of what I take to be a momentous event—the secession of the student from the institutions of higher learning on the grounds that they no longer educate and are, therefore, in his word, *irrelevant*. By making education the slave of scholarship, the university has renounced its responsibility to human culture and its old, proud claim to possess, as educator and molder of men, an *ecumenical* function. It has disowned, in short, what teaching has always meant: a care and concern for the future of man, a Platonic love of the species, not for what it is, but what it might be. It is a momentous refusal. I do not exaggerate. When the President of Cornell seriously proposes that the university should abandon liberal education so that specialization can begin with matriculation—and when he advocates this in order to *reconcile* the conflicting claims of research and teaching![1]—it should be obvious even to the skeptical that education is being strangled in its citadel, and strangled furthermore on behalf of the crassest technocracy. I find it very difficult to imagine the rationalization of these salaried wardens of a great, ecumenical tradition, who apparently view themselves and the institutions they admin-

---

[1] James A. Perkins, *The University in Transition* (Princeton, N.J.: Princeton University Press, 1966), pp. 43–45.

ister as mere servants of national and professional interests. A hundred years ago Nietzsche denounced the subservience of German universities to an inhuman scholarly technology and the interest of the Reich: "The entire system of higher education has lost what matters most: the end as well as the means to the end. That education, that *Bildung* is itself an end—and not the state— this has been forgotten. Educators are needed who have themselves been educated, not the learned louts whom the universities today offer our youth. Educators are lacking, . . . hence the decline of German culture." And what has happened in Germany is now an American story.

We, too, lack educators—by which I mean Socratic *teachers*, visible embodiments of the *realized* humanity of our aspirations, intelligence, skill, scholarship; men ripened or ripening into realization, as Socrates at the close of the *Symposium* comes to be, and therefore personally guarantees, his own definition of love. Our universities and our society need this compelling embodiment, this exemplification of what we are all presumably at, as they have never needed it before. It is *men* we need, not programs. It is possible for a student to go from kindergarten to graduate school without ever encountering a *man*—a man who might for the first time give him the only profound motivation for learning, the hope of becoming a better man. Learning matters, of course; but it is the *means,* not the *end,* and the end must always be either radiantly visible or profoundly implied in the means. It is only in the teacher that the end is apparent; he can humanize because he possesses the human skills which give him the power to humanize others. If that power is not felt, nothing of any educational value can occur. The humanities stand or fall according to the human worth of the man who professes them. If undergraduates ever met teachers of this kind, then the inhuman professionalism of the graduate schools might have some plausibility; there would be an educational base. But nothing can be expected of a system in which men who have not themselves been educated presume to educate others. Our entire educational enterprise is in fact founded upon the wholly false premise that *at some prior stage* the essential educational work has been done. The whole structure is built on rotten foundations, and the routines of education have begun to threaten and destroy what they were intended to save. There is a very real sense, for instance, in which scholarship has become pernicious to literature; the humanities as presently taught are destructive of the past and therefore of the present.

THE HUMAN MEDIATOR

I repeat: The teacher is both the end and the sanction of the education he gives. This is why it is completely reasonable that a student should expect a classicist to live classically. The man who teaches Shakespeare or Homer runs the supreme risk. This is surely as it should be. Charisma in a teacher is not a mystery or nimbus of personality, but radiant *exemplification* to which the student contributes a correspondingly radiant hunger for becoming. What is classic and past instructs us in our *potential size,* offers the greatest human scale against which to measure ourselves. The teacher, like his text, is thus the mediator between past and present, present and future, and he matters because there is no *human* mediator but him. He is the student's only evidence outside the text that a great humanity exists: upon his *impersonation* both his text and his student's human fate depend. For student and teacher alike, ripeness is all. The age of the student does not matter.

Men, not programs; *galvanizers,* not conductors. When students say that their education is irrelevant, they mean above all the absence of this man. Without him the whole enterprise is ashes, sheer phoniness. This is why students are so quick, and so right, to suspect a fatal hypocrisy in the teacher who lives without the slightest relation to what he knows, whose texts are wholly divorced from his life, from human life. What students want is not necessarily what they need; but in this case it is the students who are right and the universities which are wrong. The irony of the situation is enough to make strong men weep. Here, unmistakably, we have students concerned to ask the crucial questions—identity, meaning, right and wrong, the good life—and they get in response not bread but a stone. Here we have a generation bless-

edly capable of moral outrage, and it is the bitterest of anomalies
that the humanities should be dying among students capable of
moral outrage in a morally outrageous world. Almost without
exception the response of the universities to this profound hunger
for education, for compelling examples of human courage and
compassionate intelligence, has been mean, parochial, uncompre-
hending, or cold. Above all, *cold.* The waste in sheer human incentive, in disappointment in matters where disappointment is
destructive and fatal, is appalling. But what fills one with rage is
the callousness of scholars, the incredible lack of human concern
among humanists, the monumental indifference of the learned to
human misery and need. Why, you ask, is teaching held in con-
tempt? Because it has become contemptible by indifference.
Teaching has been fatally trivialized by scholarship which has become trivial. What, I find myself wondering, would education be
like if humanists and teachers had the courage of their traditions
and dared to face their students as men in whom their studies and
texts found worthy, or at least attempted, embodiment?

Such embodiment may be personal, rational, and contempla-
tive, or activist and public. What matters is the integration of significant life and knowledge, of compassionate study and informed
conduct. The teacher in this sense goes where the action is, where
his example is most needed. Moreover, it is by going there that he
can hope to recover the great, complex power of the text whose
custodian he is. The point is important. We must at any cost find
room in our universities for those who are capable of *living or
acting upon a pure text.* Lacking such men, the student distrusts
the teacher and the culture he represents; the culture is defeated
in the teacher's failure. I am not suggesting that teachers must be
heroes or great men, but they must understand greatness and desire it for themselves and others. Only so can they speak to the
student's hunger for the same greatness. It is important, however,
that our sense of human greatness find *varied* incarnation. One
thing a student needs to know is how men cope with the vast,
impersonal chaos of modern existence. For most of us this is a
matter of daily improvisation. We no longer have the ability to
cope together, with a collective style based upon a common set of

values, pagan, say, or Christian—it is rather an individualistic *sauve qui peut,* requiring educated hunchwork, luck, imagination, skill, and the habit of hope. This present generation has experienced drastic change, and it therefore has a drastic need for significant styles of coping, present and past and as varied as possible. What is wanted is a repertory of convincing, visible, and powerful life-styles. And this the university should, as *alma mater,* be able and happy to provide. It takes all kinds of men to make a *university*—not scholars only.

For the scholar's example is no longer adequate to educate, though at its best it may belong among the higher styles. His comparative security, his cosy enclave of learning with its narrow departmental limits, and his murderous preference for a single mode of the mind—the discursive or methodological, do not call it "rational"—with its neat problems and solutions, his stunted humanity—all this strikes the student as irrelevant and even repugnant. What he wants is models of committed integrity, as whole as they can be in a time of fragmented men. Admittedly such models are hard to find, and integrated men are not to be expected. Hence it is essential that a student be confronted with as many *different,* vivid modes as we can muster; from these he may be able to infer the great, crucial idea of all true education—the single, many-sided transformation of himself, the *man* he wants to be. These men are hard to find because nobody is concerned to find them. And meanwhile our universities are making them rarer.

BETWEEN SYLLABUS AND CURRICULUM

One point should be made. When I say that scholarship no longer educates, I am not thereby joining what Daniel Bell calls the "apocalyptic" faction against the exponents of order and reason. But I also believe that the true stature of reason is no longer visible in technical scholarship, and that the academic sense of order is inadequate because it is not related to the real chaos of existence. Finally, it is order and not instinctual anarchy that we want, and when I speak of a style of life, I mean by "style" *controlled* passion, not the free play of instinct. It is because reason and order have been so diminished in the university that we require a repertory of models before we set about constructing a curriculum. The days of the syllabus are gone forever; we are not yet ready for a viable curriculum. General education has failed, not because of its curricular inadequacy (though it *is* inadequate), but because men of general intelligence are not available to teach it. It has ended up, therefore, in the hands of specialists who always betrayed it in practice. If I had a campus to play with, my first step would be to plant there, at any price, the six or seven charismatic teachers of my acquaintance; their collective *virtù* would, I am convinced, create a curriculum that would truly, explosively educate. But it is these men we must have, regardless of their academic pedigrees—prophets, poets, apocalyptics, scientists, scholars, intellectuals, men who sprawl across departmental boundaries, who will not toe the line, individuals as large as life, irrepressible, troublesome and—exemplary. Either we must make scholarship whole and ripe and human again, or we must import into the university every conceivable variety of active, shaping, seminal humanity we can find.

At present the latter course is probably the more practicable. By usurping the whole job of education and by claiming to represent the whole mind or the only part of the mind that matters, scholarship has had the effect of destroying what education, generously defined, might provide—the basis of a common culture. We have provided men with skills they cannot meaningfully use, and by so doing we have *alienated* the laymen of any coherent future culture. R. P. Blackmur comes pat to my point: "What we have, with respect to the old forms of our culture, is the disappearance of the man who, by his education, his tradition, and his own responsive life, was the layman to all the forms of his society. The mind no longer feels omniform or that it knows its own interest. We have a society of priests or experts who are strangely alien to the great mass movements which they presumably express or control." In the profession of the teacher lies one of the few correctives to the alienation which technical scholarship has conferred upon us, since, like the artist, the teacher offers cultural skills in living and loving use.

But teaching will not easily recover its great, lost function. The forces arrayed—I will not say *against* teaching, but *for* research—are formidable indeed, composing a gigantic scholarly cartel. At its base is the department, the matrix of university power, protected from above by the graduate deans and administrators, who are more and more drawn from the research professoriat and therefore share its aims and ambitions. National structure is provided by the great foundations and the learned societies which form the American Council of Learned Societies. And now there is the new National Endowment for the Humanities, whose depressingly conventional initial programs (*inter alia* a grant for papyrological studies and historical bibliography) look as though they might have been designed by an unprogrammed computer in collaboration with a retired professor of Coptic. Even the Woodrow Wilson Foundation, designed "to attract men and women to the profession of college teaching," now seems to be tailoring its standards more and more to the pinched professionalism of the graduate schools. There is also the Cartter report of the American Council on Education; intended to assess the quality of graduate programs on the basis of *informed* opinion, it will almost inevitably have the effect of stifling innovation, if only because informed scholarly opinion is unadventurous and tyrannous as well as profoundly snobbish. My argument is this: At every level the forces making for scholarly conformity are immense, and the rewards of conformity high. If these forces are not directly hostile to teaching, they are certainly profoundly indifferent.

My point is not merely negative. If there is to be reform within the existing institutional framework, it must be radical. Teaching will not be restored by tinkering with the curriculum, by minor structural changes, or modest innovations in graduate degree programs. I offer the following observations as instances only; to my mind they represent the kind of profound structural reform that must precede real change. I believe they are practicable, but I offer them nonetheless with considerable pessimism, in the doubt that there is presently enough energy and leadership in the American university for it to be reformed from within.

ADMINISTRATION AND INNOVATION

Innovation, experiment, reform—these are crucial, and the pity is that, apart from a few noteworthy experiments, there is so little real innovation. Wherever one looks, there is the same vacuum of leadership, the same failure of nerve. For this I believe administrators must shoulder the blame, or most of it. It is idle to expect anything from the faculties, who are caught both in the hideous jungle of academic bureaucracy and their own professional lethargy. Nor can one look to the providential intervention of the foundations; they can perhaps fund imagination and courage, but they cannot, apparently, provide it. It is above all to local institutions—the colleges, the universities—that one must turn. They are funded by communities—states, alumni, student fees—and they therefore have a responsibility to the community that supports them, but above all to that general culture that I have identified with the ideal role of the teacher. But if community and faculty support is to be enlisted (and community tyranny to be avoided), there must be something more than mere management by administrators; there must be leadership, which means a sense of the whole endeavor. Chairmen of departments and deans have constituencies to represent; only the presidents and provosts can speak on behalf of the whole enterprise.

I believe that administrators fail to make anything like full, or imaginative, use of their power. As an ex-chairman I understand that administrators are not omnipotent, that hypocrisy and evasion go with the job. But I am not prepared to believe that presidents are powerless; too many instances of abuse of power convince me to the contrary. It is the margin of freedom that matters, and it is only with the failure of administrators to use this margin that I find fault. What is stunning is the universal torpor, the apparent dedication to the principle of *laisser aller*. If presidents are too harassed to provide leadership, what has happened to the provosts? Why are the deans so subservient to the departments, so supinely deferential to the research professoriat? Why don't administrators take the stump on behalf of their policies?

There is, I suspect, only one answer, and it is not powerlessness, but lack of policies and ideas, and a long habit of prostration before success. A man cannot stump for programs he doesn't have, and this is why so many administrators talk such dreary rubbish. They have, quite literally, nothing to say. Alternatively, they are the prisoners of their origins, the professoriat from which they emerged and whose assumptions and aims they share. Hence they conceive of their task as the encouragement of the *status quo* and, when confronted with the crisis of education, claim, like Clark Kerr, that chaos is positively good for us, or, like President Perkins, that we can reconcile teaching and scholarship by the simple device of abandoning liberal education.

THE COLLEGES

I can think of no more conspicuous failure of leadership than in the liberal-arts colleges. With a few notable exceptions, the record of the college is one of failure, at least if judged by its own claims. Whatever else it may be, Socratic it is not, in neither faculty nor style nor results. This I take to be a matter of fact. Certainly it is hard to imagine a more damningly documented indictment of the liberal-arts college than that of the Jacob study,[2] with its bleak conclusion that, apart from three or four colleges, the effect of college teaching on student values is simply nil, zero, and that what small change occurs comes from the student subculture. The conclusion is the more devastating because it is precisely on the claim to *teach* that the American college stakes its case. Here—in low student-teacher ratios, in college plans, tutorials, etc.—it has spent its money and ingenuity, and it is here that its failure has been spectacular. Why?

In my opinion, the colleges have failed as teaching institutions because they have been subverted from within. They have recruited their faculties heavily from the major graduate institutions, and these recruits have inevitably altered the tone and finally the function of the colleges. There has doubtless been pres-

[2] Philip E. Jacob, *Changing Values in College: An Exploratory Study of the Impact of College Teaching* (New York: Harper & Bros., 1958).

sure from the graduate schools, but for the most part the colleges have consented to the process. And they are now in the ludicrous position of proudly claiming on the one hand that 70-odd percent of their graduates go on to graduate or professional schools, and on the other of complaining that they are being turned into prep schools for graduate study. Gentility and snobbery have played a large part in this subversion, as well as the hunger for academic respectability which is now firmly linked to the business of research. Instead of cleaving to their Socratic pretensions and traditions, the colleges have tended instead to become petty universities, differing from the universities only in a slightly higher regard for the teacher and a corresponding tolerance of the student. If the wealthier colleges have managed to recruit able faculty, the poor colleges have fared badly, recruiting second- and third-rate PhD's, who for their part regard the college as an academic boondocks and lust for the day when they can return to the urban Edens of research. In the meantime, they teach the only thing they know—technical expertise—and thereby both corrupt their students and refuse their Socratic opportunities. The colleges, in short, have yoked themselves to Pharaoh's chariot and, if they regret their loss of function, they have only themselves to blame. A handful of small colleges have dared to break the bond of snobbery and respectability that binds the college to the university, and they have done so simply by daring to profess the values they assert and finding teachers who profess them, too.

Organizational energy and intelligence are crucial if the liberal-arts college is to escape subordination to graduate education. I am, of course, in violent disagreement with those who believe that "the selective liberal-arts colleges of the future must become first-rate preparatory colleges for graduate education." [3] If we believe that the liberal traditions of the colleges are viable and that the college may have a higher function than feeding professional schools, then we must set about saving it. If I am right, the trouble with the colleges is that they recruit their faculties from uncongenial sources; the well is poisoned. By imitating the universi-

[3] Allan M. Cartter, "University Teaching and Excellence," *Educational Record* (Spring 1966), p. 297.

ties, the colleges have everything to lose and nothing to gain; neither their funds nor their human resources are adequate to the competition. My solution is dramatically simple. Let the college go into business on their own, *against* the graduate universities; let them form their own league, as it were, and train the kind of man they cannot expect to recruit from the universities. I am aware that such federations are in the air, and perhaps already exist; but I am emphatically *not* suggesting federation on the principle of beating the graduate schools at their own game. It should be a *different game altogether,* designed to produce men who do not think it beneath their dignity to educate others; men in whom the general civilized intelligence survives; humanists with a concern for men; scholars convinced that the world needs humane knowledge as never before. Ideally, I think, it would seek to *involve* its students in the real world, and it would surely seek real association with the vocations and professions. But its primary purpose would be to produce truly educated graduates as well as teachers to whom it could reasonably entrust the crucial task of providing models for those who wanted to become civilized men instead of scholars. I also believe that a formidable but generous enterprise helps to summon large behavior into being, and that the immense task of building institutions worthy of his love and learning might do much to create the kind of man who is missing. Enterprises which require humanity are the first prerequisite for a greater humanity. Men must *use* themselves significantly in order to grow. That is the law of all education, all growth. Why not apply it to *education?* We need new or renewed institutions; in the act of renewing them, we may renew ourselves.

Such institutions would surely not lack for students. Those who desire further study but have no wish to be processed as professors, are, I am convinced, far more numerous than is commonly suspected. The country is rich; leisure is available; educational expectations are rising. Far too many graduates of our colleges and universities feel, moreover, that they never got an education, and it is these who go on to graduate school in the hope of getting what they failed to get as undergraduates. It is graduate *education* they want, not graduate *training.* This is why dissatisfaction with the graduate schools is so keen. There is simply *no option* available on the graduate level; everything is geared to professional training. And among those disenchanted with graduate school are precisely those from whom the colleges should in fact be recruiting their faculties—those students who are not averse to learning but who demand that it be given relevance and embodiment. It seems a cruel shame that such talent should go to waste or find no meaningful fulfillment at a time when it is so terribly needed. We are not so rich in the *higher* human resources that this source can be so tragically wasted.

Are there enough men to staff more than three or four such experimental "graduate" centers in the liberal arts? Probably not. But what matters is that there should be at least a handful of colleges in this country which dare to resist the conformity imposed by the research cartel and to distinguish themselves by putting the teacher—and therefore the humanities—squarely at the center of the curriculum. Two or three such places would, I am convinced, reinvigorate, perhaps even revolutionize, American education simply by providing convincing examples of the daring and diversity we need. The logical place for them to be established is either upon the existing base of the better liberal-arts colleges, or as a new "higher college" created by a group of colleges acting in concert. Only by some such device, by striking at the source of the trouble, can the traditional role of the college be protected and expanded. It would be a staggering loss if the only institution of higher education still committed to liberal education —that is, to the creation of civilized men, the indispensable and large-minded amateur who is the layman to any coherent or general culture—should be subverted by the demand for professionals and technicians.

THE UNIVERSITIES

Teaching is notoriously worse off in the universities than in the colleges. Not only is the university traditionally more committed to pure research, but it is particularly vulnerable to the pressures that have eroded the teacher's status. Vast numbers of students, huge classes, intense competition for federal funds and therefore for distinguished research professors, political and professional pressures—all these have operated to downgrade and even discredit teaching. But even in the university it is the creative use of the margin of freedom that matters. Something has been done, for instance, to give the multiversity a human scale—through honors programs, emphasis on individual work, residential colleges, and so on. But helpful as these reforms are, they have not succeeded in changing the imbalance. And this, I believe, is because none of the reforms really touches the nub of the problem. And that is the structure of the university itself, the way in which its physical organization determines its policies and precludes change and reform. Certainly no real change in the status of teaching can possibly occur without a radical change in the present power structure of the university.

Perhaps this is impossible, but I am not convinced that this is so. At present the heart of university power is the department. It is this departmental power that now so vehemently promotes research and is hostile or indifferent to teaching. It is at the departmental level that teaching evaluation is subverted, since chairmen apparently equate research and teaching; it is there that publish-or-perish policies are really promulgated; that the pressure for reduced teaching loads derives; from there that graduate deans are recruited; that the demand for early specialization arises, as well as the jealous specialism that fragments the curriculum into warring factions. Put a mild and gentle man of broad learning into a department chairmanship, and within two years he will either be murdered by his colleagues or become an aggressive and vindictive *mafioso* of the crassest specialism. The process can no more be resisted than the ravages of time. It is inexorable and destructive; and it is the remorseless tragedy of university politics.

This is why it is so imperative that some rival to it, some countervailing, antidepartmental force be created. Research is dominant now because teaching has no effective representation, no normalized political place or power, within the structure of the university. The departments are theoretically composed of teachers, or teacher-scholars, but actually they have been wholly captured by the research professoriat. The research scholar has *everything*—the departments, the powerful committees, the learned societies, the federal funds, the deanships, and the presidencies —and if he chooses to say that he finds teaching distasteful and unworthy of his abilities, who will say him Nay? Who speaks for teaching here? Clearly nobody except perhaps the students. If teaching is to survive within the modern university on terms of something like parity with research, it must somehow acquire institutional power. The teacher, like the scholar, must have a base, a position, a budget, students, an honored and normalized function. He cannot meaningfully exist in any other way. This, I am convinced, is simple political realism.

The obvious vehicle for such a countervailing force would be the so-called university professorship. For though this professorship is still an uncertain novelty, occupying a still undefined institutional position, it has usually come into existence because enterprising administrators felt the need for countering the effects of extreme departmental specialism. Thus, while the university professor may retain a departmental base, his appointment is a "university" one insofar as it cuts across departmental and even college lines. This "horizontal" professor has of course aroused the jealousies of departments, and they have frequently responded by cutting off the new professor's access to students. What is now needed, I believe, is a deliberate effort to expand and consolidate the university professorship with the hope of eventually creating a new professoriat of such power that it can challenge the supremacy of the research departments. I have no illusion that this will be an easy task, but the precedent exists and the principle has been established. It would seem folly not to follow it up. Clearly the problems of defining the relations of two such professoriats to each other and to the administration and students would be of exceptional and maddening difficulty, but I doubt they are insoluble. So far as function is concerned, it would seem natural to assign to the university professorship all those tasks at which the departments have proven themselves incompetent—the courses in general education, humanities, interdisciplinary programs, supervision of the teacher-oriented degree programs, etc.—perhaps even the formal responsibility for evaluating teaching throughout the university. But its overall concern would be with teaching, and with the training of teachers. It would, therefore, I hope, display that broad spectrum of high and varied human skills that can significantly claim to be called *educational,* every conceivable great style of human existence and mode of mind side by side—the prophetic, the rational, the political, the scientific, the apocalyptic, the artistic. There would, of course, be an honored place in it for scholars, too, but only for scholars whose scholarship *educates.* I suspect this proposal will strike most of my audience as fantastic, but so, when you think about it, is the present state of affairs—a vast educational enterprise built entirely upon a caste of learned men whose learning has no relevance to the young and even seems to alienate the young from both education and culture. It is a vision of madness accomplished.

PLURALISM

My argument would not be complete without a word about pluralism. Educators never tire of saying that ours is a pluralistic system and that pluralism is good since it accords with the nature of American society. I share this view, but my fear is that, where higher education is concerned, we are rapidly junking pluralism for monolithic uniformity. One can understand why this is happening, but it seems to me the process must now be resolutely opposed. If education is to become, as perhaps it must in part, an "instrument of national policy," then we must have also institutions that still perform an *ecumenical* function, that speak for man rather than for the state or the nation. Professional training at the graduate level is now corrupting all higher education by ruthlessly expelling from the curriculum everything that does not conform to professional utility. By so doing it is forcing the student—who may want to be more than merely a professor—into the streets and out of the culture. The student becomes marginal simply out of opposition to the elite which has expelled him. Alternatively, he responds by violent and often unintelligent assertions of those very values, especially freedom, which the university seems to have abandoned. His attempts at heroism thus become merely anarchic; he loses the skills of educated heroism, even while claiming to assert them. What we must have, unless we are prepared to abandon our fates to parochial technicians, is precisely the pluralism to which we are committed. We need *options, choices, alternatives;* we need to honor the diversity of human skills and needs. We simply cannot afford, except at the cost of everything, to permit the range of realization to be narrowed to one small mode of the mind, and that a mode which seems to be incapable of compassion for any other mode, which seems, in fact, to have lost respect for humanity.

One final point. I expect to be told that I am actually meeting the problem of research and teaching not by reconciling them but by divorcing them altogether. That is my intention, and one which I am prepared to risk, since the only likely alternative is to make teaching the lackey of scholarship. I think we have reached the point at which slogans like "scholar-teacher" merely darken counsel; there may have been a time when that was a viable ideal, and doubtless some exceptionally gifted men still incarnate it. But by and large its vogue passes on to the professor the two functions which the university has inherited and which it cannot meaningfully reconcile. The realities of educational practice make it starkly apparent that no reconciliation can now occur except at the expense of teaching. And I am not prepared to incur that expense if I can humanly help it. This is why I urge you to consider freshly the wisdom of separating teaching and research, with the thought that significant teaching and fresh energy in academic institutions may eventually make scholarship human again, and that an invigorated scholarship may once again accept the burden of teaching as the source of its vigor and the test of its wisdom.

◄ JOSEPH P. COSAND

The Community College
in 1980

AMONG COLLEGIATE INSTITUTIONS, the junior—or community —college is a relative newcomer. The four-year college can trace its origins to Colonial days, but the first junior college was not established until 1901, in Joliet, Illinois. Today there are some 800 two-year colleges, comprising more than a third of the institutions of higher learning in the United States (included are so-called technical institutes). Approximately 500 are public, tax-supported institutions (usually called community colleges) which charge modest fees or none. The rest are private, most of them charging substantial fees.

New two-year colleges are now being established at the rate of 50 a year, and by 1980 the American Association of Junior Colleges expects there will be more than 1,200 in operation. Growth in enrollment is just as dramatic. In September 1964, there were just over 1,000,000 students attending junior colleges—a 14 percent increase over the previous year. By 1980 enrollment is expected to be close to 3,000,000. Much of this phenomenal growth was spurred by the G.I. Bill of Rights, which enabled many veterans to attend college.

But mere numbers, however impressive, are no true measure of the value of an institution. What counts is the quality of its services and product. What are the pros and cons of the junior college? What does it offer? What is its future?

For students who expect to go on to other institutions, junior colleges offer a college-transfer program that provides the usual first two years of collegiate work. Credits earned from accredited institutions are accepted by four-year colleges and universities. Most public and private junior colleges emphasize this program. At good institutions courses are rigorous, preparing students to compete satisfactorily with those who had their first two years at a four-year college.

How good are transfer students? California—the pacesetting state for community colleges—provides a good measuring stick. Records at the University of California show that the transfer student from a two-year college does just as well as, or better than, his classmate who entered the university as a freshman.

For students who want to be educated for employment in our increasingly complex society, the typical junior college offers a technical program. Although technical programs have lagged behind college-transfer programs, the rising demand for high technical skills is spurring renewed effort among both private and public junior colleges. Assistance in planning appropriate programs is coming from advisory committees drawn from business, industry, labor, and the professions.

In the development of high-quality technical education, the comprehensive community college has assumed leadership. Already scores of excellent one- and two-year programs are offered —in such specialties as engineering technology, architectural drafting, law enforcement, commercial art, data processing, retailing, and X-ray technology. There are programs to prepare young people to work as registered nurses, dental and medical laboratory assistants, and executive secretaries.

Where school systems lack strong high-school vocational programs, some community colleges are filling the vacuum by offering programs in cosmetology, licensed practical nursing, auto mechanics, radio and television repair, welding, machine-shop work, and many other occupational areas. The programs may include apprenticeship training.

The technical-vocational programs offered by a particular college are primarily determined by the community's needs. But increasing population mobility is encouraging community colleges to prepare students for jobs throughout a state or region. This development is particularly marked where employment opportunities are limited in the area served by the college.

One highly valuable role of the junior college is to help students who have had limited success in high school and failed to realize their potentialities. These young people thus have an opportunity to continue their education—to make up deficits and repair damage.

In four-year colleges, on the other hand, the trend is to cut back on remedial work. The ill-prepared or unmotivated student will usually fail or drop out. Not all junior colleges, to be sure, have a remedial program (some have highly selective admission policies), but the truly *comprehensive* community college usually shows a real concern for helping the student to succeed by showing him how to try. While students are not coddled, they do receive help in remedying their deficiencies and developing their innate talents.

All junior colleges seek to give students, whatever program they enroll in, a sound general education. The ideal—if not always the practice—is to help the student develop the skills and knowledge that will enable him to think effectively, express himself clearly, and function maturely. Requirements for the Associate Degree—in English, mathematics, and the social and physical sciences—are evidence of junior colleges' concern with general education and with stimulating students to a lifelong quest for knowledge.

With an enlightened counseling and guidance program, the junior college can help students of diverse abilities to continue their education successfully. Counseling that helps a youngster mesh interest with ability salvages many a potential dropout or failure. College-transfer, technical, and developmental programs multiply young people's opportunities for a successful college experience. So far, so good. The ideal is edifying. But how is it working out?

Junior colleges too often operate under distinct disadvantages. As newcomers in the field of higher education, they lack the status and prestige of the older four-year institutions. Academic snobs tend to view them as a last resort—the public community colleges for dullards, a handful of fancy junior colleges as finishing schools renamed.

Prejudice aside, there is basis in 1968 for critizing junior colleges. Too many are still appendages of high schools, often sharing the same facilities and staff and with no impetus or apparent desire to develop their own identity and pride. Where the junior college is under the same jurisdiction as the lower schools, the needs of elementary and high schools are usually served first, with the junior college getting the leftovers in space, faculty, and financing. Where a junior college is governed by a separate board or is part of a state system of higher education, it is likely to fare far better.

Some communities and some junior-college faculties have a mistaken concept of the junior college. They see it as a halfway house that will eventually become a four-year college, rather than as a unique two-year institution with programs suited to the needs of varied groups of students. When the faculty mistakes the mission of the junior college, a conventional academic program is likely to be overemphasized at the expense of the technical and developmental programs. Junior colleges suffer, too, from inadequate understanding on the part of high-school teachers and counselors as to institutional objectives and programs, particularly technical programs.

Too many junior colleges are still shortchanged in every way. But enlightened leadership, both state and local, is bringing about changes for the better. In state after state there is dynamic improvement. In Florida and California, for example, junior colleges are flourishing institutions, enrolling up to 75 percent of all students in the lower divisions of public colleges and universities.

The faults and disadvantages of junior colleges are, I think, temporary. More money is available. Private and public support is increasing. Local commercial, industrial, labor, and professional leaders are giving time and service as advisers and teachers. Working in Washington with the American Association of Junior Colleges is a committee of such prominent representatives of various fields as Leroy Collins, former governor of Florida; former governor Terry Sanford of North Carolina; Ralph Besse, the president of the Cleveland Electrical Illuminating Company; and John Carl Warnecke, a San Francisco architect.

The unique promise of the junior college is that it opens the door of educational opportunity to millions of students for whom that door would otherwise be shut. It serves students whose family finances put high-cost institutions out of reach. In public junior colleges generally, tuition comes to less than a hundred dollars a semester. In some states—California, for example—there is no tuition. Where a junior college is within commuting distance, students can live at home, and the expense of room and board is eliminated.

The junior college also serves students who do not qualify for four-year colleges—slow bloomers, or students with inadequate preparation. And it serves students whose primary interest is in acquiring a marketable skill. At its best, the institution provides a variety of programs to fill students' varying needs and interests. In a well-run institution, the basic general-education program enables students to switch from one program to another as their self-confidence and achievement grow or their interest changes.

Another merit of the junior college is that it is strongly student-centered. Its faculty is employed to teach. And full-fledged teachers do all the teaching. None is left to graduate assistants. In most junior colleges, teachers of academic subjects are required to have a minimum of a master's degree in the subject they teach, as well as several years of teaching experience.

By 1980 the community colleges and technical institutes, I am quite sure, will have reappraised themselves and have decided that everyone in this country has the right to reach his full potential. If universities and four-year colleges, obsessed with academic respectability, continue to restrict admissions and programs, the community colleges of necessity must open their doors wide and say: "This is your college. This is the people's college." It will be a true center of learning, providing educational opportunities for both youth and adults, day and night, 12 months of the year.

This broad service the comprehensive community college can and must render in 1980—not in just a few communities, as at present, but all over the United States, as community leaders, boards of trustees, administrators, and faculties become committed to both a vision and a practicable goal.

In every urban center I would expect to see a major community-college campus. Here the people of the inner city will be able to find the same educational opportunities now offered in suburbia, where most community colleges seem to be located today.

In my view, the community college or technical institute will, by 1980, have accepted virtually the entire responsibility for providing the first two years of college work. By then, the four-year colleges and universities will primarily be concerned with upper-division and graduate work.

These two-year comprehensive community colleges will be, for the most part, commuter colleges where the student, regardless of his age or affluence or status will have the opportunity to pursue his education while still living at home. The support, financial and moral, will come from the local, state, and federal governments so that no student who is able to benefit from the community college's or technical institute's offerings will lose out because he is short of money. The breakthrough I foresee will be as momentous as America's commitment, earlier in the century, to universal high-school education.

The community colleges by then will be up-to-date and highly respected in every sense of the word—and not, as all too often today, marked by obsolescence in equipment, faculty, administration, leadership, or vision. Business, industry, labor, and the professions—the vital organs of the community—cannot afford this luxury of obsolescence. Luxury it is, for it results in an unbelievable waste of both physical and human resources.

With administration, trustees, and faculty working together in a new climate of cooperation and service, there will be a ferment of creativity that will bring new methods of instruction, based on the productive miracles of electronics. It will bring new sources of instructional resources, where the library will no longer be merely a collection of books, but rather a complete resource center, utilizing all kinds of instructional and learning materials. This creative climate will permit the exploitation of the individual teacher's special abilities and will eliminate the current lockstep that afflicts teacher and student alike. In 1980 we will be ready for action based upon solid research.

Perhaps the most exciting vision before the community colleges and technical institutes is a new breed of teachers and administrators, concerned with what America could be if everybody had a chance to realize his potential. The community colleges are getting some such people today, and what a thrill it is to watch them cope with problems. "There is a better way to teach—a better course—a better curriculum. There must be a better way, if we are to succeed," they say. A young physics teacher, only a few years out of Harvard's graduate school, exemplifies this new breed. He believes that by 1980, or much sooner, the joint use of television and the computer will enable hundreds of students to view a given program at the same time. But each student can respond individually. The student is required to participate, not to sit idly by wasting his and the teacher's time. The size of the class does not necessarily determine the presence or lack of personal attention—the teaching methods are the determining factors. There will be large classes and small, but students will never be lost, for each teacher will be adviser and each student will know he is important to the college, and not just a number on an IBM card. The new breed of teachers will exploit every possibility, striving to live up to Tertullian's dictum, "It is certain because it is impossible."

The community college of 1980 will search the universities for such imaginative people. They will reject the traditionalist unaware of the social revolution. They will reject the academician interested only in some narrow aspect of his discipline. They will employ only those who believe wholeheartedly in the philosophy of the community college and who are dedicated to a service for all the people.

Age is no factor in determining who these creatively discontented people are. An experienced sociology teacher, just returning from two years in Africa, can produce a "one world" atmosphere of learning—comparing America's "education for the asking" with Africa's "education only through untold sacrifices." The community college in 1980 will also have aggressive in-service training programs, stressing the importance of an exciting, stimulating educational program for every kind of student.

In the past the student has generally received individual attention when he arrived and when he departed. We wished him well on the first day, and we congratulated him when we conferred his degree. This is not enough. Many students, for lack of continuing concern, have been unable to achieve their full potential and unable to compete in the world outside school. Community colleges throughout America will, in 1980, stress the importance of advising and counseling throughout the full two years—and in the case of adults, through four, six, or eight years of part-time attendance.

Placement offices will be major centers of campus activity. Students ready for employment will be sought out by giants like Monsanto, General Motors, and General Electric, by hospitals and dentists and retailers. The technician graduating from a community college or technical institute will be recognized as a valuable acquisition.

I would hope that, by the 1980s, community colleges would help students to find values by which to live in our increasingly complex society—that students would learn to leave the world a richer place; to contribute and not to consume; to lift and not to lean; to give as well as take. This can become a people's renaissance, brought about to great degree through a people's college, and could revolutionize traditional attitudes toward the poor, the ill-fed, the delinquent. By 1980, let us hope, community-college leaders, faculty, and trustees will no longer succumb to the mesmerism of the words: Is this program of college grade? By this time they will be more concerned with questions like: Is the curriculum, the course, needed? Is it being given? If not, why not? Can we do it? By doing so, will it help to build a community that is richer culturally, occupationally, and morally?

The "college-grade" shibboleth is perhaps the worst obstacle facing community colleges in 1968. It must be surmounted. The community college is here to serve and to provide opportunity. It is not here to act as a barrier or to operate like a swinging door, gently—or not so gently—pushing out the unwanted student.

These institutions in the 1980s must react positively to community needs as interpreted by teachers, administrators, and trustees. This will be impossible if curricula are controlled by the state government, by a distant state university, or by the federal government. Local or regional business, industry, labor, the professions, and educators together can best define these needs. This is a heavy responsibility for local administration and policy-makers, for it demands vision and perspective. Narrow provincialism is just as deadly as remote bureaucratic control.

To accomplish the required goals, the teaching staff must rise above its own middle-class background and learn to understand the differing pressures upon students of all kinds—those from affluent communities as well as those from the inner-city ghettos. Both the recruiting of teachers and their in-service training need to reflect these socioeconomic factors.

The traditional liberal-arts background of most teachers must have a leavening if community colleges are to cope with the pressures of their diverse students. Administrators and teachers must come to this new world willing to admit that they are ignorant and ready to learn. The new breed of teachers and administrators must accomplish this difficult task in the 1980s. Academic presumptuousness does not work—and can never work—in a community college or in a technical institute.

In the 1980s, I believe, the communications barrier between secondary schools and community colleges will be breached. By that time we will have learned that the continuum of education cannot be broken, that a student should be helped to move along it as far and as fast as he can. The community college will be available to youth or adult, regardless of age. Education must, in the 1980s, be a continuing force, designed to provide the people with the opportunity to adjust to a changing world.

And changes will be rapid. Obsolescence will not be measured in scores of years, but perhaps only in single years. This continuing education—this articulation between the different levels of education—will permit the student to see education as something that is always there for him. It will give him hope.

Articulation between the community colleges and the four-year colleges and universities is every bit as important as articulation between community colleges and high schools. Today there is still too much feeling that a college must protect itself by maintaining traditional barriers. Students should be able to progress according to their own abilities, not according to artificial measures developed in isolated splendor.

The community college and technical institutes of 1980 will be accepted, especially in the cities, as prime institutions, where they will not be expected to operate in leftover educational facilities. These institutions will not try to duplicate the campuses of the liberal-arts college or the state university. But they will no longer be mere appendages—poor relations lucky to get hand-me-downs.

By 1980 community colleges will have an identity of their own, based upon solid accomplishments. For too long they have been obsessed with imitating the academic four-year college. Ultimately, community colleges and technical institutes will be content—and proud—to be themselves. Their campuses, built to unique specifications educationally and physically, will become centers of learning, where students, young and old, can fulfill themselves whatever their educational backgrounds.

The community college of 1980, open day and night, will serve a vast population. The person going home from work will be able to stop in for an evening class. For that matter, the person working at night—the policeman or fireman, perhaps—might well enroll for a day class, joining the regular college students who are mainly in the 18–21-year-old age group. The community college of 1980 cannot close its doors to time or to people.

The community colleges must be just as much concerned with the problems of the old as with the problems of youth. The city campus will provide sustenance for older people who are now confined to downtown apartments and who have little to live for —who sit idly by and wait for death. Yet these people can still contribute to their own lives and that of others. They cannot go out to the typical suburban campus of 1968.

Perhaps one of the most encouraging aspects of the community college in 1980 will be its secure and genuine relationship with business, industry, labor, and the professions. The equipment in the laboratories, of the latest type, will be provided by industry. There will be full cooperative use of laboratories and clinical services, medical, dental, and industrial, with consequent alleviation of tremendous personnel shortages. Even today in 1968, business, industry, and the professions have come to the community colleges for help. By 1980, they will understand that they, as well as the colleges, must contribute. A marriage cannot be one-sided; and this marriage will benefit all concerned, for it will make for a far better community in which to live.

From another vantage point, this type of cooperation will encourage faculty to stop their self-centered fragmentation. Instead, they will seek interdisciplinary action. Barriers erected by the traditional academic departments, and within departments, are ridiculous and must be eliminated—a move that is now under way. The isolation of the subject-matter specialist will be a thing of the past in the community college of tomorrow and, I hope, in all of higher education. The English teacher will be concerned with the students in technical education, the philosophy teacher with the physical-education major, the artist with the retailing student, and the mathematics instructor with the musician. A faculty should be a whole. All must work together in mutual respect if all their responsibilities are to be fulfilled.

These goals will require the highest type of leadership on the part of the administration. The new breed of administrator must be dedicated to the principles of the comprehensive community college, knowing that he is there to lead and to serve, but never to dictate. The paternalism so prevalent in past years will be definitely outmoded, if only because faculty members will have none of it. The faculty wants a voice, and they will have one—a big one, raised to support better educational programs.

These colleges will realize in 1980, I hope and believe, that there are many methods of teaching and that each teacher may have a method which is best for him. An administrator will not demand that all teachers teach in the same way, but that they make use of every accessible and appropriate teaching aid: slides, computers, tape recorders and many other audiovisual materials.

The student is there to learn, and the teacher must fill his needs by becoming the best possible teacher—not simply a dispensary of facts or a fountainhead of words, but a professional who has learned the skills of true teaching. I would expect the community college of 1980 to be staffed with professionals who are confident of their own abilities and who do not need crutches to prop up their pride. The artificiality of many of these crutches is appalling: academic rank, number of hours taught each week, and similar trivia—all mitigating against professionalism. By 1980 assistants will permit teachers to devote more time and energy to the profession of teaching.

If we expect this professionalism, we must provide a nourishing climate. Teachers and administrators alike will need to have leaves of absence from their educational responsibilities so that they can work off campus in those fields where an up-to-date knowledge of the latest techniques and equipment is essential to good teaching. Business, industry, labor, and the professions will finance this type of leave and, by this cooperative effort, the community will benefit.

The wraps will be taken off research and development in the community colleges and technical institutes. These institutions will foster research just as business and industry do today. Industry spends a high percentage of its profit on research. So does business. So do the professions. The businessman and industrialist go back to college for advanced study. The professional spends time away from his immediate responsibilities to acquire new knowledge so that he can do a better job as a surgeon, a dentist, a physician. The teacher must do the same, and will—with strong encouragement and support from the college, where the goal must always be toward better teaching.

Community colleges must take time to develop new courses and programs, and not expect this burden to be borne by teachers with their limited financial resources. This important assignment should be part of the teacher's responsibility to the college and be paid for as such. This is research and development at its best. Community colleges will gain thereby better courses, better curricula, and better teaching methods. They will know more about student characteristics and student followup. And they'll be doing all these things in the 1980s.

Such research and development will show when our equipment and knowledge are becoming obsolete. The rapid revolution now taking place in this electronic age means that every community college designed to serve the people must devote money and time to pragmatic research. The pure research taking place in the United States will and must continue, of course, but this is not a part of a community college's responsibility.

The research appropriate to two-year institutions will be an integral part of every budget—and an integral part of every community college's philosophy. With substantial support from the professional and industrial world, it will be incumbent upon these colleges to contribute time and money themselves. The college's contribution can be in-service education for the employees of the community's business, industrial, and professional groups. Classes don't have to be scheduled on the campus. Classes don't have to carry credit. Classes don't have to be only for those people who have less than two years of college education. Serving the whole community, community colleges will have to schedule classes both on and off campus, with or without credit, to meet specific needs.

The community college, serving people in a community, has to be aware of what "the revolution of automation" means, and has to be ready to meet the changes brought about in the cultural and occupational world. On "campus 1980," the community college and the technical institute will have clearly stated philosophies and objectives and will adhere to them. The best institutions will harbor no desire to become four-year colleges. They will have their own important and distinctive status. Faculty salaries and prestige will be high enough to counteract the sense of inferiority that prevails today and that tends to make the two-year college a stepping stone to a teaching position in a four-year college or university.

The stated philosophies and objectives of these comprehensive community colleges of the future will vary in detail, but essentially might read as follows:

Philosophy

The community college is concerned with the educational needs of the community or region it serves. It accepts its responsibility for leadership and proposes to develop and maintain a collegiate program sufficiently flexible to adjust to changing educational needs. To fulfill these needs it will offer academic, technical-vocational, remedial, and general cultural courses all directed toward the betterment of the student, and thus the community.

Objectives

1. Transfer education: to provide the first two years of college instruction for students planning to transfer to four-year colleges and universities for upper-division work.

2. Preparatory and developmental education: to provide each student with the opportunity to make up scholastic or subject-matter deficiencies in his educational program.

3. Advanced placement: to provide each student with the opportunity to be placed in a curriculum or in a sequence of courses according to his abilities and therefore to avoid repetition, boredom, and waste.

4. Technical and vocational education: to provide:
   a. preemployment education, and
   b. extension education for the occupational advancement of persons already employed.

5. General education: to provide—indirectly in all courses and directly in specific courses—experiences which will lead to the development of a broadly educated person who has a grasp of the interrelationship of knowledge, and who is able, through learning, to think effectively, communicate his thoughts, make relevant judgments, discriminate among values, and make appropriate applications of what he has learned.

By 1980, I would expect a different procedure for earning an Associate in Arts degree from a community college. Today we are mired in the tradition of a required number of units, regardless of how much a person has actually learned. Advanced placement will be almost a commonplace a dozen years from now.

It is about time we begin to analyze, through counseling and through advanced placement, what a student needs, rather than continue to impose upon him a required number of courses which are repetitious and often dull. We are approaching the time when the student will rebel, and educators will finally realize the absurdity of requiring a specific number of college credits. The degree will then reflect measurable learning, rather than reward the mere compilation of credit hours. Today's practice is a carryover—like the lecture with no discussion—a selection based upon grades only for admission to college, a blind adherence to college-entrance tests even though the results of such prognosis are dubious. We have tolerated many such traditional rites established over a period of years. The comprehensive community college can lead the way out of this wilderness.

◀ A. A. LIVERIGHT

Learning Never Ends: A Plan for Continuing Education

> We have a comparatively decent system of common schools, school for infants only; but except for the half-starved Lyceum in the winter, and latterly the puny beginnings of a library suggested by the state, no school for ourselves. . . . It is time that we had uncommon schools, that we did not leave off our education when we begin to be men and women. It is time that villages were universities, and their elder inhabitants the fellows of universities with leisure—if they are indeed so well off—to pursue liberal studies the rest of their lives.
>
> HENRY DAVID THOREAU,
> *Walden*

IN 1968, 112 years after Thoreau called for the establishment of "uncommon schools," his dream is still largely unfulfilled. But some seeds have been sown, and the shape of the future is already discernible.

Social developments such as the technological and cybernetic revolution, increasing leisure, affluence and longevity, along with the federal government's new concern for the arts and humanities, its support for nonvocational and nonagricultural adult education,

149

and the war on poverty are having an important impact on the educational establishment.

As the need for a new problem-solving approach to metropolitan problems becomes accepted, the importance of multipurpose, community-oriented, urban universities will be universally accepted. In some communities it will be the private university which fills this new urban educational responsibility. In most communities, however, it will be the urban branch of the land-grant institution, or a newly created, independent, but publicly financed urban university which will emerge as the "urban-grant" university (to use the term coined by Chancellor John Ryan of the University of Massachusetts in Boston). Whether central responsibility is lodged in the public urban universities or not, the private institutions of higher education—both within the cities and in the peripheral areas—will be called upon increasingly to participate in consortium arrangements for providing for the growing and varying needs for continuing education in the ever-growing metropolitan complexes. And, as adult education in its own right responds to the social pressures with additional research and further professional development, it may well by the 1980s have matured from a peripheral, low-status, expendable activity to a basic, integral, subsidized part of the university.

These trends suggest that there may well be a new institutional form—a College of Continuing Education—in each urban university. First, let us pay a brief visit to Metropolis University in 1980 and later examine in more detail its "uncommon" College of Continuing Education.

As a result of the organization of the College of Continuing Education, we find that a new force and a new style of life have been developed in Metropolis, and that there is a new look and attitude at Metropolis University itself.

Most important, the entire community of Metropolis constitutes the potential student body of the university, and its faculty is drawn from all facets of the community. The Metropolis University Alumni Association includes the key leaders in the community (who have participated in advanced specialist and liberal-education programs both as students and leaders), many civil servants, the teachers and doctors and lawyers and the poor people in the inner-city community who participated in various local leadership-training and community-education programs. This close identification with all levels of the community has not meant any diminution in the respect for Metropolis U. nor has its academic respectability been sacrificed. Rather, by dint of this total community involvement, the university and the idea of education and lifelong learning have become accepted by all persons and classes in the community.

From an operational point of view, Metropolis University has become accepted as the central spot for initiating the problem-solving processes in the city. Both organizations and individuals know that they can discuss their problems with either the "urban agents" of the university or faculty members in the College of Continuing Education, and that the best brains and resources not only of Metropolis U. but of all the institutions of higher education in the area, both public and private, will be brought to bear on solving their problems. In like manner, adults who want to continue their education know that they can come to the inner city campus (or utilize it through satellite centers) and secure immediate and effective advice and counseling about how their educational needs and interests can be met—whether directly through Metropolis U. or through other institutions. By 1980, the College of Continuing Education has become the nerve center for mobilizing, planning, and cooperation in continuing education in Metropolis.

Also, the inner-city campus of the College of Continuing Education has become the new cultural center of Metropolis. Built around the core of a Learning Center and a Public Museum, both of which are integral parts of the College of Continuing Education, are clusters of little theatres, motion-picture houses, coffee shops and restaurants, and both transient and permanent residential quarters. More and more older persons have moved back to the city, attracted by the cultural and educational resources centered in the inner-city campus and a new, richly endowed, exciting, alive, integrated community has developed in an ever-growing area around the inner-city campus.

Probably the greatest impact of the "uncommon college" is upon its students. Women attending the various special daytime programs carried on by the various institutes bring their babies to the college, where they are cared for by students from the School of Education. Older and retired persons, who have increasingly moved into the apartments surrounding the inner-city campus, take part in a wide variety of educational programs and so, both on the inner-city campus and on the main campus of Metropolis U., the age of students covers the entire spectrum. As far as the undergraduate is concerned, he no longer thinks of college as a special preserve or club for himself and his contemporaries who are merely marking time there before they move on to serious pursuits such as work or graduate school. He realizes that for hundreds and thousands of adults in Metropolis, the university and education are a way of life. As older students are increasingly referred to the regular campus classes, they bring an important ingredient of practical experience to heretofore purely theoretical discussions and enrich the discussions by their observations and experiences. In turn, the participation of younger students in seminars, discussion groups, and classes on the inner-city campus provide a fresh, dynamic, and inquiring facet to the discussions which might otherwise be too pragmatic and earthbound. This intermixture of all ages at Metropolis University not only acclimates younger students to an atmosphere of lifelong learning but also, in many classes, improves the quality and nature of the learning experience itself.

Just as the new College of Continuing Education has an impact on its students and the community, so also does it affect the university itself. Faculty members who take part both in the regular campus intellectual life and in planning, teaching, and research at the College of Continuing Education discover new facets to their teaching and research and a relevance which many of them never imagined before. An "adjunct faculty" recruited from industry and government—at first looked upon with some suspicion—has become increasingly integrated into the faculties and departments. Their practical and sometimes hard-boiled attitudes and approaches provide another important dimension in faculty discussions and in developing research—enriching rather than limiting the nature of teaching and research on the campus. Although initially involved primarily in the continuing-education program, these adjunct-faculty members increasingly teach regular undergraduate and graduate courses. In turn, members of the adjunct faculty bring back to their industrial and governmental tasks new insights, a new approach, and an interest in applying the latest campus research and scholarly findings to their regular jobs and tasks. By dint of the presence of the members of the adjunct faculty and of mature students, the former stuffiness and isolation of the university have been broken down and a new air of inquiry, cooperation, and involvement in the community has developed. Metropolis University, without in any way sacrificing its scholarly attainments and research skills and concerns, has become a vital and essential part of the planning, thinking, and education of the community. It is in every sense an "open" rather than an isolated and closed university.

Needless to say, this has had an impact on the attitudes and habits of the administration and faculty. Top scholars and teachers who welcome the openness of Metropolis University and who realize the value and importance of a university which combines a vibrant, relevant, and varied mission and a student body with the persistent values of scholarship and contemplation have increasingly been attracted to Metropolis University. The new faculty also were attracted by the emphasis on independent study, by the use of teacher's aides and by the resources of the new learning center which provide them with both the leisure and the resources for their own independent study and research.

As far as community acceptance and support are concerned, the "uncommon college," with its close community identification, is looked upon as an essential ingredient in community advancement. It provides an answer to the former town-gown division and is an important factor not only in marshaling financial support for its own activities but also for the total university program.

In every sense of the word, Metropolis University, by 1980, is the core of the learning society in the city of Metropolis and thus the prototype for the new and pioneering urban university of the future.

Although the College of Continuing Education at Metropolis University is a mythical unit in a mythical university, its component parts already exist as programs in operation or on the drawing board around the country. To document and clarify this important point, the footnotes in the following discussion refer the reader to the prototype programs in each case and will be found in the Appendix at the end of this essay. Virtually all these specific proposals—for physical location and plan, development of faculty, involvement of the community, flexible use of new and old techniques and methods, organization and administration, and financing—have roots in some program under way or being planned in 1968.

Metropolis University as projected here is located, let us say, in an important city and is one of the state's two largest universities.

When it was founded, the original organizers recognized that a sound program of continuing education and community service was an essential ingredient for a responsive urban university. A policy committee consisting of representatives of key community groups as well as the faculty and administration of Metropolis University was given major responsibility for developing this program. The committee adopted the following guidelines for the college:

> Opportunities for lifelong learning and continuing education are a basic function of Metropolis University, and its responsibility to its students does not end with graduation. The research and teaching resources of the university will be applied to problems in the community as well as to programs of continuing education. In carrying out these responsibilities, Metropolis University will identify and make maximum use of existing resources in the community, instigating programs itself only if they are especially

appropriate to a university or can serve a germinal or demonstration purpose.

Early in its discussions, the policy committee agreed that, if graduates of Metropolis University were to become lifelong learners, certain conscious efforts would have to be made during the undergraduate years to firmly establish curiosity and interests and to provide skills for independent study. This resulted in changes in the methods of undergraduate teaching and the addition of several courses.

Teaching methods were revised to place greater emphasis on the identification and understanding of significant questions and dilemmas than on achieving final answers. Faculty members felt that students would be more likely to continue their study and learning if, at the end of a course, they were left with open-ended questions rather than a sense of closure. Since teaching is one of the most effective ways of learning, opportunities were made available for undergraduates to lead discussions and to teach both within the regular college and in the College of Continuing Education. Honors programs and independent research provide students with skills and habits which will stand them in good stead after formal schooling is completed.

To this end, the university added such courses as a seminar dealing with human and personal development, which permits students to examine their emerging needs and problems in small peer groups. These seminars continue after graduation as a major activity of the alumni association and assist in the transition from college to work.[1] Another required course concerns the development of learning and study skills utilizing new techniques for information storage and retrieval and the increasing number of opportunities for individual study. This seminar is given once to orient freshmen to opportunities within the university and again to orient seniors to facilities in the community.

A cooperative work-study program was instituted by the committee for young people who could not attend college for financial reasons. Employers hire workers in pairs over a year's period, thus permitting two students to alternate between work and school.[2]

Although originally developed to meet a community problem, this program was so successful in motivating students and increasing their ability to combine theory with practical experience that it was extended to non-needy students as well.

After making these changes in the undergraduate curriculum to provide a climate for lifelong learning, the policy committee identified six elements which they felt to be essential for a sound program of continuing education and community service. These were:

1. A curriculum especially for adults.
2. A readily accessible campus built to meet adult needs.
3. The best possible faculty for continuing education with a clear identification with the College of Continuing Education.
4. Clear-cut administrative responsibility for planning and conducting the program.
5. Community participation in planning and executing the program.
6. Imaginative and effective use of new educational technology.

The policy committee of the College of Continuing Education agreed that a curriculum developed along traditional departmental and disciplinary lines would not meet the needs of adults. As the basic motivations and interests of adults fall normally into four primary roles—worker, family member, citizen, and self-realizing individual—it was decided to develop the curriculum of the college along these lines. Four institutes were established, each with its own planning committee composed of community members with relevant experience, together with representatives of the administration and faculty of the College of Continuing Education. The four institutes are:

1. The Institute for Occupational and Professional Development, to answer the needs of the adult as a worker.
2. The Institute for Personal and Family Development, to assist the adult to achieve maximum effectiveness in family and personal relations.

3. The Institute for Civic and Social Development, to prepare him for participation in community, national, and world affairs.

4. The Institute for Humanistic and Liberal Development, to encourage self-realization and personal fulfillment.

Each of these institutes, under the guidance of its planning committee, undertook to assess the needs for continuing education and community service in its area of concern; identify and secure information about activities and programs already established to meet these needs; allocate responsibility for various levels of the program to the different educational institutions; stimulate cooperative planning to link together these facilities; and develop such programs as should appropriately be carried on by the College of Continuing Education.[3]

THE INSTITUTE FOR OCCUPATIONAL AND PROFESSIONAL DEVELOPMENT

A community survey of community needs and facilities identified many programs for "man as worker." As a matter of fact, there were proliferation and duplication in this area, with the public and proprietary schools, the colleges, and business and industry offering varied opportunities for occupational and vocational training. The major task, therefore, was to secure some agreement as to the program most appropriate for each educational institution as well as to divide responsibility between the schools and industry. Certain gaps and needs did, however, become apparent which could most properly be met by the College of Continuing Education. The following programs were consequently developed:

1. Special Degree Programs for Adults: An AB degree especially for adults could be secured through a combinaton of independent study credit for knowledge gained outside the classroom (awarded on the basis of nationally accepted examinations),[4] a series of interdisciplinary seminars, and a scholarly project.[5] Because of its flexibility, this special program enrolled hundreds of housewives as well as people in business, industry, and the armed

forces. Adults who wanted simply to round out their education and who were not interested in a degree could take the seminars and independent study in the humanities, the social sciences, or the natural sciences. A special MA for adults was established as a terminal degree primarily for specialists who wish to enlarge their horizons. An MA degree in the humanities[6] was offered primarily for scientists and an MS in scientific areas, for humanists. Employers, increasingly interested in ensuring a broader point of view among their middle and top personnel, provided annual one-month sabbaticals[7] to permit their employees to participate in the seminars as a capstone to independent study throughout the year.

2. For workers who wish to go beyond the preparatory and on-going job training provided by industry and government, the College of Continuing Education offered a wide variety of courses both on a residential basis at the inner-city campus and on an evening or weekend basis in cooperation with nearby liberal-arts colleges. These courses covered all the disciplines relevant to the interests and needs of the workers and involved theory and broad concepts rather than limited occupational training. By 1980 the conventional evening college of the 1950s and 1960s had pretty well disappeared. The regular undergraduate and graduate courses formerly offered by them had been taken over by the regular campus divisions, thus placing the responsibility for such education where it belongs.

3. In cooperation with professional associations (lawyers, doctors, engineers, etc.), the College of Continuing Education helped to set up and house—at its inner-city campus—a wide variety of seminars, institutes, and conferences to keep the professionals abreast of new findings in their fields. The professional societies themselves provided most of the technological and operational information and recruited students, while the college made available the appropriate faculty to provide theoretical background, either from Metropolis U. or from other institutions.[8]

4. Building on the experience gained in the Cooperative Extension Service in the late nineteenth and early twentieth centuries and growing out of the Technical Services Act passed by Congress in 1965, the Institute for Occupational and Professional Develop-

ment carried on an active industrial, scientific, and social-service demonstration and field program. Its staff members interpreted the latest developments in engineering, science, and the social sciences to practitioners in the field, who utilized these findings in their occupations and professions.

By 1980, responsibility for all of the more technical aspects of specific vocational and occupational training had been allocated directly either to business, industry, or the government,[9] or, where appropriate, to the public schools and junior colleges. The university was free to concentrate on the kind of education for "man as worker" which logically falls within its educational orbit.

THE INSTITUTE FOR PERSONAL AND FAMILY DEVELOPMENT

The assessment of community needs and resources revealed a vast array of associations and organizations which were already carrying on programs in the community or which had national resources and programs which could be brought to the community.[10] The main task was therefore one of attempting to orchestrate the total program and of training appropriate leadership. To carry out these functions, this institute included the following activities:

1. A special task force made up of representatives from the Medical School, the School of Nursing, the School of Social Work, and the social sciences as well as from community agencies was set up to establish a broad curriculum for personal and family development and to determine the extent to which these needs were being met in Metropolis. The set of goals which grew out of this study serve as guidelines for a community-wide program.

2. To implement the community-wide program, the institute conducts a continuing educational TV program utilizing the Public Affairs Network, described later.

3. A special program aimed at recruiting and training adults for subprofessional and volunteer jobs in family and social welfare and for service in a variety of community agencies was developed.

4. A family counseling service was operated in connection with

the psychology department—primarily on a group-counseling basis.

5. Pioneering programs for pre- and post-retirement were available primarily through counseling prior to retirement and referral after retirement to the most appropriate kind of educational activity or volunteer service.

6. Training programs for leaders, teachers, and administrators of educational programs carried on by other agencies were offered by the institute with emphasis on educational techniques and methods, human relations, and sensitivity training.[11]

INSTITUTE FOR CIVIC AND SOCIAL DEVELOPMENT

Loss of important municipal bond issues, the poor quality of local government, the lack of understanding of local, national, and international issues all pointed to a great need for education in this area. Programs to meet the need were almost nonexistent. As a result, major responsibility for creating such programs fell clearly to the College of Continuing Education.

The proposed curriculum developed by the institute planning committee is aimed at increased understanding of metropolitan, state, and national government as well as of typically urban problems such as urban planning and development, housing, civil rights, crime and law enforcement, pollution, education, etc. Understanding of international affairs was also agreed to be essential. The following were among the programs developed:

1. A field seminar aimed at creating an understanding of the metropolitan area and its government, carried on in seminars at the inner-city campus and field trips around the community. The community, its resources, and its activities were the textbook and laboratory for the program, and the bus, its primary classroom.[12]

2. Extension of the field seminar to state and national government, again with great reliance on field trips and observation.

3. Assignment of adult interns to various branches of the metropolitan, state, and national governments, thus providing retired persons with a second occupation and assisting governments

to carry on special studies and activities which could not be done with regular personnel.

4. A continuing public-affairs institute to discuss crucial government issues. The program was carried on in cooperation with the local education-television station (the Public Affairs Network) and a series of "listening posts" for small discussion groups throughout the area.[13] In this continuing "teach-in," top faculty present the facts and background information while politicians, officials, and citizens provide special points of view.

5. Continuing education for officials and other employees of the city, state, and federal governments through seminars and independent study arranged by the appropriate agencies in cooperation with various departments at Metropolis U. or other universities.[14]

6. Special programs of study in depth for government employees, leaders of community organizations, and individual citizens, either through seminars or independent study which would include substantive information as well as the more traditional leadership and sensitivity training.[14]

7. The international program would include field seminars to the United Nations and to various embassies, discussion of international issues over the Public Affairs Network, internships in international agencies, and training of leaders.[15] In addition, the College of Continuing Education would sponsor the development of "sister-relationships" between Metropolis and comparable cities in Europe, Asia, Africa, and South America, and develop programs of area studies at the college and followup field visits and study tours to the various "sister" communities.[16]

INSTITUTE FOR HUMANISTIC AND LIBERAL DEVELOPMENT

As in the civic and social development field, the special institute committee found great need for continuing education in this area and almost no programs to meet the needs. Again, major responsibility fell upon the College of Continuing Education.

The committee made a basic decision with respect to content

and curriculum. It agreed that, to be truly humane and literate, a nonscientist must be conversant with the new technology and the scientific method, just as a scientist must have minimum literacy in the arts.

1. As a base for a program of scientific humanism, a new Museum of Popular Science, established and operated by the College of Continuing Education in cooperation with the scientific societies and private industry and aided by the National Science Foundation, served as the nerve center for most of the scientific programs for the layman.[17] A modification of the Deutches Museum in Munich, West Germany, and the Museum of Science and Industry in Chicago, this museum was developed to permit scientists and technologists to interpret new developments, inventions, and theories to the public. Science seminars, demonstration-tours, and lectures given at the museum were carried to the community by the Public Affairs Network.[18] Both the educational program and the museum were aimed at adults, though younger people could also use the facilities and participate in the seminars. The varied museum program also provided opportunities for adults to participate in the science sequences in the special MA and AB programs, to engage in individual study, to carry on experiments through take-home kits, and to study in depth through participation in regular on-campus classes.

2. In the arts and humanities, major reliance was placed upon the arts and cultural institution in the community and in the various universities. The following were some of the specific programs instituted:

(a) A program of educating audiences in which the College of Continuing Education in cooperation with the arts institutions attempts to develop in citizens a broad understanding of the arts in general, a commitment to and experience with one particular art form, general knowledge of others and a sense of responsibility as a citizen-patron of the arts. This program combined seminars, visits to museums and theaters, discussions with artists, actors, and playwrights, and some actual experience in "doing"—reading plays, painting, playing an instrument, etc.[19]

(*b*) More advanced workshops for persons interested in a particular art form—including courses in appreciation, writing, dance, and art,[20] master classes in music.[21]

(*c*) Participation in the arts and humanities portions of the special AB program and in the terminal masters program as well as special on-campus courses and independent tutorial studies in depth in a particular area of arts or humanities.

(*d*) Opportunities to participate—after completing various study and seminar programs—as volunteers in the various art and cultural institutions in the community.[22]

In addition to the institutes, three centers were established: a Center for Counseling and Community Referral, a Center for Research and Professional Development, and a Center for Metropolitan Studies and Problem-Solving.

According to the committee's plan, the centers, an integral part of the College of Continuing Education, cut across the four institutes and provide services and research to all of them.

CENTER FOR COUNSELING AND COMMUNITY REFERRAL

This center, operated in cooperation with the Counseling Program in the School of Education and the Psychology department and responsible for identifying and assembling information about continuing-education resources in the community and for counseling adults about those opportunities, carried on the following activities:

1. It brings together in one convenient and accessible location complete information about available and potential resources for continuing education of all kinds in the community. It makes such information readily available through modern information storage and retrieval systems and an annual directory of continuing-education opportunities in Metropolis.[23]

2. It provides a counseling service both for individuals and for groups and organizations interested in continuing education. It refers individuals to the most appropriate program or tutor (whether at the college itself, in regular classes at Metropolis U.

or elsewhere in the community) and identifies the agency, institution, or college institute which would be of greatest help in organizing a program.[24]

3. It helps to establish and house a Central Volunteer Bureau in cooperation with the local Council of Social Agencies and the Institutes of Civic and Social Development and of Humanistic and Liberal Development so that individuals can be referred to appropriate volunteer jobs.[25]

4. In cooperation with the various institutes, it organizes individual tutorial service whereby persons interested in independent study can be referred to tutors either at Metropolis U. or at other institutions.

CENTER FOR RESEARCH AND PROFESSIONAL DEVELOPMENT

This center, operated in cooperation with the Adult Education Division of the School of Education and responsible for research and training of professional and semiprofessional adult educators and for evaluation of continuing education in the community, carries on the following activities:

1. Research in adult learning and teaching, adult motivation and participation, community organization, and other areas directly related to continuing education.

2. Graduate programs in adult education leading toward a master's degree or a doctorate for persons who devote full time to adult education as either teachers or administrators.[26]

3. A special research and study unit in comparative international adult education to provide background for American adult educators in international activities in the field, to familiarize foreign adult educators with activities in the United States, and to develop a small cadre of adult educators with a sound basic approach to international adult education in the United States.[27]

4. Training seminars and courses for part-time and lay leaders involved in various kinds of continuing education in the community.[28]

5. Fellowships and internships whereby graduate students in the center may have an opportunity for practical experience work-

ing both in the institutes and with other continuing-education organizations.[29]

6. Constant evaluation of all continuing-education programs conducted by the College of Continuing Education. Educational objectives are established in cooperation with the program planners for every program in each institute so that the effectiveness of the various programs may be objectively evaluated.[30]

CENTER FOR METROPOLITAN STUDIES AND PROBLEM-SOLVING

This center, operated in cooperation with the Social Sciences Division and/or a Center for Urban Studies, stimulates and facilitates studies and research in the community by means of the following activities:

1. It assists the various institutes in carrying on their assessment of community needs and resources by involving appropriate faculty and research assistance within the university.[31]

2. It assists in identifying crucial community problems through the institutes and the network of urban agents, described later, whose job it is to analyze these problems and recruit appropriate faculty members to help solve them. In reverse, it assists faculty in identifying and locating appropriate problems and locales for research programs in the community and in securing funds for such study.[32]

3. In cooperation with the Center for Research and Professional Development, it arranges for evaluation of the social impact of continuing education conducted both in the institutes and elsewhere—and it sets up continuing public-opinion studies to determine the impact of the program on attitudes and activities in the community.

The following is a brief outline of the physical, organizational, administrative, and financial arrangements which the policy committee agreed were required to implement the program of lifelong learning at Metropolis U. in 1980.

A READILY ACCESSIBLE CAMPUS FOR ADULTS

Metropolis University has an inner-city campus for continuing education located in a formerly deteriorating section of the city. Property is acquired as part of a total urban-renewal plan—by a metropolitan planning agency and sold, at low cost, to the university.[33] The campus itself is surrounded by a privately developed "complementary campus" which includes theaters, motion-picture houses, museums, parks and facilities for other performing arts as well as housing for both permanent residents and transients involved in university activities.[34]

The inner-city campus consists of a learning center for adults (a modern atheneum for continuing education), a fairly small residential unit, and the Museum for Popular Science.

The Learning Center includes offices for tutorial sessions as well as small discussion rooms and lounges, used both for regular seminars and for special programs and study groups arranged by the adults themselves.[35] It is equipped with a modern system of information storage and retrieval whereby groups or individuals may have shared-time access to printed materials, films, TV tapes, history tapes, reproductions of paintings, recordings, programmed and computer-aided instruction, and other visual teaching aids.[36] Special tutors from the institutes help students use these new technological resources and provide courses in independent study.[37] Although the Learning Center is the nerve center and major repository of educational resources in the metropolitan area, satellite centers and individuals outside of the center city have ready access to its materials by means of two-way communications devices. The Learning Center houses the studios of the Public Affairs Network and is equipped to receive reactions from "listening posts." It also includes administrative and faculty offices for the full-time and adjunct staff and appropriate lounges and faculty meeting rooms.

The Residential Center—a small one as great reliance is placed on the transient residential facilities in the complementary campus[38]—provides housing for several hundred persons with small discussion rooms and study carrels in each of the sleeping rooms.

This residential center—as differentiated from the residential facilities in the complementary campus (which also has telephone tie lines to the Learning Center)—is used primarily in connection with studies and research being carried on by the Center for Research and Professional Development.[39]

The Museum of Popular Science, which was described earlier, is located on campus and includes seminar, study, and tutorial rooms for group and independent study in addition to the permanent collection and many changing exhibits.

The combined college and complementary campus emerges as the new cultural center of Metropolis. In 1980, such inner-city campuses are increasingly becoming a crucial factor in the rebuilding and renaissance of cities.

FACULTY ARRANGEMENTS

The ever-present problem of securing enough quality faculty to meet expanding educational needs is solved by the College of Continuing Education at Metropolis U. through two new developments.

The first is a reverse "lend-lease" arrangement with industry and the government in Metropolis. Well qualified natural and social scientists as well as humanists are made available to the College of Continuing Education as an "adjunct faculty" on sabbatical leave from their regular jobs.[40] These outstanding people (including at least as large a percentage of PhD's as the campus faculty) are screened initially by members of the regular faculty. After appointment, they become an integral part of the academic community of Metropolis U. with regular faculty rights and privileges. They have access to a special faculty lounge at the Learning Center, belong to the campus faculty club, participate in institute faculty meetings, and are clearly identified with the university in every possible way.

The second method for dealing with the faculty problem is through the increasing use of "faculty aides." These are adults who are active in the program of continuing education and who assist leaders and teachers in the community and tutors at the College of Continuing Education. In addition to being carefully selected by the faculty of the various institutes, these faculty aides must complete a special training and education program in the Center for Research and Professional Development.

ADMINISTRATION AND ORGANIZATION

The four institutes and the three centers, the satellite centers,[41] a group of urban agents and the alumni association (which by 1980 has become primarily an arm for the continuing education of Metropolis University graduates) constitute the College of Continuing Education. The college is headed by a vice-president or provost for Continuing education and community service.

Each institute is staffed by a dean, a small core of regular campus faculty members on leave from their departments, and one or two members of the adjunct faculty on sabbatical leave from their employers. Additional seminar leaders and faculty for the programs carried on directly by the institute are recruited primarily from the adjunct faculty, assisted by faculty aides.

The centers are staffed by a director and staff associates—regular faculty members conducting research in the community as well as graduate students from counseling, education, and urban studies—again assisted by faculty aides.

In addition to the staff of the institutes and centers, the College of Continuing Education has a corps of urban agents assigned to different communities in the metropolitan area.[42] They are reoriented and retrained Cooperative Extension field workers and county agents and are by now intimately familiar with the community, where they establish relations with committees, administrative bodies, and various other resources for continuing education in the community. Their function is to identify educational and research needs and to marshal programs and resources to meet them.

Unlike its faint prototypes of the 1960s, the College of Continuing Education in 1980 is not expected to be a moneymaker for the university.[43] Consistent with its commitment to continuing education and community service, Metropolis University provides the salaries for the core staff, key faculty, and basic office help as an integral part of the regular university budget. Additional salaries are paid out of the operating budget of the College of Continuing Education: income from tuitions, grants, and contracts.

Financing, beyond that for the core staff, is highly diversified and varied. A consultant firm assumes responsibility for building, financing, and operating the "complementary campus" (the residential housing, the related cultural facilities, eating places, etc.). It also handles the maintenance and food services. Costs are greatly reduced by coordinating construction of the regular and the complementary campus.

Basic financing for the Learning Center is secured from various kinds of government loans, from the city government (in the form of reduced land costs and bond issues), and from private industry (in loans or donations of the required technological equipment).

The Residential Center—on the campus—is also financed by a combination of federal loans, operating contracts with the development firm, grants and contributions from individuals and foundations, and a minimum special charge to all conferees.[44]

The Museum of Popular Science is financed by the National Science Foundation, aided by contributions from NASA, from private industry, and from private foundations. Operating costs are covered by the city government, private industry, the university, and fees for special events, seminars, and projects.

The bulk of the operations of the various institutes—the faculty costs—are covered by tuition paid both by individual students and by their employers.[45] Research activities in the various institutes and centers and in the college in general are financed primarily through federal grants from the U. S. Office of Education, Housing and Urban Development, the departments of Commerce and Labor, and the National Endowment for the Arts and Humanities.

COMMUNITY COOPERATION

Throughout the entire development of the College of Continuing Education, community participation in developing the basic program and in planning and carrying out the program of the institutes has been emphasized. In addition, the active adjunct faculty and the faculty aides provide a meaningful and integrated relationship between the college and the community. The satellite centers both in the city and in the suburbs, as well as the effective use of urban agents (selected where possible from indigenous leaders in the various communities), bring the college directly into the communities and, through community advisory groups, responsibility for program development is shared with the students. The entire concept of community participation and involvement has been so completely built into the planning, staffing, and evaluation of the program that it is part of the structure rather than a separate and special activity.

USE OF NEW EDUCATIONAL TECHNOLOGY

Through the use of the most up-to-date information storage and retrieval systems in the Learning Center—which is the physical core of the college—the development of individual learning carrels, two-way communication between the inner-city and satellite campuses, and, eventually, tie-ins with home learning carrels,[46] as well as through the Public Affairs Network, the College of Continuing Education will, from the outset, make maximum use of the new technology. A special technological advisory committee, working with a Director of Innovation and Planning (in the Vice-President's office), keeps the college *au courant* with the newest developments. At the same time, the college will not overlook traditional teaching and learning methods. Independent study, assisted by the new technology, will become a major way of learning. Responsibility for the teaching and tutorial tasks will be widely shared by faculty aides with the more experienced tutors.

Dangerous and difficult as it is to predict the future, this attempt to say what continuing education will look like in 1980 is not entirely utopian and imaginary. It is important to underline again that almost all of the specific proposals—for physical location and development, use of faculty, involvement of the community, the flexible use of new and old techniques and methods, organization and administration, and financing—have roots in some program already under way in 1968.

Whether the "uncommon college" for continuing education becomes an accepted part of universities in 1980 or not depends on the extent to which universities subscribe to the concept of lifelong learning in the next decade and the degree to which they plan for a truly comprehensive program rather than merely providing, as they did in 1968, bits and pieces of a total program. The auspices are excellent. The seeds have already been planted and nutrition is being increasingly provided by the federal government. Thoreau's dreams and hopes for an "uncommon school," although too long delayed, seem likely to be realized before the end of the century.

APPENDIX

Examples cited here are not all-inclusive. They suggest only one or two programs or activities to illustrate material in the text. Many other examples could be cited, but the following will serve as a starting point for readers who desire to look at ingredients of the College of Continuing Education.

1. Oakland University, Rochester, Michigan.
2. Rochester Institute of Technology, "Earn-Learn" program; Drexel Institute of Technology, Philadelphia, Pa.; Antioch College, Yellow Springs, Ohio, etc.
3. Urban Extension Center, Buffalo (in re Poverty Programs);

planned coordination of adult education activities at St. Louis, Mo.

4. National system of college-level examinations now under development by Council on College-Level Examinations of College Entrance-Examination Board.

5. Prototype programs "especially for adults" in operation at University of Oklahoma, Norman, Okla.; Syracuse University, Syracuse, N. Y.; Goddard College, Plainfield, Vt.

6. Master of Liberal Arts, Johns Hopkins University, Baltimore, Md.

7. Thirteen-week sabbaticals with full pay now included in contracts for some thirty thousand steelworkers with seniority each year.

8. Large proportion of programs offered at residential centers such as those at Michigan State University, East Lansing, Mich.; Universities of Nebraska, Lincoln, Neb.; Oklahoma, Norman, Okla.; and Georgia, Athens, Ga., are of this type.

9. U. S. Chamber of Commerce estimated that, in 1964, in-service training and education programs operated by business and industry cost between five and 15 billion dollars annually.

10. Figures provided for a study of adult education in the U.S. conducted in 1965 (with only a fraction of the voluntary agencies reporting) indicated that some 52,000,000 adults were reached by programs carried on by health, welfare, and social agencies.

11. Lists of scores of such training programs at universities can be secured through National Training Laboratory and Leadership Resources Institute.

12. "Laboratory College" operated cooperatively by Northwestern University, Evanston, Ill., and Center for Study of Liberal Education for Adults, Brookline, Mass., 1959.

13. Metroplex Assembly program, Washington University, St. Louis, Mo., 1957 to 1960.

14. University of Wisconsin, Madison, Wisc., training program for government employees.

15. Foreign Policy Association programs including "Great Decisions."

16. Detroit Adventure, Wayne State University, Detroit, Mich., 1918; Study-travel programs at Syracuse University, Syracuse, N. Y.; Brigham Young University, Provo, Utah; etc. Cooperative University summer study programs: University of Rochester and Hull University, England; McMaster University and University College of Rhodesia at Salisbury (until 1965). Cooperation between extension divisions: University of British Columbia and University of Rajasthan; Michigan State University, East Lansing, Mich., and University of Nigeria at Nssuka.

17. Partial steps in this direction, Oregon Museum of Science and Industry; Natural Science Museum, University of Nebraska, Lincoln, Neb.; museums in connection with colleges in the Soviet Union.

18. Station WGBH, Channel 2, educational TV station in Boston.

19. Fine Arts Program, University of Chicago, as well as several additional programs now operating or projected under Title One of the Higher Education Act.

20. University of Wisconsin, Madison, Wisc., general extension programs including theatre and writer's workshop; University of Michigan, Ann Arbor, Mich., statewide art and writer's program.

21. Master programs in music offered by University Extension, University of California.

22. Chicago Art Institute and other art museums in major cities.

23. Radcliffe College, Cambridge, Mass., *The Next Stop: Educational Opportunities of Greater Boston—for Adults,* compiled by the Education Exchange of Greater Boston.

24. Sarah Lawrence, Bronxville, N. Y., Continuing Education Programs for Women.

25. Chicago Welfare Council, Volunteer Bureau.

26. Full research and graduate programs in adult education now offered in 16 universities in the U.S.

27. Several proposals now in preparation for submission under International Education Act of 1966.

28. Indiana University, Bloomington, Ind., and Florida State University, Tallahassee, Fla.

29. Internships in general extension divisions at University of Wisconsin, Madison, Wisc., and in the residential center at the University of Chicago.

30. Preliminary work relating to evaluation of informal programs developed by Center for Study of Liberal Education for Adults, Brookline, Mass., 1961.

31. University College, Syracuse University, Syracuse, N. Y.

32. Center for Metropolitan Studies, American University, Washington, D. C.; Center for Urban Studies, Rutgers; the State University of New Jersey.

33. Hyde Park–Kenwood land-clearance and urban-renewal program, Chicago.

34. Plans developed for area surrounding San Francisco State College (and Berkeley) by a private development corporation.

35. Institute for Retired Professionals, New School for Social Research, N. Y.

36. Florida Atlantic University, Boca Raton, Fla.

37. Bachelor of Liberal Studies, University of Oklahoma, Norman, Okla.

38. University of Wisconsin Conference Center depends entirely on adjacent commercial housing for its conferees.

39. Michigan State University, East Lansing, Mich., residential center is equipped with one-way windows and arrangements for taping discussion for research purposes.

40. U. S. D. A. Graduate School, Washington, D. C., and Consortium of Universities in Washington, D. C., offer graduate programs.

41. Burlington Center for Adults of Northeastern University, Boston.

42. University of Missouri, Columbia, Mo., West Virginia University, Morgantown, W. Va.—former cooperative extension field staff retrained to represent the entire university.

43. State subsidies for general extension in land-grant colleges now vary from zero to over 40 percent of budget. All state cooperative extension programs financed by federal and state governments and local counties with no tuition charged.

44. Projections for university campuses under State University of New York provide for such mixed financing.

45. Tuition refunds for successfully completed courses are offered to employees now by most major national industries.

46. Plans are now underway for home-learning carrels in Davis, Calif., and other "new cities."

The College Student of 1980

In 1980, as now, our society will still be troubled and far from having reached any kind of perfection. Then, as now, a not insignificant proportion of our young people will reject "the system" and find alternative value orientations and styles of life. The "hippie" phenomenon in its present form, however, will not be highly visible. Fashions change. The major values of the "hippies"—honesty, community, tolerance, pleasure—will be embraced by such large segments of "square" society and the more manifest features of the hippie style will have been imitated by so many thirteen-year-olds that seriously disaffected young people will have to create new styles. What these will be is beyond prediction; but we may be sure that social scientists and journalists will be studying the new communities and religious groups, becoming honorary members of them, and reporting back to a fascinated public.

When I read the autobiographies of Princeton men collected and published by Otto Butz[1] in 1958, I was sharply reminded of the autobiographies of undergraduates that had been collected at the Harvard Psychological Clinic in the mid-1930s.[2] This year, in my class in personality at Stanford, students were asked to prepare case studies of "someone they knew well." About a quarter of the class wrote autobiographies, and many others made studies of

[1] Otto Butz, *The Unsilent Generation: An Anonymous Symposium in Which Eleven College Seniors Look at Themselves and Their World* (New York: Rinehart and Co., 1958).
[2] H. A. Murray, et al., *Explorations in Personality* (New York: Oxford University Press, 1938).

contemporaries at college. I was reminded of the Butz collection and of the earlier Harvard autobiographies.

Reexamining some of these documents from the 1930s and 1950s confirmed my impression that, when students of different generations are considered as individual personalities, they show many similarities. Their problems, preoccupations, and concerns are, rather overwhelmingly, the perennial ones of young men in Western societies: establishing independence of their parents, coming to terms with authority, maintaining adequate self-esteem while achieving a more or less accurate evaluation of themselves, deciding on a vocation, discovering members of the opposite sex and learning how to relate to them as individuals, adapting themselves to the requirements of student culture while revealing themselves enough to make friendships possible, and attaining a perspective on our society that will permit them to see and to oppose its ills without lapsing into cynicism or total withdrawal.

In writing autobiographies, students usually show themselves in a worse light than is quite justified by the facts. They naturally dwell, sometimes overdramatically, upon their conflicts and dilemmas rather than upon their achievements and virtues; and feeling a need to explain themselves, they resort to psychology, whose terms are anything but flattering. Nevertheless, the autobiographies of which I have spoken leave the same general impression as do the intensive studies of individual students, by means of interviews and other, more specialized techniques that some of us have carried out in each decade since 1930[3]: below the surface of style—in behavior and dress—of conformity with the ways of their peer groups, of meeting the role requirements of their particular institution, at the level of inner needs and ways of

[3] For studies conducted in the 1930s, see Murray, et al., *op. cit.;* for the 1940s, see T. W. Adorno, Else Frenkel-Brunswik, D. J. Levinson, and N. Sanford, *The Authoritarian Personality* (New York: Harper, 1950); for the 1950s, see N. Sanford, *Self and Society* (New York: Atherton Press, 1966), pp. 40–52 and 168–191; N. Sanford, *Where Colleges Fail* (San Francisco: Jossey-Bass, 1967), pp. 79–88; and C. Bereiter, and M. Freedman, "Fields of Study and the People in Them," in N. Sanford, ed., *The American College* (New York: Wiley, 1962); for the 1960s, see reports recently and soon to be published by Joseph Katz, Harold Korn and Marjorie Lozoff of the Institute for the Study of Human Problems, Stanford.

confronting the perennial problems of growth, in other words, at the level of personality, students of different decades have much in common.

Before turning to the differences among students of different generations and looking ahead to 1980, let us give further attention to their similarities, viewing the matter in the perspectives of both personality theory and social theory.

Looking at students in the perspective of personality theory, as I have done in the paragraphs above, one is impressed by their diversity as well as by their complexity. Personality is a vast and intricate structure formed on the basis of myriad experiences, the most important of which occur during childhood in the context of family life. What happens to the child in interaction with family members depends on the personalities of his parents and siblings, the economic and social circumstances in which they live, the parents' memberships in various ethnic, racial, religious and other social and subcultural group, and a range of accidental events. And when we consider that personality is also shaped by events outside the family, beginning, usually, when the child enters school and continuing through his college years and possibly beyond, it appears that there are enough sources of variability to make it a truism that each personality is unique. This, however, does not prevent us from observing the characteristic behavior of many individuals and inferring the existence of common, more or less uniform dispositions or elements of personality, or from deriving, on the basis of intensive studies of individual through time, general principles of personality organization and growth. Among these latter is the idea that growth is progressive—that certain events must occur before other events become possible and that the occurrence of the given first events create in the individual a state of readiness which will lead to further growth once appropriate stimuli are brought to bear. Thus a number of writers—e.g., Freud,[4] Piaget,[5] and Erikson[6]—have conceived of stages of

[4] Sigmund Freud, *An Outline of Psychoanalysis* (New York: Norton, 1949).
[5] Jean Piaget, *The Language and Thought of the Child* (Cleveland and New York: The World Publishing Co., 1955).
[6] Erik H. Erikson, *Identity and the Life Cycle* (New York: International Universities Press, 1959).

development, each with its characteristic achievements, crises, and tasks. Among these stages is that of late adolescence or young adulthood, as described by Erikson,[7] White,[8] Sanford,[9] and Freedman,[10] the major problems and tasks of which have been listed above.

Besides looking at youth in its psychological aspects, one can look at youth in its social aspects—as the state of people who are ready to take vocational, marital, parental, and citizenship roles but have not yet committed themselves to them. (According to this conception, there is no youth in those village societies in which boys go to work at age nine and girls are married at eleven.) Youth, so conceived, are free to try various styles of life, to test the prevailing systems of value and belief, and to advocate or promote what is new or contrary to established ways. It is thus that youth have always had an important role in the initiation of social change.

Conflict between generations and their mutual misunderstandings—what is nowadays called the "generation gap"—seem to be compounded of both psychological and social factors. It is not only that youth are free to embrace the new but it is often precisely by doing so that they may establish their independence of their parents—or punish, or rebel against them, if the nature of the relationship has created the need to do so. It takes two to make a generation gap, however; and there are good psychological reasons that parents often respond in irrational ways to the impulsive or radical or deviant behavior of young people. Such behavior creates anxiety because it arouses impulses, usually sexual or aggressive ones, that were never effectively controlled. If such impulses are strong and close to the surface but yet unrecognized, they may falsely be attributed to youth, as in fantasies about the "goings-on" among them or in gross overestimations of the amount of aggressive, sexual, or drug-taking behavior in

[7] ———, *Youth: Change and Challenge* (New York: Basic Books, 1963).

[8] R. W. White, *Lives in Progress* (New York: Holt, Rinehart and Winston, 1952).

[9] N. Sanford, *Self and Society, op. cit.; Where Colleges Fail, op. cit.*

[10] M. B. Freedman, *The College Experience* (San Francisco: Jossey-Bass, 1967).

which they engage. Indeed, it seems that nowadays there are many adults who are willing to believe anything about young people, using them as scapegoats in much the same way they used Negroes and Communists in the recent past.

Such scapegoating would not be possible, of course, without a lack of communication between the generations. Unfortunately, this lack is strongly favored by both youthful fears of adult criticism or ridicule and adult withdrawal from encounters that provoke anxiety. Many parents seek to "live through" or "wait out" their children's adolescence by not noticing what they do, hoping thereby to avoid experiencing painful emotion. (There is also a good measure of parental indifference.) Young people, of course, react to this strategy either by further withdrawal on their part—lapsing into silence or just disapproving whenever possible—or by behaving in a way that will *"make* them pay attention."

Parents, in one way or another, relive their own adolescence in that of their children. If they do not withdraw, they are likely to interfere—and they will certainly be accused of doing so. It is not only that they would suppress in their children what is barely suppressed in themselves and try to insure that their own mistakes are not repeated, but there is the persistent hope that their children will make up for their own failures to seize opportunities. This kind of hope on the part of adults sometimes takes the form of egging the youth on, pushing them into activities for which adults have neither the courage nor the energy but in which they may participate vicariously. Sometimes adults make awkward attempts to join in the fun; disliking to be rejected by youth, they seek to fraternize with them, or, dissatisfied with the prevailing culture, they identify themselves with the youth—as in the case of the middle-aged social scientist who, in the course of his studies of youth, copies their manner of dress and adopts their vocabulary, using their inventions as he does the latest monstrosities of his technical lexicon to put down his less sophisticated colleagues.

The youth, of course, regard all this with scorn and go their way. But, sad to say, adults, if they are wise, still have the last laugh; for the way of youth turns out to be deeply influenced by what their parents say and do, and by what they are. There is enough of his parents inside the young person, by virtue of early identifications and later positive and negative modeling so that his "independence" will often be, in reality, opposition; his delinquency or deviance, an acting out of parental fantasies; his noblest actions, the practices of what his parents merely preached. By the time a person is truly independent of his parents, he is himself adult—and ready to make a different contribution to the generation gap. Meanwhile, more good than bad will have come of the struggle of youth to find their own way: original ideas, values more suited to the times, and socially valuable actions that could be carried out only by youth.

There will be a generation gap in 1980. Also, in 1980, there will be one or more youth movements. And these movements, since they will be of *youth,* will have something in common with that of the present and those of the past. Rudolph[11] has shown that the current student movement is not unlike other major efforts at reform by American students in the past, and Lipset[12] has shown the similarities of American student movements to (as well as their differences from) student movements in other countries. Kohn[13] has stated that all youth movements have in common "a deep dissatisfaction with the existing intellectual, moral, social or political order, a desire to change this order, and a confidence in the power of youth to change this order." Katz,[14] in his review of the literature on the student activists of the 1960s, writes:

> There are recurrent themes in youth movements. Among them is the opposition to the impersonal organization of human life; opposition to the sacrifice of moral, emotional, intellectual, and aesthetic values to material expansion; and a desire for greater closeness with other people.

[11] Frederick Rudolph, *The American College and University* (New York: Vintage Books, 1965).
[12] S. M. Lipset, "University Students and Politics in Underdeveloped Countries," *Comparative Education Review,* 1966, 10, pp. 132–162.
[13] Hans Kohn, "Youth Movements," *Encyclopedia of the Social Sciences* (New York: Macmillan, 1935).
[14] Joseph Katz, "The Student Activists: Rights, Needs, and Powers of Undergraduates," in *New Dimensions in Higher Education* (Washington: U. S. Office of Education, 1967).

Those who will be concerned about the generational conflicts and the student movements of 1980 must above all, then, have an understanding of youth *per se*. The same holds for all who will have responsibility for planning and carrying out programs in higher education and for work with individual students. Such an understanding will have to be acquired mainly through the study of personality and human development, with special attention to the period of late adolescence. By 1980 educators will see much more clearly than they do today that the major aim of college education is the fullest possible development of the individual personality, and that the only basis for planning an educational environment is knowledge of how students actually develop.

Fortunately, by 1980 far more such knowledge will be available than there is today. Psychology, which is mainly focused now as it was in the 1920s upon the experimental study of narrow areas of behavior from a predominantly behavioristic point of view, will return to the interests and outlook of the 1930s and 1940s, that is, to a concern with complex processes and the person as a whole and to a comprehensive, holistic, and dynamic approach to investigation. This last will embrace theoretically oriented longitudinal studies of personality development; and hence educators will not have to depend, as they do now, on a mere handful of investigators for speeches before their professional associations and for hastily written articles about college students. Instead, there will be literature on college students respectable and attractive enough so that even college teachers will be able to read it without fear that their sensibilities will be assaulted or their status lowered. Indeed, by 1980, counselors, deans, and other specialists in student personnel will have discovered that one of the best things to *do* about students—singly or in the mass—is to study them; accordingly, these professionals will be producers as well as consumers of knowledge about students.

THE STUDENT AND SOCIAL CHANGE

All this said, let it now be stressed that people brought up in one period will naturally differ in some ways from people brought up in another period—particularly in a society that changes as rapidly as ours does. Here it is fundamentally important to distinguish between differences in *personality* and differences in *behavior*. Since personality, as indicated above, is a structure of dispositions largely determined by the child's experience in his family, we have to account for personality differences from one period to another mainly on the basis of differences in the social factors influencing family life and child training in the two periods. Behavior, on the other hand—even the consistent behavior of an individual over time—is always partly determined by the situations of the moment. Thus, in explaining the distinctive behavior of a group of individuals—student activists for example —we have to weigh the contributions of personality and situational factors, allowing for the possibility that, in a given case, one or the other type of factor might have been by far the more important. We evoke the concept of personality to help explain why *these* students and not others are activist; we evoke situational determinism to help explain why student activism became pronounced in the middle 1960s but not before.

This general approach can be illustrated by the use of various studies of student activists that have recently been carried out. The members of the Berkeley Free Speech Movement, particularly those arrested during the Sproul Hall sit-in of December 1964, have been studied by Block, Haan, and Smith,[15] Heist,[16] Katz,[17] Lyonns,[18] Somers,[19] and Watts and Whittaker.[20] Student

[15] Jeanne H. Block, Norma Haan and M. Brewster Smith, "Activism and Apathy in Contemporary Adolescents," in J. F. Adams, ed., *Contributions to the Understanding of Adolescents* (Boston: Allyn and Bacon, 1967) (draft chapter).

[16] Paul Heist, "Intellect and Commitment: The Faces of Discontent" (Berkeley: Center for the Study of Higher Education, University of California, 1965) (mimeographed).

[17] Joseph Katz, "Personality Characteristics of Students Arrested during the Berkeley Sit-in of 1964," in *Personality Development and the Impact of the College* (forthcoming report to the U. S. Office of Education and the Danforth Foundation, 1967).

[18] Glen Lyonns, "The Police-Car Demonstration: A Survey of the Participants," in S. M. Lipset and S. S. Wolin, eds., *The Berkeley Student Revolt* (New York: Doubleday, 1965).

[19] Robert H. Somers, "The Mainsprings of the Rebellion: A Survey of Berkeley Students in November, 1964," in *ibid.*

activists and demonstrators at the University of Chicago have been studied by Flacks[21]; those at Pennsylvania State University by Westby and Braungart.[22] Katz,[23] in summarizing and evaluating these studies, writes, "The amazing fact is that the results of all these studies converge, that they do not contradict each other in major findings." Among these findings are a great many pertaining to differences in personality between activists and other students at the same university. According to Katz:

> Activist students measured by a variety of personality instruments consistently score significantly higher not only on the dimensions of theoretical orientation and esthetic sensitivity as already reported, but also in their degree of psychological autonomy, social maturity, tendency to express feelings and impulses directly, and lack of authoritarianism. This means that activists, according to these measures, tend to be more flexible, tolerant, and realistic; less dependent upon authority, rules or rituals for managing social relationships; less judgmental; tend to express impulses more freely either in conscious thought or in overt action; have an active imagination; tend to be independent of authority as traditionally imposed through social institutions, and oppose infringement of the rights of individuals. In one study where personality data for the arrested students as freshmen were available, the activists turned out to be significantly different in these personality dimensions from their classmates upon entrance. In their values, activists tend to be concerned with self-expression, intellectual orientation, sense of community with and responsibility for their fellow men; while the non-activists tend to be more success-oriented, self-denying, conventional, competitive, self-controlled, foresightful, and orderly. Activists tend to express a much greater dedication than do non-activists to work for national and international betterment and to humanitarian objectives. They score lower on ethnocentric prejudices.[24]

---

20 William A. Watts and David N. E. Whittaker, "Free Speech Advocates at Berkeley," *Journal of Applied Behavioral Science,* 1966, 2, pp. 41–62.
21 Richard Flacks, "The Liberated Generation: An Exploration of the Roots of Student Protest," in *The Journal of Social Issues,* 1967 (in press).
22 D. Westby and R. Braungart, "Class and Politics in the Family Backgrounds of Student Political Activists," in *American Sociological Review,* 1966, 31, pp. 690–692.
23 Joseph Katz, "The Student Activists: Rights, Needs and Powers of Undergraduates" (Washington, D.C.: U. S. Office of Education, 1967) (in press).
24 *Ibid.*

Consistent with this picture are the findings that activists scored significantly higher in verbal but not in mathematical aptitude, and that their grade point averages were significantly higher than those of nonactivists. Concerning socioeconomic and family background, Katz summarizes as follows:

> The activists' parents are higher in income, occupational status, and education than the parents of non-activists. They tend to be politically more liberal. Their child-rearing practices were more permissive and the parents had closer affective relationships with their children than parents of non-activists. At the same time, disagreement was more openly expressed in activist homes than non-activist ones. Jewish students are overrepresented and Catholic students tend to be underrepresented in activist samples.
>
> These findings put into question the "conflict between generations" thesis that has been advanced as one explanation of the activist protest. Many activists seem to be acting in conformity with their parents' values, but they want to express these values in a purer, less compromising, and more energetic way than they think their parents do. Moreover, they seem to be using the freedom of dissent and the affection they have experienced at home as a yardstick by which to measure the behavior and attitudes of the authorities at school and in the society at large.
>
> The overrepresentation of Jewish students may be ascribed— among other factors—to the often high degree of intellectual motivation among Jewish students, which . . . is a distinguishing characteristic of the activists, too; and it may also be ascribed to their experience of minority status and discrimination, which may have made them more sensitive to social injustice, and given the high morale found among American Jews, prone to work actively for its eventual eradication.[25]

Now let us examine the hypothesis that differences in personality among students of different generations are due in part to differences in upbringing. In order to support this hypothesis on the basis of the studies of student activists, we must first, of course, have evidence that the differences in personality actually exist—that more students of the activist type described above entered the universities in question during the four years beginning in 1960 than entered them during the four beginning, say, in 1950. There are no hard data on this. Katz, however, offers the opinion

[25] *Ibid.*

that less extreme forms of the dispositions that distinguish the activists exist fairly widely on the college campus today. He writes:

> Informal evidence gathered from student newspapers and observations of campuses across the country seem to suggest that more students have become sympathetic to the activist ideology, that more expression has been given to these attitudes on more campuses, and that formerly non-reform-minded student leaders, such as newspaper editors or political office holders, have espoused activist causes—often in a quieter manner than that of the outright activist.[26]

This is in line with the common view that, in general, the current generation of students differs from the "privatistic" ones of the 1950s (Riesman; Goldsen, et al.). And when Katz reports, on the basis of his own studies, that the personality differences between activists and nonactivists were already present when these students entered college, there is a presumption—assuming constancy in recruitment by, and selection of, the universities under study—of a change in the personality processes of a segment of the college-going population.

The activists, as we have seen, differ from other students not only in personality but in major determinants of personality, i.e., in socioeconomic and family background. This leaves us with the intriguing possibility that, among parents of the sort who send their sons and daughters to leading universities, there was less authoritarian upbringing of children born in the middle and late 1940s than of children born in the middle and late 1930s. It makes sense to suppose that this was actually the case for, as the studies of activists show, nonauthoritarian child training is associated with higher incomes and occupational statuses and with more education—circumstances far more common in the late 1940s than during the depression years of the 1930s. One might speculate further and suggest that the decline in the Protestant work-ethic and in the American dream of economic success was more advanced in the 1940s than in the 1930s, and this made for less strictness and rigidity in child training.

But all this is not to suggest that the student activism of recent

[26] *Ibid.*

years and of the present is primarily an expression of student personality. On the contrary, it seems to be primarily a matter of students' responding, in a youthful way, to the social conditions under which they live, both in the university and in the larger world.

The *Report of the Select Committee on Education* at Berkeley[27] offers an eloquent account of how our society is seen by "intelligent nonconformist students":

> As these students see it, while the dominant group claims to champion freedom, religion, patriotism, and morality, it produces and condones slums, racial segregation, migrant farm laborers, false advertising, American economic imperialism, and the bomb. In private life, moreover, the students find as much immorality and injustice as in public life. They commonly explain it as the product of an all-pervasive hypocrisy.
>
> To succeed in this society, they believe, you must mask your real feelings and become an organization man, wear what you're expected to wear, say what you're expected to say, and praise the product of your company when you know it has been built to wear out. It's all a game, playing a role; and these young people find that Americans in this other-directed age have been conditioned to accept without a thought or a murmur their own falsity. They accuse Americans of sacrificing conscience to the quest for status. In this society, they say, those who claim to be moral are really immoral and those who claim to be sane are truly insane.
>
> All this these students condemn. What terrifies them is their conviction that the failure of the individual sense of responsibility, in combination with technology and cybernation, is producing a bureaucratized, machine-run society. They find themselves in danger of losing both their freedom and their humanity to IBM machines and to those who use them. They say that a man must fight hypocrisy to live in a moral world, but he will have to halt the computers if he is to remain a man at all.

Although one can detect in this outlook something of that youthfulness discussed above, one would be hard put to it to prove these students wrong. But probably one would find it equally difficult to show that the situation in our society today, even with the Vietnam war in progress, is worse than it was dur-

[27] Charles Muscatine, chairman. *Education at Berkeley: Report of the Select Committee on Education* (Berkeley, Calif., March 1966).

ing the time of the Korean War and McCarthyism—when there was little apparent student unrest. Katz and Sanford[28] have suggested that the "student revolution" of the middle 1960s would not have occurred had it not been for "positive factors" such as the civil-rights movement, the Peace Corps, and domestic social-service programs, all of which gave students the feeling that they counted for something.

These writers have argued that the student revolution was prompted not only by positive and negative forces in the larger society but by conditions on the campus itself—conditions related, of course, to events on the national and world scenes. Katz and Sanford write:

> As is well known, the conditions of the post-Sputnik era have led to a tightening of standards of academic performance and an increased demand upon quantity of work by students. The resulting pressure is felt by good students as well as poor ones. In the more selective schools, all the students are able and well prepared, yet they still feel an enormous amount of pressure, because of the grading curve and the inclination of the faculty to assign more reading than anyone can do. People usually ascribe these pressures to the intellectual competition of the Cold War, but another factor is the higher birth rate, which has considerably increased the number of students applying to colleges and has thus provided both an economic and a moral base for increased selectivity.[29]

These writers then go on to suggest other factors that seem to have had a determining role in the student revolution: increasing specialization in higher education, imposing on students a great deal of work that is essentially meaningless to them; faculty efforts to raise standards, arousing in students a sense of being forever tested and evaluated and generating competitiveness that inhibits friendship and results in a lack of community; the growing involvement of the university in our technology, with a resulting depersonalization of campus life; a decline in the nurturing function of the college-as-parent while the control and punishment functions remained intact; the tendency of graduate students to

[28] Joseph Katz and N. Sanford, "Causes of the Student Revolution," in *Saturday Review*, Dec. 18, 1965, pp. 64–67.
[29] *Ibid.*

find their situation increasingly frustrating and to side with the undergraduates; and finally—on the positive side—increased sophistication and knowledge of the world on the part of entering students, resulting from improved schools and the opportunities for travel afforded by our affluent society.

IN 1980

Looking ahead to 1980, then, we have to ask ourselves what kind of society and world, and what kind of college or university, our students will inhabit, and what kinds of responses can be expected from late adolescents who may differ in personality from students who are in college today.

I am going to offer two major predictions: (1) There will be an expanded, and expanding, universe of students—more different types of students, greater ranges of variation on all the factors we ordinarily use to characterize students; and (2) this whole universe will have moved, and will be moving, in the direction pointed to by the student activists described above.

From the point of view of Americans, the world of 1980 will not be radically different from that of the present. All of our major current problems will still be with us, some in intensified form, others near solution. Most of these problems will center around technology and the efforts of people to participate in its benefits while avoiding or overcoming its ills. Technology will continue to develop, increasing the power of those individuals, groups, and nations that have access to it, without much change in the relative position of those which do not.

In our country there will be increasing efforts by young people, and older people as well, to get the education necessary to participation in our productive system; and these efforts will be largely successful, owing mainly to increasing government aid. But there will still be large numbers of people who are not needed, or are unable to participate, in production. Many welfare and even public-works programs will be directed to improving the lot of these people, but not enough to prevent poverty in the midst of our plenty. There will be a continuing rise in the gross national product, enough to raise even further the level of our general affluence but, owing to conservative economic policies, the rate of growth will not be high enough to put an end to poverty. The long range trend is toward a more equitable distribution of wealth, but we have to allow for a period of political reaction at some time during the next 12 years; whereas radical economic reform will be hotly debated, and the guaranteed annual income will be a lively possibility, 1980 is too soon to expect an end to our economic ills.

While we and a few other highly industrialized nations will grow richer, most of the other nations of the world, unable to control population growth, will become poorer. Meanwhile the spread of American influence, particularly the material aspects of American culture, throughout most of the world, will continue; and, as in the technologically less advanced nations arrangements for the distribution of wealth are not highly developed, a disproportionate amount of our material aid to a given nation will go to those of its citizens who are already relatively well-off, while creating rising expectations in the others. Thus, despite vigorous efforts by our government to ameliorate this state of affairs, there will be, in 1980, revolutionary situations in many countries of the world (including Vietnam, for although the fighting there will have quieted down—owing to the efforts of a Republican president who argued that the war was fine but too expensive and that in any case the boys should be brought home—a revolutionary situation will continue). Thus, an American military "presence" in many areas of the world will be called for, and will be seen to, although the question of who are the "good guys" and who the "bad" in various countries will be a subject for much debate in this country. This means that some kind of draft of military manpower will probably still be in effect.

THE EXPANDING UNIVERSE OF STUDENTS

This is a glimpse of the world which, in 1980, some 12 million college students will be preparing to enter. The diversity of these students is clearly indicated by present trends. So far we have spoken only of the activist students—a highly significant group as we shall see. It remains to be pointed out that these students not only differ significantly among themselves (Block, Haan, and Smith distinguish among the "alienated," the "activists," the "constructivists," and the "anti-social"), but they constitute only a tiny minority of all the students in American colleges and universities: Katz[30] has stated that student activism at Berkeley was never more than 15 percent while Peterson[31] concluded from his 1964–65 survey that, the country over, student protests were more like a "flickering candle" than a "conflagration." We may expect that, by 1980, differences in age, ability, background, value orientation, and personality that are now apparent will have become much greater.

Age. It now appears that nineteen-year-olds are to be drafted first, leaving older men free except in a national emergency. This change will affect college men (and their girls) in ways too numerous to be gone into here, but it can be assumed that many students who went into the armed forces at age nineteen would return to college after their service, thus increasing the average age of college students and creating a situation like that obtaining in the late 1940s when the college population included an army of veterans. It is not expected, however, that these students will be as vocationally oriented as were those of the late 1940s; indeed, it would not be surprising if many of them joined the ranks of the student activists.

In addition to students who leave college temporarily because of the draft, there will be many others who leave for a time, continue their education elsewhere, and then return to college. This will be a more common pattern in 1980 than it is now, for by that time there will be more evidence that experience of the real world, intervening at some time during the course of one's formal education, is beneficial to the individual's development.

A greater age range will also be caused by an increasing tendency for adults to return to college or to enter college in the pur-

30 Katz, "The Student Activists: Rights, Needs and Powers of Undergraduates," *op. cit.*
31 R. E. Peterson, *The Scope of Organized Student Protest in 1964–65* (Princeton: Educational Teaching Service, 1966).

suit both of necessary skills and of means for improving the quality of their lives. By 1980, a majority of all adults in the United States will be receiving some kind of education, though only a limited proportion of them will be in institutions now called colleges; the great majority of college students will still be in the phase of development that we have called late adolescence or young adulthood.

Ability. Pearson[32] has recently pointed out that the total range of ability found among high-school graduates in this country is represented in the population now in college. As many as five percent of the students who entered college in 1960 scored in the bottom fifth of the aptitude distribution and as many as 21 percent scored in the bottom half. Interestingly enough, 72 percent of the students in the bottom quarter of distribution were performing satisfactorily at the end of one year of college. It can be predicted that, by 1980, the proportion of students of very modest ability who enter college will have increased to a point where it exceeds that of high-school graduates of the same ability who do not enter college. At the same time, students at the top of the aptitude distribution will continue to be pushed ahead rapidly in school, so that the range of ability found in college students will be greater than it is now.

Value orientation and personality. While the values and personality characteristics found among the student activists will be even more common in 1980 than now, the great mass of college students will be cut of a different cloth. One might say that, for every student from an affluent home who enters college with a view to finding himself or to reexamining our society's purposes, there will be as many as 20 who enter college with the primary object of acquiring a vocation and going up in the world. The diversity of the college population will have been greatly increased by a continuing influx of students from backgrounds more characteristic of those young people presently not in college. In other words, differences between students of 1980 and students of now will be

32 Richard Pearson, "Admission to College," in Earl J. McGrath, ed., *Universal Higher Education* (New York: McGraw-Hill, 1966).

due in considerable part to the fact that more different kinds of individuals will then be entering college.

At the same time, differences in value orientation will be increased by tensions generated within the institution itself. The increasing radicalism of some students will be countered by the conservatism of others, which will in turn generate even more radicalism. For example, at the University of Hawaii in April 1967, the students elected a very conservative student-body president. His campaign promises concerned mainly covered walkways and an improved image of the football team. In his first speech after election, he said the faculty were "100 percent for the students" and that everybody should cooperate. The liberal students, who now tasted defeat for the first time in some years, reacted badly, proposing the creation of a "disloyal opposition," and they were barely headed off by an energetic counselor. Thus, the issues have been sharpened at this university and students have taken up more extreme positions than in former years. It seems obvious that the University of Hawaii, a high proportion of whose students are commuters, vocationally oriented, and from homes in which neither parent went to college, is far more typical of American universities than are those places, such as Berkeley or Chicago, which have seen much student activism in recent years. This will still be so in 1980. Although these institutions will have their share of activists (the University of Hawaii is not unlike Berkeley of 30 years ago), counterbalance will be provided by students coming up from below.

There will, of course, be a tendency in this country for institutions of higher learning to become more alike, as ordinary institutions imitate the more successful ones. This will not, however—at least not in the next 12 years—result in any great reduction in the diversity of students. Catholic colleges and other church-related colleges, for example, now striving to improve themselves through greater secularization, will not be so much like our present leading institutions as one might think, for the impact of a liberating kind of education upon young people brought up in religious homes will not be the same as it is for other students. In fact, we may anticipate greatly increased vitality on the part of the better Catholic institutions during the years ahead. This will be reminiscent of the period 30 to 40 years ago when the colleges of the major Protestant denominations were discovering science, becoming secularized, and, according to Knapp and Goodrich,[33] producing the bulk of American scientists.

THE UNIVERSAL TREND

Indications that the whole universe of students will have moved, and will be moving, in the direction pointed to by the student activists come not only from studies of the particular students described above but from observations of larger samples of students. It is not only that many students in leading universities sympathize with the activists, as Katz[34] pointed out, but they show in less extreme form a similar value orientation.

This is shown, for example, in the vocational-choice pattern of National Merit Scholarship semifinalists during the years 1957–1963, as reported by Nichols.[35] There was a sharp increase in preferences for teaching, government service, and—particularly since 1961—the ministry; science and engineers barely held their own despite the material inducements to go into these fields; and preferences for business declined. The proportions of students intending to major in social science and the humanities increased steadily while the proportion intending to major in science, engineering and business gradually declined. In general, it seems that these highly intelligent young people have been becoming increasingly interested in working with people and being of service to them, less interested in the physical world and in practical affairs.

These findings conform closely with our more recent (1966) observations at Stanford University, where less than three percent

[33] R. H. Knapp and H. B. Goodrich, *The Collegiate Origins of American Scientists* (Chicago: University of Chicago Press, 1952).
[34] Katz, "The Student Activists: Rights, Needs and Powers of Undergraduates," *op. cit.*
[35] R. C. Nichols, "Career Decisions of Very Able Students," in *Science*, 1964, 144, pp. 1315–1319.

of the entering freshmen men expressed a preference for business. (Business may have increasingly great difficulty in recruiting the most talented young people; at San Jose City College, where students generally showed a greater interest in security than did Stanford students, only 12 percent intended to go into business.) These findings on career preferences are, generally, in keeping with observations on the general values and attitudes of current students. In the Student Development study at Stanford,[36] students were given a comprehensive questionnaire in their freshman and senior years. They were asked to rank in order various "concerns" of their lives after college. Both in their freshman and in their senior years these students gave the highest ranks to "emotional well-being," "being liked and respected by others," and "love and affection." Thirty-three percent of the men and 40 percent of the women stated that "developing a personal identity" would be a major task in their future lives. All of these concerns ranked ahead of social and political ones (we are here reporting on students in general, not activists), and well ahead of wealth and the pursuit of intellectual or activist goals. These students seem to be seeking a kind of psychological and social, as opposed to material, wealth, as if they had been impressed by the psychological poverty that characterizes many of their elders who, products of the Depression, made material wealth their major objective.

That students who have shifted their concerns from getting a living to self-development, to the larger issues of society, and to making contributions should take longer to choose a major and, in increasing numbers, finish college without having decided upon a career is to be expected, and this is what the Student Development Study finds. Going into the Peace Corps or into graduate school is in many cases a further means for postponing a final vocational commitment. The draft is, no doubt, a factor in this change in student outlook, but we should attach more importance to affluence and the general shift in orientation that we have been discussing. It may be suggested, too, that students who are re-

[36] J. Katz, et al., *Personality Development and the Impact of the College* op. cit.

laxed about their future vocation are likely to be open to the genuine educational influence of their college, and thus to be "shaken up," to be made aware of many possibilities, and to take the time they need to settle upon an identity.

That these trends in student value orientation and personality will continue and be very pronounced by 1980 is indicated by what is known of the economic and family backgrounds of student activists. Student activism, and very probably the trends just described, are associated with affluent and highly educated parents. Probably the safest prediction that one can make for the next 12 years is that levels of affluence will continue to rise and that increasing numbers of students will come from highly educated families—hence more and more students of the types we have been describing.

The fact that student activists were in the majority of cases acting in accord with their parents' values shows that what was involved was no transitory adolescent rebellion but, more likely, a deeply based social trend. The students knew very well what they were doing, could be quite explicit about their values, and were able to connect their actions with a searching analysis of their university and their society. Many of the leaders of the Berkeley revolt had been advocating educational reform for several years, and we know that some of them are of the same persuasion still. Students who are working for change in the system at Stanford have read and discussed the educational literature, often more thoroughly than the faculty members and administrators with whom they argue their case; they have an intellectual as well as an emotional interest in better education. Some of these students have already determined to enter graduate schools of education, from which position they will make common cause with undergraduates.

Not only will students of this new breed be around in greatly increased numbers in 1980, but there will still be plenty for them to protest against. On the national and international scenes students will constitute a strong and increasingly effective force for more democratic and more human policies, while on the higher-education scene student demands for better education and for a larger role in determining their own affairs will have spread to virtually all institutions in the country. Whether or not there will be crises or highly visible demonstrations at a given institution will depend, of course, on what this institution does to meet the changes in the student body. Colleges or universities whose authorities can listen to students and that can adapt in reasonable ways to reasonable demands, will avoid serious trouble. The next 12 years will be a period of much experimentation and innovation on college campuses, and many of their officers will learn to enjoy stimulation and change.

I am not predicting more demonstrations of the Berkeley type. It is not only that things become "old hat" very fast in this country, but students will have found other ways to promote change on their campuses. Student interests in larger political and social issues and problems will be at a high level in 1980, and they will be using campuses as forums and rallying points for social service and organized political activities. Campus authorities, by then well-seasoned, will take all this for granted, and, although there will be in some states and at some institutions dramatic confrontations of radical students and a conservative opposition, things will rarely get completely out of hand.

As suggested above, there will be a significant amount of disaffection among young people in 1980 but it will take new forms. The "hippie" phenomenon will have almost disappeared, and the use of LSD for kicks or for religious purposes, already past its peak, will not be attracting much attention. The public will have become bored with reading about it, the hard core of desperate people eager to try anything will already have been involved, and serious "seekers" will have learned that it is not possible to bypass the ego. With marijuana there will be a different story. It will not be legalized by 1980, for it will be known to be not altogether harmless, but it will have for a great many young people somewhat the same functions that alcohol now has for many adults and will generally be regarded in much the way alcohol was in the years before the repeal of Prohibition, that is, with growing indifference by everyone except official and unofficial watchers over public morals.

Student activism will be flourishing in 1980 not only because more students of the new breed will have been produced, but because it will have many of the features of a successful social movement. It will gain strength from its successes. At places where there has been no activism in the past, students who have reformist zeal by virtue of their personalities will have to take the lead, but as the movement develops it will become increasingly easy for ordinary students to join in. Meanwhile, as time goes on, more and more students of the activist persuasion will be in graduate schools, where, encouraged by the presence of people like themselves, they will lend support to the reformist efforts of undergraduates. Indeed, by 1980, it will be possible for people who were activists as undergraduates to retain their youthful orientation even as assistant professors. They will be joined by formerly "suppressed activists" among the older professors and together they will supply the leadership that activist students want and need. Also by 1980 large numbers of students of the new breed will have taken their places in society, where, finding each other, they will offer outside support for reformist tendencies inside the college and universities. In these circumstances a great many parents of college-age youths will be discovering that the kind of education being promoted and offered by the new alliance of undergraduates, graduate students, assistant professors, and older professors with a new lease on life, is exactly what they want for their sons and daughters; and a great interest in humanistic education, long latent in our society, will be touched and released.

This general trend will, of course, be most pronounced in the older, richer, and more cosmopolitan institutions, but it will have spread to most colleges and universities in the country. In many of these it will still be encountering strong opposition in the form of vocationalism and political conservatism, but the direction for the more distant future will be clear.

It would be tempting to go on from this to visualizing a Utopia. Eventually perhaps, but not by 1980. There can be no Utopia in this country while huge areas of the world sink deeper into poverty. As a result of the trends I have described, we will have in our colleges and universities by 1980 the will and the intelligence to come seriously to grips with this situation and to begin to correct it. Unfortunately, however, the world is run largely by men who are still preoccupied with the issues and the modes of resolution that excited them in their youth, and they will not have surrendered their power by 1980. There will be plenty of excitement and plenty of promise at that time, but no Utopia.

The Future Undergraduate Curriculum

THE FUTURE undergraduate curriculum in American colleges and universities can assume one of at least three possible forms. It can, in 1980, resemble in most details its present style. And there is strong historical evidence that this may be its future. In 1934 a student was faced with such alternatives as attending a small (500 students) or a large (14,000 students) institution, electing a professional or a liberal-arts program, joining a Greek-letter organization, or renting a room, funding the college years through family support, summer employment, work during the academic year, college loans, or scholarships, or even through federal funds (the $26.00 a month paid to ROTC students was a welcome subvention), and attending a four- or a two-year institution. Having made such decisions, the undergraduate of 1934 faced placement tests, lecture courses, college requirements concerning personal conduct, bull sessions, football weekends, experimentation with alcohol, fuzzy courses on sex hygiene, reading lists of master works, and grade point averages necessary to remain in school. Not much different from student problems in 1964 and conceivably not much different from what may be true in 1974 and even 1984.

Or, the undergraduate curriculum can gradually change its character, assimilating the innovations which presently work best so that, by 1980, the substance of the curriculum will be as different as the Yale curriculum of 1828 (completely prescribed and classical) was from the Harvard curriculum of 1870 (after the free elective system had had time to take effect). Educational developments do spread slowly and only after testing and considerable discussion. The general education ideas of Erskine and Carman in the 1920s and of Hutchins and Woods in the 1930s became widely accepted and attempted only in the 1950s (after the Harvard Report[1] gave the movement respectability). The cooperative work-study concept did not gain general recognition and legislative legitimacy until 40 years after its first trials at the University of Cincinnati and at Antioch College. And the free-university type of course, demanded by dissenting students in the late 1960s, is but a new expression of the unstructured curriculum which Bennington College attempted in the 1930s.

Or, the undergraduate curriculum can suddenly change as a result of such powerful forces as population growth, exponential increases in knowledge, the social revolution of the nonwhite populations of the world, the technological revolution—especially cybernation and the revolution in weaponry which makes major warfare unthinkable. Other parts of the academy have changed as abruptly. Although the concept of university preoccupation with research had existed since the last decades of the nineteenth century, the actual implementation of that concept could happen only after the lessons of World War II had been learned. The financial plight of college teachers had long been recognized but the shift of the profession into an affluent one required the demographic revolution of a low-birthrate generation called upon to teach a high-birthrate generation and the shock of Sputnik to emphasize the importance to the society of those who educate its future leaders.

Although college faculties are conservative with respect to educational matters (being against all changes made during their careers) and colleges and universities are conservative norming agencies as an important part of their socially assigned roles, the

[1] *General Education in a Free Society.* Report of the Harvard Committee, with an Introduction by James Bryant Conant (Cambridge, Mass.: Harvard University Press, 1945).

current rate and direction of change within the larger society are of such magnitude that perpetuation of the undergraduate status quo does not really seem to be a viable option. Of course, there will be colleges and universities which will not change, and a few of these may even prosper. But for the majority, whether their faculties, administrations and boards approve or not, the imperatives of economic needs, of student demands, of technological requirements, of changes in other levels of education, revolutionized conceptions of work and calling, and of altered moral values and their sanctions are simply too great to resist. Thus, it seems reasonable to suppose that typical college students attending college in the 1980s will find considerable change as compared to what their predecessors did in the 1960s. It becomes necessary, then, only to anticipate whether the changes will have been evolutionary and deriving from present practice, or revolutionary to an extent that the entire character of undergraduate education will have been altered.

Even if changes are evolutionary from the innovations of the immediate post-World War II decades, these have been sufficiently varied and numerous to anticipate a substantially different undergraduate program by 1980. Students must expect typically to attend large, complex institutions. The tendency here is clear. Currently, for example, one-fourth of the total number of colleges and universities educate approximately three-fourths of the five and one half million students who will enroll in September of 1966. By 1980 the average size of a college will be 20,000 students and it will be located in an urban or metropolitan area of 100,000 population or more. Gone will be the day when the stereotyped vision of a college as being a small, tranquil place set in a pastorally romantic small town, far from the temptations of the city, has any basis in reality. And this large institution will be multipurposed in character. Whether it be a state or a private university, a former teachers' college, a former technological institute, a liberal-arts college or a two-year college, it will offer a wide variety of programs to a wide variety of student needs and will offer courses of a wide variety of complexity and abstractness. Junior colleges will offer work now commonly taught in the upper division of bachelor's level programs, and liberal-arts colleges will offer master's degrees and programs in such specialties as Inter-American Trade. This means that small colleges of 800 to 1,200 will have grown to well over 2,000 students and that a few single campuses will have become virtual cities with over 50,000 students enrolled. Probably Michigan State University, the University of Illinois, and the University of Minnesota will have reached that condition.

But large size will not always be achieved through location on a single campus. Most of the private liberal-arts colleges which dot the Middle West, the East and the Southeast will have become complex institutions through cooperative and federative arrangements. Such organizations as the Great Lakes College Association, the Associated Colleges of the Middle West, the organization of private institutions in Colorado, and yet to be formed unions of such institutions as the four private colleges located in Minneapolis will have developed centralized admissions, faculty recruitment, library acquisition, and curriculum allocation policies so that a student enrolled in any one college may obtain the full advantages which the entire federation can offer. Such unions will maintain a full faith and credit stance. Nor will distance be a bar even for associations of colleges located in several different states. Some courses will be offered commonly through amplified telephone or television from the college best able to support them. Students having been reared in a mobile society will not find it inconvenient to move from college to college during their undergraduate years. The old worries about transfer credit will be gone. And short-range, inexpensive jet airliners will allow professors to cover courses at several different colleges each week. Since their salaries by 1980 will be high enough, the peripatetic professor will not feel the need to demand extra fees for these visits. The economies of scale which a federation will allow will provide the resources with which to pay highly qualified specialists.

The reverse of this phenomenon will characterize the large single-campus institutions. Where smaller colleges spread over a region will federate to provide richness of program and financial resources to augment their already developed potential for small group relations, large institutions will feudalize themselves to add a personal element to the urbanlike wealth of resources their size has already given them. The patterns of the University of the Pacific with its cluster colleges, the Santa Cruz branch of the University of California, which will divide its 20,000 students into colleges of no more than 1,000 students, the Michigan State University perimeter of many colleges ranging in size from 600 to over 3,000 students will be widely copied. A few universities, because of specialized problems, will not subdivide completely, but even these, such as the University of Michigan or the University of Massachusetts, will maintain at least one cluster college to serve as an educational experiment station.

This decentralization of function will also characterize urban institutions located in or close to the central city. Colleges of this sort, especially junior colleges, will have found that the Colonial concept of the college campus as something walled off from the rest of the world no longer allows the college to be of service as the society expects it. Rather, urban colleges will sprawl amoeba-like through large parts of the largest cities, expecting that, as students go from class to class, they will pass through and profit from the variegated richness of experience which renovated cities provide. Public, high-speed transportation will have reduced the significance of distance as have the subway systems in New York and Boston. Further, the arms of the college will reach to places where people live. The college thus will do in the urban setting what land-grant colleges did in a rural age, i.e., bring education to the people rather than force the people to come to the college. As with so many innovations, this conception of a college is not a new one. The University of Paris has enriched centuries of Paris life and in turn has been refreshed by Paris through just such a form.

While most colleges will have become multipurpose, they will differ from each other in how they structure themselves to achieve their purposes. In a few, patterns of two-year colleges designed to feed into upper-level two-year colleges will emerge. These are not likely to become widely popular because of their tendency to segregate students by levels of education and because of such practical problems as the four-year-college need for the financial support which the lower two years so often provide. But there will be some, especially in those states whose population has reached saturation levels and whose needs for vigorous planning are so enormous. Several regions in Florida and possibly several in California may elect this option. In many more institutions, whether historically residential or commuting, another form of decentralization will be employed. This is the living-learning unit perhaps best exemplified by the House Plan at Stephens College. Facilities will be available so that students can live in a residence hall which also contains classroom space, faculty offices and a stock of learning resources. Students will work on a circumscribed curriculum for at least a portion of the time they spend as undergraduates. And even commuter colleges will find that some students can live as cheaply in such a college facility as by commuting to the campus each day. Then, a few campuses will have followed the example of Oakland Community College and Oklahoma Christian College. These institutions, especially Oakland Community College, have attempted to develop a new kind of college—one which minimizes formal course work and which, through the use of individual study booths, tape recorders, film-strip machines and programmed textbooks, seek to individualize instruction. Students generally are expected to work on their own most of the time on programmed tasks, but a tutor is always close at hand to check student work, to test performance, or just to give moral support. Without doubt, more institutions will attempt such a structure, particularly as computers become even more popular, but by 1980 none of the better-known undergraduate colleges or universities will have taken this route. But for institutions serving people without a high intellectual tradition, the automated college will be an effective means of providing a basic education in a number of the skills needed to survive in a complex society.

Just as most colleges will have become multipurpose institutions, so will almost all have become coeducational. While the separate-sex colleges and universities have been important in higher education in the past and still have much to commend them, the tendency for a more natural mixing of the sexes is currently so irresistible that by 1980 even such venerable bastions of single-sex education as Princeton, Yale, Vassar and Smith will, in one way or another, have become coeducational. The patterns will obviously vary. Colleges such as Hamilton and Colgate may create a women's branch, located part way between the two older schools. A few women's colleges will enroll a relatively few males to strengthen certain departments. And most will simply accept men and women on terms of equality. Further, they will make greater use of coeducational residence halls which will enable men and women to interact at meal times, in lounge rooms and libraries, and in each other's rooms. The problem of differing rules for men and women will by 1980 have generally disappeared.

Although institutions will resemble each other in the complexity of program and in size, there will still be important differences between the 2,700 colleges and universities which will exist in 1980. Several states will maintain highly selective, moderately selective, and unselective institutions, each with a somewhat discrete role, and within the private sector a few will be highly selective and will concentrate on the training of a limited number of future graduate students and students in advanced professional schools. But generally, by 1980, the construction of new facilities and the production of college teachers will have caught up with the demand. Thus, prestige colleges will generally not be in such a favorable market situation, and the trend, already discernible, of a widening of the ability band accepted by selective institutions will, by 1980, be quite pronounced. Most colleges and universities will have relatively heterogenous student populations with respect to academic aptitude, talents, ethnic background and socioeconomic origins. While some of the predominantly Negro institutions will still exist, it will be a gradually disappearing form.

Into such institutions will flow perhaps 60 percent or more of the age group seventeen–twenty-two. But the patterns of flow will be significantly different from those existing in 1968. To insure that students find and are admitted to the best institution for their purposes, a national admissions center will be maintained, linked by computers to regional centers or, in the case of populous states, to state centers. These massive banks of information about students and colleges will provide each college with lists of students judged appropriate for it, and each applicant with lists of colleges in which he will be accepted. This system will not preclude individuals' seeking admission outside the system, or colleges' similarly acting independently. But most students and colleges will utilize the college-student matching service because it will eliminate the period of tension and uncertainty which, in 1968, characterized the admissions process.

Data concerning each of the five million or more freshmen who each year will be entering higher education will include elementary- and secondary-school records, statements of personal interest, financial information and other similar material. They will not, however, contain information from counseling, from personality testing, results of disciplinary or legal action; for by 1980, the dangers of invasion of privacy will have become sufficiently clear that legal safeguards will have been enacted. This availability of large amounts of relevant information will suggest differential readiness of students to enter college. Thus, the present advanced-placement program and the few experiences with early entrance into college will be expanded so that perhaps ten percent of all high-school sophomores and 15 percent of all high-school juniors will be identified and offered admission into college. Similarly, the centralized admission centers will allow students to leave and re-enter college, to transfer from one college to another with relative ease. The concept of a normal progression from high school through two or four years of college, thence into the world of work will no longer be regarded as typical. Instead, students will regard early entry, a year's leave of absence, a year at each of three or four different institutions, or a ten-year program to receive a bachelor's degree as all quite normal. States will, by 1980, have finally recognized that out-of-state students represent a net gain to state-supported colleges and to the state itself; hence, the tendency of 1965 to increase barriers to out-of-state students will have been reversed so that easy transfer will be facilitated.

An important part of each student's education will be some form of off-campus experience. The Peace Corps, Youth Corps, Cooperative Work-Study, Youth Camp, and even national-service

concepts will be widely accepted. While students will not be compelled to participate in such activities, the experience will generally appear so valuable that most late adolescents will want to
have them. And colleges will generally finally have worked out
ways so that reasonable academic credit for such nonacademic
activities can be granted. Nor will parents regard leaving school
for one or several years as sinful or disgraceful. They will generally have accepted the fact that childhood or youth, defined as not
fully self-sustaining, will have extended from the nine or ten years
of age at the beginning of the nineteenth century to thirty to
thirty-five years of age in 1980. Life expectancy will still allow the
student who finishes the first phase of a lifetime of education at
age thirty to anticipate forty-five years of some form of productive
adult activity.

While some parents will still cling to the notion that students
should finish school in a hurry so that they can enter the labor
force, most will have accepted longer childhood as being normal.
They will be motivated to accept the change since, by 1980, a
national scholarship program will be so well entrenched that
every student will be assured of needed financial support. Parents
having adequate incomes will be allowed substantial tax
deductions for educational expenses and students from less well-
endowed homes will be entitled to full scholarships just by establishing that their parents earned less than a stipulated amount.
The amount will be considerably above subsistence levels so that
children from such homes will not feel compelled to seek employment to help support parents.

All of this means that there will be a much greater mix of generations in undergraduate colleges than now exists. There will be
fourteen- and fifteen-year-old early entrants in classes with thirty-
and forty-year-old returnees. There will be young married couples
in college, women whose children are full grown and men who at
the age of fifty will be seeking reeducation in an undergraduate
college to prepare for a second, third, fourth or even a fifth career
—a career which can be for work, retirement or leisure.

These students will be exposed to a variegated curriculum from
which to fashion programs suited to their own needs and condi-

tions. The program lockstep which in the past had limited most students to formal course experiences, arranged in symmetrical patterns of hours and days of the week, will have been broken by the computer. Each college will have its own computer center linked to central data banks. Through these, the detailed administrative work of getting students assigned to unusual experiences, of accounting for them and of locating educational opportunities, will be accomplished with minimum human effort.

Most students will be provided some form of foreign experience. Some will routinely be sent to overseas campuses such as those currently maintained by Stanford. Others will spend a year abroad, traveling and studying on their own. Still others will spend each summer for three or four years working on a project in a foreign country for which they had prepared during the previous academic year. And their foreign experiences will be reinforced by the existence, on their home campuses, of large numbers of foreign students and foreign professors. In many respects, higher education in 1980 will be as international in flavor as were the medieval universities of the thirteenth century. Of the 20,000 or more students enrolled in a single college, 1,000 will be natives of other lands, 5,000 will be abroad at any given time, and another 1,000 will be concentrating on preparation to go abroad to travel, study, or help a developing society grow.

This same worldwide vision will permeate formal courses as well. While in 1968 the Western European tradition characterized the bulk of American college course offerings in the humanities, social science and even in the sciences, that will substantially be changed by 1980. Every student will do some work on a non-Western subject. This may include Asian languages, African history, Oriental philosophy, or a combination of all of these. Each institution will concentrate its efforts on a few regions or specialities and its own students may take courses there or go to another institution to pursue a desired pattern of non-Western courses and experiences. And the non-Western emphasis will be enhanced by extracurricular activities and cultural events which will be as likely to feature non-Western as Western art displays, speakers, concerts, or ballets. And most of the professors will have had foreign experience to enrich their own understanding and teaching.

Not that the American or Western European tradition will be neglected. For one thing, secondary schools will have enriched their general-education effort, and students will come to college with a firm command of American and English literature, American government, and international affairs. And educational television will have brought significant elements of this culture into the homes of students while they were growing up. But in addition, the undergraduate college itself will devote considerably more time to the general education of students—defined as providing a common universe of discourse for people, especially in their non-vocational lives. This general education will comprise the bulk of undergraduate training and will be so organized that all students will do intensive work in literature, philosophy, history, science, mathematics, and the social sciences. These may be offered in either an interdisciplinary or a single-subject form. But they will be taught chiefly for their general-educational value rather than for any specific vocational outcomes.

The time in the undergraduate curriculum will be freed for these purposes because vocational training will gradually cease being a major preoccupation of the undergraduate schools. Much of the technical training needed even in such complex fields as electronics will be provided by employers who alone will be able to provide the newest equipment with which to conduct training. These industries will be able to use programmed instruction, to develop quickly complex skills. In a very real sense 1980 will witness a return of a form of the apprentice system, applicable not only to the skilled trades but to the service and managerial industries as well. For the highly skilled professions and callings for which long periods of preparation are needed, formal education will be handled in graduate and professional schools. Whether it be education, business, medicine, law, dentistry, journalism, or nursing, the specific educational preparation will normally be received after the bachelor's degree. Such a development will have had enormous consequences for colleges such as liberal-arts colleges which, in the past, have been actively involved in teacher preparation. Some, perhaps as many as 300 or 400, will have created master's programs in teacher preparation and in several other vocational fields requiring advanced education. Others will simply give up professional training and will concentrate all of their efforts on the liberal arts and sciences, conceived in the broadest of terms.

Lest such a concept seem too Utopian, it should be pointed out that the survival values of the future developed society—and that is clearly what the United States has become—are not the same ones needed in the past. Time was when the essential skills needed to survive were those of a hunter, or warrior, or herdsman, or farmer, or manipulation of heavy equipment. The time is rapidly approaching when cybernation will have developed so far that possibly five or ten percent of the adult population can man the entire productive enterprise. When that time comes, then the skills needed will be those to utilize well the vast amounts of free time which increased longevity and decreased need for productive work will make available to most Americans. As Edward Gordon points out, the phenomenon is already far advanced with adults using their time for gardening, boating, chauffeuring children, home craftsmanship and the like. By 1980 the skills most needed to survive will be those of communication. The management and conceptualization of knowledge will become much more important, because the rate of increase in knowledge will be so rapid that concentration on specifics will be futile. Ways by which to use leisure to insure personal growth and satisfaction must be found. And these are the skills or values to which the liberal arts and sciences can contribute most.

But although all students will work generally in the area of the humanities, social sciences, natural sciences and communicative arts, they will not necessarily do so in formal courses organized in orthodox groupings of one teacher and 30 or 40 students. Much of the formal curricula will be offered through independent study which will begin during the freshman year. Students will select a topic which is of interest to them, gain approval of a teacher and then spend considerable time developing it. The project may be a library project but it could as well be a mapping expedition to the

Cascades, a teaching experience in a deprived part of the country, the creation of a poem or musical composition, or an ecologically oriented float trip down the Mississippi River. And the reporting —for reporting and synthesis are important parts of education— may be a written paper, a series of photographs, tape recordings or unique artistic statements. As a general rule, the concept of independent study will be so well entrenched by 1980 that every student will spend as much as a third of his undergraduate years working on his own. And he will be aided in his efforts by libraries linked to central information centers, equipped with individual carrels for each student and organized so that books and other sources of information are equally respected.

This individual effort will also extend to the acquisition of many of the skills needed for independent work. While high schools will have come a long way in teaching students the basic skills of reading, writing, arithmetic and the like, students will continue to enter college deficient in one or more of them. They will be provided with programmed materials, computer-based teaching machines, and spaces in which to develop the needed abilities. And the same approach will be extended to some of the higher skills. A student needing statistics will be able in a relatively few hours to acquire enough knowledge about sampling probability and correlation to handle the data he assembles. A student anticipating a trip to France will be able to use a language laboratory, on his own time, to gain sufficient competency in French to enable him to begin to function on his own once he arrives in France.

Another recognition of the needs of individuals will be the inclusion of "free university" courses within the structure of the undergraduate college. Until approximately 1964–65, college courses were typically bound by the definitions of specific disciplines or combinations of disciplines. They were based on the assumption that firm grounding in principles was essential before students could use a subject to examine the big, perplexing questions of mankind. Undergraduate students thus experienced considerable frustration as they wanted a course in psychology to provide them with insights about themselves but were given the structure of the eye instead. A few universities began in the 1960s to try to rectify this condition. Harvard College developed seminars which did attack large problems, and the University of California created *ad hoc* courses in response to specific student demands. By 1980 most colleges and universities will have worked out procedures so that a group of students commonly interested in a problem can locate a professor who will work with them in a courselike setting. The titles of courses will, of course, change from year to year.

Perhaps the most impressive change in the content of undergraduate courses will be a shift from disciplinary courses during the first several collegiate years to courses designed to help students expand their impulse life. Nevitt Sanford has stressed the particular problems of late-adolescent students in learning to accept and use emotion. But many of the courses taken in college were once organized so as almost to deny affective concerns. Freshmen would normally take a foreign language, rhetoric, a beginning science course, mathematics and a history-survey course —all skills- or fact-oriented. Gradually, however, under such influences as a no-grade system, student demand for a more personal education, and an acceptance that a longer time in college was appropriate, students were allowed and even encouraged to take courses in poetry, music, philosophy and the applied arts during the freshman year. In a number of colleges every student was expected to take at least for one semester a studio course in one of the fine arts, perferably one in which he was not particularly competent. Art finally reached the state where it was no longer regarded as an ornament but an essential way of knowing reality.

Finally by 1980 colleges and universities will have reached the conclusion that, if students took too many courses, their gains were likely to be superficial and of short duration. Thus, as a general rule students will not be allowed to take more than three courses at any one time. While a few courses may extend over a semester, most will be year-long efforts, thus allowing enough time for students to become more deeply involved.

Techniques of teaching and instruction will generally reflect the changed curricular emphasis and the tremendous technological development of aids to instruction. While few colleges will have attempted to base the bulk of their effort on the use of technology, most will have adopted a number of devices for specific problems. And professors finally will generally have overcome the subconscious fear that the machine would replace the human.

Almost all colleges will have followed the lead of the Universities of Michigan and California, which have created offices for the improvement of instruction. These centers experiment with new techniques, teach professors how to use them, and supply funds and equipment for professorial experimentation. Such college centers will be linked to the large research and development centers on college teaching and will receive a steady flow of reports of new approaches. These, in turn, will be interpreted to local faculty members, who will be encouraged to use those which are relevant. And professors will have enough time to experiment for, by 1980, they, as well as students, will have discovered that teaching too many courses results in superficial teaching. Further, salaries will be sufficiently high that the motivation for professors to take on extra consulting or speaking responsibilities will have diminished. Since the supply of professors will have caught up with the demand, the pressures on professors from government and industry will also have lessened.

Each college will maintain a learning-resources center which will have books, tapes, slides, pictures, recordings, video tapes, programmed courses and a wide range of devices with which to use these materials. Students will be able to have access not only to the local collection of materials but also to those of the largest repositories, for the electronic computer will allow transmission of full texts over long distances with a small copying device for reproducing the text at the receiving end.

Obviously each student will have his own tape recorder just as, in 1968, he had his own pen and notebook. Thus, in place of going to a special language laboratory (although each college will maintain several), he can practice a programmed lesson in his room, hear lectures and recall the contents of a group discussion. Equally obviously, students will be able to talk with computers even as they now use a telephone, in order to obtain digests of research, answers to specific questions and guidance as to what they need to know in order to solve a problem. And it is possible that each student will have a small transistorized television set, operating on ultrahigh-frequency channels so that he can receive some instruction in his own room or study carrel.

However, the even more significant changes will not lie in the realm of technology but in the domain of attitudes and approaches to teaching. The psychology of poverty will finally be replaced by one of affluence. In place of the assumption that only a limited number of students can actually profit from college work, the assumption will be that every student can grow and develop. The significance of grades will have diminished, although not have disappeared, for the college still must certify the achievement of students. But failing grades will normally not be used. Rather, students will persist with a course until they finally have mastered it. Further, the college will expect almost all students to succeed and will reflect these expectations in the attitudes of faculty, the assumptions of counselors and the tone of catalogs and other materials about the college. By 1980 no president will dream of telling a freshman class to look to either side of them because one of each person's neighbors will not be around in June.

Large-scale examination programs will finally be seen not as a threat to students or teachers but as one of the best ways to allow individual progress through college. To the advanced-placement, college-entrance, graduate-record, and professional examinations will have been added well-prepared batteries of college-level examinations which colleges can use to determine whether or not students can proceed to the next level. And each college will maintain a testing office to create examinations with which to augment those prepared nationally.

Although individual study will be widely used, there will still be need for formal class work. But the middle-sized classes of 25 to 50 will finally be abolished. Rather, students will expect to receive some instruction in quite large groups—500 or more—and more instruction in quite small groups—five to ten. The large group lectures may be live, televised, or received via amplified telephone. These will be intended to stimulate or inform and professors giving them will have sufficient time to prepare so that they are truly fresh expositions of new knowledge. Within the small groups, students will have opportunity to express their own ideas and to probe in detail those of their teachers or fellow students.

But these formal class activities will not be rigidly scheduled. Rather, through flexible scheduling, large group sessions will be offered whenever all students are ready to receive it. This means that, between one large lecture on recent U.S. foreign policy and the next, some students will not need to do any further work; others will rehear a taped version of the lecture, while still others will go to small groups to develop greater understanding of the concepts earlier presented. The combination of computer storage of student-achievement data, a more limited number of individual courses and a changed primary mission for the undergraduate college makes flexible scheduling plausible.

Not only will the supply of college teachers be such that there will be professorial time for new approaches, but also additional teaching time will be provided by students themselves. By 1980 colleges and universities will finally have accepted the validity of what every teacher has long known—if one wants to learn something well, the surest method is to teach it. Every student will have built into his program at least one experience with teaching others. While some of this teaching will be done to noncollege groups, the bulk of it will be on the college campus itself. It is possible that much of the small-group discussion work will be handled by students, not in the sense of their being slave or low-cost labor, but in the better sense that a teaching experience is a part of their own education.

For these new approaches to teaching to be used will demand new conceptions of what a college teacher is. It will demand the abolition of a number of myths such as that of "publish or perish" and the invention of new roles for college teachers. It will also require the creation of a system of ethics applicable to a definite profession of college teaching as contrasted with the system of ethics which grew out of the professor's role as scholar and researcher. Of all the changes possible between 1968 and 1980, those regarding the nature of college teaching will be the most difficult to contrive. College teachers have long been noted for their conservatism with respect to educational matters. But there are some signs that change is in progress. The student demands of the mid-1960s have stimulated discussion of college teaching. The fact that several universities have created new degrees for well-trained people who do not want to do research but who do want to teach is indicative of change. And the fact that fifteen universities have already created offices for the improvement of instruction suggests that institutions are finally taking seriously ages-long criticisms of college teaching.

Thus, by 1980 there may be acceptance of the fact that most colleges and universities are not and have never been research centers. They are educational institutions for which the teaching role is the most significant. And it is possible that those institutions which are research centers will finally do what William Rainy Harper and David Starr Jordan advocated long ago—separate the undergraduate college from the university. By 1980 this split will not be far advanced, but there may be strong tendencies in that direction.

Within the teaching institution, professors will have accepted that their chief duty is to help young people change. They will come to see that teaching goes on in a counseling situation just as much as in a formal class. They will accept the fact that they earn their salaries as much through not teaching in an orthodox fashion as in delivering formal lectures. This shift will come hard for professors who are products of the Calvinistic ethic of work. But gradually a teacher will accept the notion that a well-developed one-and-one-half-hour class each week, when combined with thorough preparation and with counseling and advising students, is a full-time job.

And with this shift will come the creation of a new system of ethics, which will be not unlike those of the medical or legal professions. College teaching will be viewed as a helping profession to which the interests of students are of first consideration. No longer will a professor feel that his own work comes first and that work with students is an infringement on his own valuable time. Work with a student will have come to be of greater worth than the preparation of a research paper or the acceptance of a consulting assignment.

The antecedents for all of these structural, curricular and instructional developments are already in existence. And since social institutions evolve, the likely course of events is such that an evolutionary rather than revolutionary development will take place. But it may be that events and knowledge are crescendoing at such a rate that a radically different undergraduate college must be envisioned in 1980. Predictions here would almost take the form of science fiction. But in the past, science fiction has been prophetic; hence some speculation is in order.

The undergraduate college could go out of existence, as secondary schools and the graduate and professional schools divide up between them the educational responsibility for people from twelve to thirty. Jacques Barzun has hinted that this could happen. Or each home could have an educational room with a full range of electronic devices so that the bulk of education would take place in the home. Or narcopedagogy, self-hypnosis, subliminal perception could develop so that learning would normally take place while individuals were doing other things. Or books and printing could be eliminated with knowledge and insight acquired through auditory and visual, nonverbal, or even extrasensory means. Or each home could be equipped with a computer linked to national or international—via Telstar—banks and every educational need met just by asking the computer the relevant questions. But these seem quite remote. Rather, the educational scene in 1980 could be etched in tones, words and concepts already in limited use.

An eighteen-year-old in 1980 will very likely attend a large college which is subdivided into quite small units. Let us imagine the possible educational career of a young man entering college that year. During his first year he will do an independent study project, take a course on Western civilization and another on the philosophy of science and religion. He will acquire intellectual skills as the need develops through individual effort expended with the guidance of a faculty member who serves as his adviser. The next summer he will go to South America to live in a village where he will spend his time helping the villagers adapt new technology to old ways of doing things. Intrigued, he could elect to stay for another year but will have been in conference with his college advisers so that he could work on an anthropological study of the village. The needed resource materials he will receive from the nearest Latin-American university via electronic transmission from the library of his home institution. After returning from 18 months in Latin America, this student will take a year-long course in mathematics, one in psychology, and will do an independent study survey of the history of China. The following year he will marry a fellow student and move into a married-students apartment. He and his wife will form a research team for a joint project of teaching preschool children in a nearby community and will at the same time take courses in religion and theology and in the fundamentals of biological science. That year, as an extracurricular emphasis, they will attend the 15 lectures and concerts dealing with and deriving from Indian civilization. During the next year, as their first child will be born, the student couple may decide to drop out of school for a year. To insure adequate income as well as to continue educational progress, the husband will accept a year's work-study experience in an electronics firm where he will be taught the skills of advanced programming. As both he and his wife want to gain some understanding of sociology, a friend will have tape-recorded all lectures given in the subject and they will play and discuss them during the evening. So successful will this experiment be that they each will take and pass a comprehensive examination, and hence be awarded full academic credit. Finally, during the next year they may decide to receive their bachelor's degree and to leave college. They will take an integrative philosophy course, a course on modern European literature and a course on the uses of history. After graduation the husband may accept a position with an airline company as an aircraft controller. His first six months he will spend receiving training and then begin to fill his full shift.

This is how it might be in 1980 for people living in a developed society in which the knowledge industry has become the main concern of the majority of the people.

◀ ELIZABETH PASCHAL

Organizing for Better Instruction

EVERY GOOD TEACHER, including Socrates, has known that instruction should emphasize learning, not teaching. A problem arises as soon as formal education requires the instruction of many students of diverse interests and abilities in a group. Schools and colleges need to provide experiences that will help each individual student to learn and make him want to continue learning. How can institutions make instruction individual? And how can they clearly define the successive goals of learning and properly appraise a student's progress and ultimate achievement?

There is very little satisfaction in any quarter with our efforts thus far to meet these exacting requirements. But there are exciting prospects of greater success in the 1980s, because we have now at hand or under development the technical means of individualizing collegiate instruction even though our colleges and universities will then enroll more students than there are now in high school. The patterns of instruction predicted in this chapter will not, of course, be universally adopted. However, there is enough experimentation already in process to indicate certain directions for the future and ensure that many institutions will take these paths.

Other chapters in this book have focused attention on the dimensions of change in curriculum, in types and numbers of institutions, in the numbers and competencies of students seeking higher education, in the responsibilities of colleges and universities to their communities and the world—changes that will remake the campus of 1980. The instructional patterns which were tolerable on the smaller, more homogenous campuses of the first half of the twentieth century must change radically, too. The closed community, sheltered from the outside world, prolonging the adolescence of its students and fostering in them a romantic attachment to their chosen schools, has been invaded and exploded. As Rosemary Park, then president of Barnard College, said not long ago at a convocation on the university in America, "Alma Mater is dead."

Within the next 15 to 20 years many other symbols and arrangements of the conventional campus will follow Alma Mater to the grave. Traditional "classes"—freshman, sophomore, junior, senior—will, in the better colleges and universities, live only in the memories of old grads, though, of course, some laggard institutions will still cling to the old, outmoded patterns.

When, as at present, students must count credit hours to earn a degree, the four classes jog into an academic lockstep. If 120 semester hours add up to a degree, 30 hours must make a sophomore, 60 a junior, etc. In the 1950s and 1960s we have seen some breaking of the lockstep. Programs of early admission to college or admission with advanced standing have interrupted the academic tramp-tramp. In *early admission,* students not yet graduated from high school are accepted as college freshmen and are not required to make up such entrance requirements as they lack. The student admitted with *advanced standing,* by virtue of special courses taken in high school, can sometimes enter as a sophomore. More frequently, however, though exempted from certain freshman requirements and allowed to proceed to more advanced work, he still must amass the standard total of credit hours for graduation.

Despite these useful programs, we have not progressed very far toward a clear definition of the educational experiences appropriate to the college years, as distinct from the school years. Early in this century, bright children were sometimes allowed to skip one or more grades in elementary school. This crude device for permitting a student to move forward at his own pace has given way to ungraded classes in some schools. Like skipping a grade, the early-admission program advances the student faster. But it leaves gaps in his learning and requires him to take a giant step in all his subjects at once. Admission with advanced standing, like the ungraded class, permits a smoother progression in learning and allows different rates of achievement in different subjects. Both programs suffer from the drag of the credit-hour approach to learning. They offer some escape for the capable student, but within narrow limits. Academically, they are more respectable than the noncredit remedial courses which many universities and colleges used to offer—some still do for students from segregated schools and educationally deprived homes.

These are small steps in the right direction. But the big task for higher education now is to abandon the credit-hour criterion, to make clear what a student must achieve in growth of knowledge, judgment, and intellectual competence to warrant his getting a degree, and to devise means to assess his achievement. It seems probable that within the next 20 years the baccalaureate degree will cease to represent completion of senior college work. The rapid growth of knowledge and higher employment standards will increasingly require at least that mastery of a field of study represented today by the master's degree. The success of the three-year master's-degree programs and the introduction of new programs, such as Yale's Master of Philosophy, are returning to the master's degree the academic respectability and status it has largely lost. The faculty of many good liberal-arts colleges are already pushing their institutions into offering master's degrees. By 1980 the baccalaureate will have lost status just as the master's has in universities which offer the Ph.D.

Eventually, the baccalaureate could become the terminal degree for junior or community colleges, which will also be faced with the problem of defining the competence required for graduation. However, given the present weight of academic prejudice against permitting community colleges to go beyond the Associate of Arts degree, probably only the stronger, more experimental community colleges will confer baccalaureate degrees by 1980.

When degree requirements are defined in terms of learning instead of credit hours, there should be better coordination of a student's major field with his general liberal education. When colleges face the problem of evaluating a student's achievement in terms of his knowledge and understanding rather than time spent in classes, they will not be able to consider his comprehension of his major field complete unless he sees its place in the whole of human learning; and the student's "mastery" will be suspect if he has learned only a vocation. Newly defined, a college degree will also reflect the graduate's capacity to exercise his responsibilities as a citizen, to make good use of his leisure time, and to continue learning.

In the past, the growth of knowledge has fragmented the curriculum and hampered effective interdisciplinary instruction. Paradoxically, the remedy is at hand in the ever faster growth of knowledge, which already is beginning to disclose the interrelation of disciplines and the indispensability of men who are not merely learned but also wise and humane.

How will colleges organize instruction to produce such graduates? Each entering student, with help from his faculty adviser, will lay out a program that will bring him to the point of competence required for the degree he seeks. Throughout his college career, he will work with his adviser to appraise his own progress and to change his program when desirable. There will be no uniform sequence of courses, and the extent to which any student learns from books, from lectures, and from laboratory experience will depend on him. Only the goal will be fixed: the competence required for the degree.

Resources for study will not be limited to the college in which the student is enrolled. Already colleges are sharing information. By 1980 every first-rate college will extend its command over resources it does not own. And each campus will make its own resources more readily available to its own students.

No longer will faculty members spend class time giving factual information or attempting to discover what facts students have accumulated. It will be up to the students to acquire, outside class, all the data upon which to base understanding. Resources will be at hand in books, taped lectures, films and filmstrips, records, photographs, programmed texts, and computerized programs. Large regional libraries will form a network with computer systems for storage and retrieval of data, and transmittal systems that will make it possible for a student to get rapid access on his own campus to information available any place in the country. Microcopiers will put original manuscripts within reach of every student.[1] Already the campus library is becoming a learning-resources center with electronic equipment supplementing its collection of books, and with a large part of its space and resources arranged for individual or small-group study. This is the direction all libraries will follow by 1980.

Faculty will depend on these technological developments to free them from routine work for the more important tasks of helping students develop their capacity to organize knowledge, apply it to solving problems, and grow in wisdom. Since another chapter in this book deals in detail with new technology for teaching, only brief reference is needed here. Among the future resources available on all campuses will be taped lectures by the world's outstanding scholars, to be shown over television to large groups or a single student. The conference telephone hookup, with conferees' seeing as well as hearing one another, will make it possible for groups of students to ask questions and get immediate replies in conversation with outstanding persons in many fields of scholarship, the arts, government, industry, and organized labor. Pioneer work by Stephens College with a group of smaller institutions has demonstrated the feasibility of extending the campus in this manner.

For individual study, computers will provide programmed materials far more varied and flexible than those available today. The machine can answer questions put to it by the student, discern gaps in his knowledge, and present him with appropriate materials or questions for his consideration. Properly programmed, the computer can be used not only for drill, but also for tutorial work.

[1] The revolution in copying techniques and transmission systems has already sparked controversy over the copyright law, which protects writers, publishers, and others from unauthorized use of original materials. Clearly, a solution must be found which will assure the writer of a fair return for the use of his work but at the same time facilitate the widest possible dissemination of materials.

The techniques for programming such tutorial systems are known. Further development will be rapid.

There is no question that, by 1980, computer technology in instruction will make it possible for students of different abilities to arrive at the same level of competence in basic skills by different routes and in different lengths of time. When a student's faculty adviser discusses his progress and helps him plan his next steps, no time need be spent examining his grasp of material he has studied alone. The student's own knowledge of his accomplishment, which keeps him working at the material until he has mastered it completely, will allow both individual conferences and group discussions to concentrate on developing techniques of solving problems and encouraging creative thought.

The student will spend much of his time in independent study, guided in direction and purpose—but not closely supervised—by the adviser. Recent experiments in offering independent study to students far below the honors grade, with less than the usual faculty direction, justify the belief that by 1980 such programs will be an important part of the instructional pattern. In some, the student will study by himself; in others, groups of students will share the exploration of a common problem. By 1980 the experiments now in process with student-conducted seminars and laboratories, between-term noncourse study, reading periods, and the like, will have succeeded in refining the techniques and identifying the limitations of such programs. Hence, the faculty adviser can guide the student to the best mix of classes and independent study. Eventually a student may spend between 40 and 70 percent of his time in independent study.

In 1980, nearly every student will spend time away from his home campus, and not only in academic work. The spectacular growth during the 1950s and 1960s in the number of colleges and universities permitting students to earn credit for study abroad, and in the number of students going abroad, reflects the educated man's concern with the world today. This concern will continue to grow as faster means of travel and communication shrink the time-space between nations and by 1980 will color the education of every student. Particularly for the study of non-Western cultures, experience abroad will be essential. In the instructional pattern of 1980, in which the student plans his complete program from the start to attain recognized goals, the role of foreign study will be defined in advance, and the student will prepare for it carefully. The guilty or frustrated reaction that many students have today on returning from a year abroad—that they did not study so hard or learn so much in academic courses as they might have done at home on their own campuses—arises from failure to understand what can be learned from diverse experience and to examine what sort of learning a student needs most at a given stage of his education.

In the future, some students will leave their campuses to study in other American colleges or in research laboratories such as the Argonne National Laboratory, whose resources are now open to faculty and students of the Associated Colleges of the Midwest. Cooperative arrangements among groups of colleges have grown rapidly in the past decade and are augmenting resources of each campus, large universities as well as small colleges. The huge college enrollment of 1980 will make cooperation among institutions even more important to survival and success.

Off-campus *work* experience, paid or volunteer, will play a larger role in the educational programs of 1980 than today. Work-study plans have been incorporated in some college programs since the first such plan was organized by the University of Cincinnati in 1906. Many of the programs developed since have placed more emphasis on the general education of the student than on acquisition of vocational skills. This concern will become increasingly marked in the future, as technological developments decrease dependence on simple human skills and increase the need for emotionally mature and intellectually alert men and women who are prepared for change in both their work and their leisure. The importance of preparing for these changes is emphasized by a recent estimate that 70 percent of the children now in elementary school will eventually work in occupations that do not now exist, and also by the steady decrease in the length of the work week under union contracts.

Off-campus work, intelligently chosen and related to broad

educational goals, undeniably promotes intellectual and emotional growth. The sticky problem of how much "course credit" to give for such work will disappear in the organizational plan of the 1980s which eliminates credit hours. Any off-campus experience, study or work, will be included in a student's program for its expected contribution to what he must learn before he can claim a degree, and it will be evaluated accordingly.

When a college program puts on a student the responsibility for learning outside class a large part of all he must master before its conclusion, one may well ask what the faculty are doing to make it worth his while to be enrolled in college. The student revolt in the 1960s has been attributed, in part, to the isolation of students from senior faculty, particularly in large universities. Professors are now in great demand as consultants to government and business, and often put their own research and outside work ahead of teaching. The problem has been most acute in the undergraduate colleges of universities, especially among students in the social sciences, who tend to be acutely aware of the gap between what is going on off campus and what they are doing in classes taught by graduate students little more experienced than themselves.

The flexible program envisioned for 1980 will help restore the important faculty-student relationship. It will make the professor not a purveyor of information, but rather the senior scholar in a joint intellectual adventure, and the adviser who helps direct the student's organization of his learning. The professor's experience off campus and his research interests will add to his value in this partnership, and the flexibility of his program of teaching will permit longer absences from the campus with less disruption of instruction.

Certain colleges have already discovered that even a limited approach to more flexible programs, such as a morning freed from classes and other meetings to give students and faculty uninterrupted time for study, has paid large dividends. The hold of the regular class meeting is hard to break, but new curricula and the move toward year-round operation of institutions are shaking it loose. To provide a faculty adviser for each student in 1980 will mandate the reduction of hours spent in class and the grouping of class meetings to permit large blocks of free time. For example, a professor might give a series of lectures or conduct seminars several days within one week and not again for six to eight weeks. The lectures will be principally demonstrations of problem-solving in the professor's field. Students will then spend some weeks applying the demonstrated methods to problems on which they are working independently. Seminars will be devoted to criticism of the students' efforts. Thus, class sessions adapted to permit large numbers of students to get help in their individual programs of study will make an excessive number of individual conferences unnecessary. Experiments already undertaken by Antioch, Lake Forest, and other colleges offer assurance that independent study need not mean the substitution of 20 individual conferences for one class meeting. The new organization of instruction rests on a new role for the faculty.

Recognizing individual differences among faculty members as among students, institutions will not expect every professor to lecture, to meet classes, and to advise students. However, in undergraduate institutions, most faculty members will have personal contact with students as advisers. Each faculty adviser will help his group of students plan and revise their programs, appraise their progress, relate their new learning to their objectives as educated men and women, and above all grow in ability to ask the essential questions, solve problems, and make discoveries. In this faculty-student relationship rests the essence of the scholarly partnership—the apprenticeship of a young learner to a more experienced one, a true scholar-teacher.

Indeed, when instruction is organized in this manner, activities off campus will be as important for faculty as for students. Participation in the larger community—as consultant, member of a research team, lecturer on other campuses, or citizen actively engaged in political affairs—contributes to the professor's understanding of the place of his specialty in human knowledge. The cross-discipline approach to solution of problems, which is usual in the world of diplomacy, business, and industry, will become more common in colleges as professors continue their learning in applied as well as pure research. Freedom from inflexible class schedules will allow professors to use the community for their own education as well as to serve it with their specialized knowledge, and to give students the example of truly liberal education, continuing throughout a lifetime.

Institutions will arrange for faculty as well as students to study and work abroad, and the campus will increasingly benefit from the experiences and insights of students returning from study abroad and of foreign students who will come to American colleges in increasing numbers. Too often, up till now, the student from one culture has been antagonized or baffled by his experiences in another country. When foreign experience is truly integrated into the whole learning pattern, the hopes for its beneficial effect on the student and the institution are more likely to be realized.

As projected, the college of 1980 will give the student great flexibility in how he reaches his goal and how long he takes. But the student's goal will be much more clearly defined than it is now in terms of knowledge, competence in using the knowledge, and maturity of judgment. This projection raises the question of how the student's achievement in relation to the goal set can be appraised. How does one equate the educational value of working for two months for a business concern in Quebec while living with a French Canadian family (as in Goddard College's comparative-cultures program) with that of a student-led seminar, a period of concentrated study in which the individual uses all the resources available in a well-equipped learning center, or class attendance on a regular basis for the same period of time? How does one decide that one student has achieved what is expected of him in two years, but another, not even in four? What weight should the student's own evaluation of his progress have, as compared with that of his adviser or of professors previously unacquainted with him who are asked to sit on his examination committee? Clearly, the function of examinations will be different in the 1980 educational structure.

One unlamented casualty of change will be the final course examination, made out and graded by the professor who taught the course, and whose recorded grade attests the student's completion of three or five hours of the required degree work. To some extent, examinations in separate courses have already been subordinated to the comprehensive examination. The comprehensive is usually limited to a student's major field, and the student is still required to complete a given number of credit hours and pass individual course examinations. In some cases, more frequently for the ablest students, passing an examination on the content of a course he has not taken may give the student credit hours for that course. This procedure has introduced some flexibility into the instructional pattern. However, the practice of exempting from certain required courses any student who can pass an examination has been more common than that of awarding course credit on the basis of the examination alone. Faculties have generally been reluctant to admit that a student can do work worth credit without attending, or at least enrolling in, a class.

The difficulty of constructing examinations for credit purposes is in part responsible for the limited opportunity students have to move toward a degree by this method. Since 1963, the Educational Testing Service and the New York State Education Department have developed certain comprehensive and course examinations which colleges may use for assessing credit. Colleges in New York State, stimulated by the College Proficiency Examination Program, have given more thought to the use of such examinations than most colleges elsewhere. The experience gained in the use of tests of this kind and the increasing recognition that valid education takes place outside classrooms will ease the road to the flexible instructional patterns of 1980.

A number of years ago I sat in a convocation called by the president of one of the leading women's colleges for an important announcement. She said: "I congratulate the members of the freshman class, who will be the first members of this institution privileged to take comprehensive examinations." The hall was quiet for a moment. Then, in unison, the student body sighed, the noncongratulated in relief and the privileged freshmen in dismay.

Perhaps the student who enters college in 1980 will also doubt, at first, the privilege that will be his: to earn a degree dependent on examination of his total educational achievement at a given time. But by this means he gains freedom from the lockstep of credit hours. And it will create a better atmosphere for joint intellectual inquiry by students and faculty. No longer will the student study the professor rather than his subject, in order to feed back on tests the answers he believes the professor will consider worthy of good marks. No longer will his sole motive for attending classes be the knowledge that some professors refuse a passing grade to a student who cuts classes. And no longer will professors have the uneasy feeling that some students seek conferences and ask questions not because they are interested in learning, but because they wish to make a favorable impression. A number of experimental colleges have observed improvement in the student's expectation and accomplishment when he assumes new responsibility for his own learning.

When instruction is organized to achieve the defined objectives in knowledge and understanding for which the degree stands, through programs designed by students in conference with their advisers, achievement should be determined by a comprehensive examination administered by scholars other than those whose courses the student attended. The adviser will, of course, sit with the examiners and have a voice in the appraisal, but he must not be handicapped in his relations with the student by being the determiner of "pass" or "fail." He and others called in from time to time at his suggestion will have made informal reports of the student's progress; and the student, appraising himself as he goes along, will have learned to do a better job of it by comparing his own estimate with those of his adviser and other professors. He will learn to criticize his own work intelligently and more honestly, freed as he will be from the bugaboo of grades at each stage of his progress. Since he will be able to choose the time for his degree examination, without regard to years spent in college, wisdom in self-appraisal will be a necessary part of his education.

The scope and content of the examination will depend on both the definition of the degree and the student's major field. For a liberal-arts degree, it will be broader than the present departmental or even divisional comprehensive examination. The objective of the examination will be not to discover the student's accumulation of facts, but to determine how he organizes his knowledge in dealing with new problems and situations—whether, in short, his education has prepared him to assume adult responsibilities commensurate with his ability, and to continue learning throughout his life.

One might ask whether a person who has never attended college classes might not, on the basis of his experience and independent learning, stand for examination and receive a degree. Probably, by 1980, there will not be much demand for this privilege, because there will be relatively few people desiring a college degree who have not taken some class work. However, we may expect some experimental colleges to open their comprehensive examinations to any person whose learning, achieved by whatever means, is worthy of a degree. The faculty in such cases would probably want the applicants to spend an extended period, perhaps a fortnight or a month, on the campus in order to gauge their abilities properly. The campus of 1980 will be accustomed to the coming and going of its scholars, undergraduates, and faculty, and the presence of adult students in degree programs will cause no surprise.

By way of summary, we might follow the course of a high-school graduate of 1980. Let us assume that our candidate, Joe, chooses a liberal-arts college which has been in the vanguard of educational improvement.

Joe will be assigned a faculty adviser, chosen if possible from the field of his chief interest. The adviser may be changed later, on his own initiative or Joe's, if the change seems likely to further Joe's education. He will spend the first week or two in consultation with his adviser and in learning what will be expected of him before he can be awarded a degree. He will begin to plan a program to meet those expectations. He will enroll in some courses designed for entering students. If his previous learning and experience in a given field warrant it, he may enroll in advanced courses.

He will meet professors who follow different patterns in teaching, but probably none will meet classes three times a week for 15 weeks. Each will make clear to Joe and his colleagues what the course is intended to accomplish, what resources are available in the learning-resources center, and what knowledge they must bring to class sessions if they are to profit from what will be done there. In class, students will not be reviewing or repeating information, but will apply their knowledge to exploring new problems and to learning what questions are critical in the advancement of their education. If Joe finds the class meetings contribute less to his educational program than study outside of class, he will be free to cut them all. For most of Joe's fellows, however, the pattern will include some class instruction, especially in their early college years. Joe will need considerable experience before he can proceed entirely on his own, even though some of his previous schooling or work has prepared him for such independence.

Joe will have the option of staying on the campus throughout the year or of spending some time away from it in work or study, domestic or foreign. Probably before he takes his degree, he will have spent between one-fourth and one-third of his time off campus. Normally, vacation will be no longer than one month a year. The old pattern of summer-long vacations, laid down when most people were farmers, will have been buried by 1980.

Since the campus will be operating on a year-round basis, but with nearly all students away at least a quarter of their time, Joe will not march in step with all those who entered college when he did. He will attend lectures or seminars occupying different periods of time, some running for six weeks, others for ten or more. The irregularity in hours of course work will not create a problem because he will be working much of his time independently and can adjust to the classes he wants to attend.

Joe and his colleagues will learn to judge their progress, and examinations will be available by means of computer-based programs to help them determine gaps in their knowledge. Joe will not hesitate to test himself or to reveal his deficiencies to his professors, because there will be no record of grades to be held against him when he enters graduate school. Consequently, he has no incentive to cheat on examinations. When he has mastered one part of his program, he will move ahead without delay. He may be ready for his degree examination in three years, or in five, whenever he can demonstrate the broad general education and mastery of one field which the college requires for its degree. This demonstration must satisfy scholars whose concern will be not with facts learned but with the student's ability to use his knowledge in unfamiliar situations and to relate his major field to learning as a whole.

Is this an impossible dream for 1980? Not at all. The changes between 1950 and 1965 in methods of teacher education, the use of new technology in instruction, the growth of off-campus experience, and attention to the needs of the more able students would have seemed equally impossible at the start of that period. Students who have had flexible and challenging programs in elementary and high school do not readily adjust to the college lockstep. They increase the pressure for change. Furthermore, changes forced on higher education by the rapid development of new knowledge and the greatly increased demand for education beyond high school will make change inevitable in methods of instruction.

In some institutions, the seeds of the future are already germinating, from extended emphasis on independent study to the use of television as a teaching tool. As noted earlier, the acceptance of the full range of technological aids to teaching—taped lectures by the greatest scholars of the world, programmed materials teaching all basic data and technical skills, original documents microfilmed and available by computerized retrieval systems for transmission to a student on any campus, language laboratories, telephone communication between small groups and persons too far away to be consulted face to face—will so free faculty from the chores of instruction that they can at last concentrate on the essential function of a teacher: helping the student develop his powers of thinking. It will be the chief occupation of faculty advisers in the 1980 pattern of instruction.

Under this pattern, the small college will not be at a disadvantage in its appeal to students and faculty members. With its resources extended by technology, by cooperative arrangements with other colleges and universities, and by its use of the off-campus community, domestic or foreign, faculty can engage in research without sacrificing their teaching role. Similarly, the university can recapture the advantages of the small college, allowing students access to senior professors as advisers.

Colleges and universities can, through the use of technology and flexible arrangements for instruction, accomplish the "dual-purpose revolution" described by Frank Bowles in an address to the Annual Conference on Higher Education on March 14, 1966: the maintenance of high educational standards and the simultaneous democratization of higher education. When institutions define their degrees so as to make clear what each graduate must accomplish, and when, at the same time, each student follows his own path, long or short, to any given degree, colleges and universities can, with no sacrifice of educational standards, accommodate a flood of newcomers whose interests and abilities are widely different.

Abraham Lass, a high-school principal, recently said: "The joy has gone out of learning." The chief reason is that, at each stage in his program, the student is overhung with anxiety about admission to the next stage, about making grades high enough to keep him ahead in the competition for place. In a system which puts the emphasis on learning rather than on grades, with a faculty given time and motivation to help students achieve understanding and creativity, that joy can be recovered and the individual's continued learning assured.

◄ C. R. CARPENTER

Toward a Developed Technology of Instruction 1980

I BEGIN WITH certain assumptions about the future of American higher education.

First, the trends of demands which are now affecting colleges and universities will continue and increase in strength. New and unpredictable demands will be added to these before 1980.

Second, the traditional and conventional methods and procedures for operating colleges and universities will become critically inadequate under the weight of the cumulative demands during the 1970s; a real emphasis on teaching will increase, and the needs for a developed technology of instruction will become slowly evident to educational planners, decision makers, and administrators.

Third, the relative advantages and limitations of special parts and systems of instructional technologies will be supported by reliable and valid evidence from expanded and improved research, and a wide range of types of vivid or even dramatic demonstrations and models will be developed during the late 1960s and 1970s to show the merits and emphasize the real functional advantages of developed technologies.

Fourth, the introduction of new technologies in any field always requires both training and retraining of the *"peopleparts"* of the technology, and the field of higher education is no exception to this generalization. We will make progress toward a technology of instruction in direct relation to the extent that college and university faculties are informed, trained, and retrained. Faculties need to become personally skilled in and committed to efforts to insure that innovations, new approaches, and advanced methodological configurations are made to match the complex and demanding tasks of instruction.

Fifth, the introduction of new technologies requires new kinds of buildings and facilities, new equipment, and new networks of communication apparatus; and therefore it is assumed that planning, architectural design work, and construction will be done in such ways as to accept and accommodate new instructional technologies rather than to lock in old methods and to lock out new developments.

Sixth, it is assumed for the next 12 years that the plans and programs launched during the 1950s and 1960s by foundations, by federal and state agencies, by educational institutions, and by private enterprises will begin to yield significant results in terms of the developmental and extended uses of advanced and effective technologies of instruction. The equipment and apparatus that is now in various stages of development will have been perfected and proved in field tests to be operationally dependable.

Seventh, during the 1970s the systems-theorists in economics will include educational enterprises in their conceptualizations of the nation, and included also will be calculations of the resources required by education. Detailed analyses will be made of cost factors, flow systems of products and people, and the socioeconomic results. It will be made clear that complex and advanced education is essential for a high level of economic activities. It may become possible to change the emphasis in the "academic marketplace" from high-intensity investments in salaries and wages to an adjusted and better balance with instrumentation and equipment.

Eighth, increasingly, as costs and expenditures of higher education grow to levels that exceed all previous public estimates, it is assumed that emphasis will increase on demands for institutional efficiency, effectiveness, and economy. Requirements will be developed for assessing the returns or yields on funds committed to education. In brief, the economics of education will become a serious consideration during the late 1960s and during the 1970s. As colleges and universities grow larger, the necessity will become evident for administering them by the best-known business-management practices.

Ninth, the developers of equipment and facilities for higher education will evolve a better balance than now exists between the functions served or the jobs done by their products and the full range of functions or operations of complex instructional tasks or instructional cycle. The highly emphasized display and distributive functions (as in one-way televised instruction) will be balanced with the undeveloped provisions for learner responses, "feedback," reinforcement, and the assessment and testing of performances.

Tenth, gradually over the next decade the design characteristics of expanded and extended colleges and universities and systems of these institutions will become compatible with new and emerging technologies of instruction.

NEW BUILDINGS AND FACILITIES FOR A DEVELOPED
TECHNOLOGY OF INSTRUCTION

Special buildings, equipment, and apparatus should be provided to serve as a basis for developing and using a truly modern technology of instruction. Already there are parts of what is needed dispersed thinly over many campuses. Unless needed buildings and facilities are provided, a technology of instruction cannot develop. But by 1980 it should be possible to have what is required for developing and using advanced technologies of instruction.

Instructional-Resources Centers: The major complex which is already available in whole or in part on some campuses is the instructional-resources center. Such a center may consist of information and knowledge stores, the main libraries of books and journals and branch libraries, special collections of books, collections of *realia* in laboratories and museums, exhibits, photographic collections, demonstrations, materials, art galleries, music studios, and dozens of variations of sources, centers, and collections which have materials for direct use in instruction. There are not likely to be fewer but more of such resources for learning; the assemblies are not likely to be smaller but larger by 1980 than those observable in the best institutions on the campuses of the mid-1960s. What may be new by 1980 will be the organization into integral systems of the varied and appropriate materials needed for planning, organizing, producing, and recording programs for stimulating and guiding learning activities.

A principal barrier to a mature technology of instruction is the failure to integrate the different kinds of resources and materials that are needed into common pools with accessibility for efficient use. Having what is needed readily accessible to those who have the responsibility for developing units, blocks, sequences, areas, courses, and curricula of instruction could be one of the results of reorganized future libraries and informational sources.

A family of facilities that is usually associated with the library provides necessary support for any kind of technology of instruction. This family, often called the audiovisual services, consists of still- and motion-picture photographic and sound-recording laboratories and studios, and graphics services. In those institutions which have closed-circuit and broadcast television, some parts of these services may be included in television activities. Radio facilities can be closely related. More and more often in the mid-1960s, video-tape recordings and services are beginning to be provided to support the instructional programs. This kind of medium along with films will continue to be used as thermoplastic carriers are introduced.

A second facility that is already in place and is sure to expand is the family of digital and special-purpose computers. There is no tool for which more uses are being found and predicted than the computer, and there are promising applications in the area of instruction as we shall describe later.

Throughout the country new buildings are being especially designed for teaching and learning. These structures are wide departures from the old rectangular classrooms. Of special interest are new kinds of instructional auditoriums for large classes and for multisection courses. These facilities are currently characterized by adequate provisions for the projection of motion pictures, slides of various standard sizes and large-screen television images. Usually these display assemblies are arranged for rear-of-screen projection from central core areas that serve a number of surrounding classrooms. Generally, the design is such as to provide for sets of two or more pictorial displays to be projected simultaneously on a screen to aid in making analytical comparison. Standard transparencies are projected from the classroom and onto the front of the screens and sometimes motion pictures are similarly presented.

In properly designed rooms with elevated floors, interior climate control, excellent lighting and acoustics, classes may range in size up to 500 or more students. Now supplied with abundant display facilities, soon these buildings will be provided with individual responders for use by students. These will be connected with computers for rapid processing of the responses of students. Feedback or reinforcement will be provided to the class and perhaps even to individuals if future research proves this to be an advantage. These buildings, when completely equipped as outlined, will provide alternative means to closed-circuit television for handling large classes or many sections of large courses in small rooms.

Television as a way of mediating instruction has developed during the past dozen years and in all probability will be expanded and, one hopes, improved. When signals are distributed over cables or microwave links, instruction can be made available throughout an educational community, over a campus or a county, for a state or indeed for the entire nation. The instructional programs can originate live in television studios, or the materials can be prerecorded on motion-picture films, usually 16mm videotapes or on thermoplastic carriers. When programs are prerecorded, then distributions can be made, even though awkwardly, by mailing or expressing tapes. This procedure is now used by National Educational Television (NET) and by the Mid-West Airborn Television Project, the closest primitive model to satellite transmission. Currently the production of instructional television is done both by simultaneous live distribution and by recording on tapes for later distribution to points of use by individuals and by classes.

Telephonic networks, long lines that span the nation, microwave transmission, all forms of broadcasting and satellite retransmission and reflection provide vast capabilities for distributing information, programs, and instructional materials. However, there is a growing and serious deficit in instructional and educational programs of the right kinds which have high qualities and effectiveness for instigating learning and understanding the formation of sound attitudes.

The proposal of the Ford Foundation, which was first made in August 1966 and more fully presented in December 1966, to the Federal Communications Commission, argues that there should be launched four synchronous communication satellites, and perhaps a fifth for Hawaii and Alaska. These satellites would provide a very greatly expanded distribution potential for educational, instructional, and commercial communications. The awkward video-tape distribution arrangement that is being used by the NET and The National Center for Instructional Television would be antiquated as well as some of the ground-based distribution arrangements now being used by the commercial television networks. The Foundation's proposal includes the suggestion that the savings between the cost of distribution as now paid by commercial networks and the cost of satellite distribution should be collected and invested in the production of more and better education programs. If the estimates of the Ford Foundation are correct, 25 million to 30 million dollars annually will be available for producing instructional and educational programs. For this purpose the Joint Council on Educational Telecommunications is suggesting that about 25 production centers be established in the United States.

The development of reliable video-tape recording machines has made it possible to separate the activities of planning, producing, and testing of instructional programs from the activities of distribution and use. Conditions are favorable, therefore, for the construction and use of new kinds of separate and special instructional-materials production centers.

Production Centers: Centers to produce instructional materials of varied kinds and sizes are urgently needed by this country's colleges and universities. These centers as presently conceived can serve as physical bases for the work that is absolutely necessary to provide needed instructional materials for television and other media. The improvement of its instructional qualities and effectiveness to levels of desired excellence depends on the availability of special-purpose and well-manned and -equipped production centers. What would be the components of such centers and how will they work?

The centers can be located in places that are favorable for the concentrated efforts of groups of very competent subject-matter specialists, teachers, educational psychologists, writers, programmers, media and measurement specialists as well as engineers and technicians. The centers also would provide favorable conditions for the work of selecting, creating, organizing, and producing instructional materials in whatever media and modes of communication may best be used to accomplish the specified performance objectives for the designed instructional materials.

The instructional-material centers of different types and configurations should be designed and operated to provide space and working arrangements for a wide variety of content specialists. Successive groups of these will flow through the center and be served by the permanent staff of the center.

A center would consist of a number of subdivisions and would be committed continuously to one or more "course development" tasks. Therefore, for each content area being served there would be readily accessible collections of the best library, museum, laboratory, or field resources for the area. There would be collections of books, journals, and reports on teaching-and-learning, educational psychology, reports of research on instructional communications processes, media programmed instruction and other related subjects. Laboratories, studios, and general-purpose work areas would provide space and facilities for a wide range of functions and operations including all of those arrangements of teaching-learning conditions which are shown to be best for specific contents and related student performances. Provisions for photographing and recording stimulus materials and situations will include television and video-tape assemblies of the highest necessary qualities, 16mm motion-picture sound-tape facilities that are both studio-based and in mobile units, still photography and slide and graphics studios, and arrangement of spaces designed with on-line computer services for both individual and group testing of the instructional materials that are being developed. Testing and evaluation of materials in terms of student performances with progressive revisions will be done during productions. These spaces, the equipment and furnishings, and the way they are used should simulate the conditions which will prevail when the instructional materials are distributed and used in the field with populations of students.

The center should be carefully designed, with limited space and laboratories for photographic processing, duplicating of photographic and graphic materials and print. The main jobs of processing, duplicating, and printing should be done in central or commercial laboratories and printing plants.

The building and using of instructional-materials production centers raise once again a number of important questions:

Will it be possible to have the necessary interinstitutional cooperation for producing the materials? The reply to this question is that professional academic groups like the physicists, chemists, biologists, and mathematicians have already demonstrated that they can cooperate and importantly increase the amounts and quality of instructional materials available. These professional groups have even revised whole curricula on the secondary-school level. The Course Development Division of the National Science Foundation has demonstrated, also, what can be done successfully in the sciences on the secondary-school level of our educational system. However, it remains to be demonstrated that the same kind of intensive cooperation can be proposed, financed, and accomplished successfully in higher education, which ranges from junior colleges to professional and graduate schools.

The second question is of equal importance: Will instructional materials, other than printed materials, be used sufficiently by enough different colleges and universities to justify the great effort and high cost of production, duplication, and distribution? In the past the answer to this question has been a dismal "No." A case study of lack of cooperation in the use of video-taped course materials and the difficulties and barriers to the production and use of recorded courses on a cooperative basis by the universities of a state has been reported by Carpenter and Willis.

The following suggestions may increase the chances that the cooperative production and use of the recorded instructional materials can be successful:

1. The systems approach should be used in all core-of-course and special-purpose productions.

2. The materials should be planned and cooperatively developed by *prestigious and competent professional men in the subject-matter fields* supported by competent professional and technical staffs.

3. The *core-of-courses—and not complete courses—*should be produced. The core-of-courses should consist of that material of instruction for which there is professional consensus that it is of basic importance and has the lowest possibility of early antiquation or has the longest anticipated period of use.

4. The proved and demonstrable quality of the materials in terms of effects on learning performances should be very superior compared with other alternate choices, and this quality should be clearly evident without complex statistical analysis. There is no substitute for high quality in instructional materials.

5. Limited use should be made of teachers as performers for recordings, whether on film, video tapes, or other carriers. It is a reasonable hypothesis that recordings of teachers, when injected into classrooms, threaten the teachers who must work directly with students.

It is a reasonable assumption that the combined effects of these suggestions may make nonprint instructional materials acceptable for use on a broad enough basis to justify the high cost of production and distribution.

One final question needs to be asked and it is this: Should the production of the instructional materials that are needed for launching and sustaining the development of technologies of instruction be done primarily by the private-enterprise system? This should be as feasible in the future for electronic and other kinds of instructional materials as it has been in the past for books, and the analogy is especially close for textbooks. The cold facts seem to be that the production of the kinds of materials that are needed in 1968 simply involves too much risk of large amounts of capital for not enough gain or profit to interest private industries. The demand on levels of higher education is not only slow to develop but relatively limited compared with that in the public schools. Furthermore, there are serious problems of copyrights on instructional materials. Generally, it has been true that the intent of producers of films, tapes, graphics, displays, slides, etc., has been merely to supplement the instructor and the textbook. The challenge has not been often accepted to produce the basic core materials of programs of instruction and then let the teacher supplement, if and when necessary, the core-of-course materials.

There are other reasons that commercial enterprises have not filled the rapidly expanding void for more and better instructional programs. The investments needed are very large indeed compared with the relatively small investment and low risks involved in publishing textbooks. For some "courses" or blocks of curricula, the costs may amount to as much as five million dollars. Then, too, colleges and universities normally have on their staffs the people who are most needed to produce the material, that is, experts in the content areas, and they are most difficult for industry to employ. Finally, if private industries are, before 1980, to produce what is needed in the quality required, as compared with publishing, new strategies of procurement, production, and marketing must be developed and put into effect.

Equipment and Facilities: Industry has produced an abundance of equipment types and facilities for an advanced technology of instruction. That the available inventory is unbalanced has already been indicated; there are phases of the instructional cycle that still need to be instrumented. Nevertheless, it would appear to be useful to review briefly some of the equipment that is available and make inquiries about its uses in instruction.

There are available many highly developed sets of facilities and equipment which can record, distribute to points of use, and serve important teaching-learning functions. Prominent among these are audio facilities. Sound equipment is economical, practical, and reliable, and yet, with the exceptions of language-laboratory apparatus, much of the sound-only technology has been unduly neglected in instruction.

Let us call the roll of some of the types of audio equipment:

1. Radio—both broadcast and wired arrangements for campuses and educational communities.
2. Telephones and associated apparatus.
3. Language or learning "laboratories."
4. Listening situations including programmed laboratory and "prep-laboratory" work.
5. Tape recorders and reproducers.
6. High-fidelity stereo recorders and reproducers.

There are surely other types; however, these will illustrate the kinds of audio instruments.

It can be observed that this list refers to two categories of equipment; that which can be used within arm's reach and that which serves communications at a distance—telecommunications.

Often in our affluent society we need a restatement of Gresham's law: *The simple mechanism is displaced by the complex one and the more expensive displaces the less expensive.* For example, television has displaced radio for many appropriate uses in mediating many kinds of instruction.

Instruction which almost exclusively involves sound can appropriately depend on sound recordings, transmission, and reception for creating the conditions needed for some kinds of learning. Therefore, parts of language instruction, given the motivation of students to learn, can be mediated as adequately by radio as by the more complicated media because, except for print, the visual stimulation is relatively unimportant in speech sounds. Where needed, reciprocal or two-way communication can be provided more easily by radio, or even the telephone, than by television, although audio feedback can be used here. Furthermore, when the instructional task requires several media, there are the interesting possible linkages of print-radio, television-print-radio, radio-telephone, radio-telephone-print, and there are many other combinations of kinds and proportions of the multi-media "mix."

Very great engineering and technical advances have been made in developing many varieties of sound recording, distribution, and reproduction equipment. This has been manufactured in large quantities and sold in almost every home in the land. Great areas of the earth, furthermore, are blanketed by radio broadcast signals.

The compelling facts on sound-only media are these:

1. Sound-handling machinery is available and capable of serving important educational-and-instructional purposes with complete adequacy as far as media functions are concerned.

2. Educational possibilities of sound-handling media and equipment have not been charted, exploited, and used as extensively or as intensively as might be done in terms of the potentialities of these media.

It is paradoxical to observe that the powers and potentials for extending instruction are available for vast domains of sound communication—but only limited educational uses are being made of these powers and potentials. Even among professional educational broadcast people, more excitement and interest can be generated in 1968 by discussions of synchronous communication satellites than by discussions of educational radio or audio tape for regulating and learning.

The same problem exists in both the developed and the developing countries of the world. Failure to solve the problem is regrettable in all countries, but it is most deplorable where radio transmitters and distribution networks are already available, where television has not yet been established nor is now practical, and yet the available potentials of radio are either not used or are misused. The magnificent All-India Radio Network is both not used and misused relative to vast educational and instructional needs and opportunities in that great subcontinent.

At this point it can be observed that advancement toward a technology of instruction by 1980 does not solely or principally require the development of new products. Rather the advancement in the main depends on using apparatus and equipment that already exists. The main problem is to employ new and useful configurations of elements such as transistors which have already been invented and are in production. There are, however, some promising new products and, as always, new product possibilities.

Probably the developments which will have the greatest effects in communications and therefore on instructional technologies are thermoplastic materials for recording, storing and reproducing pictures and sound. On the distribution side, synchronous satellites interconnected with proper land-based equipment are more useful for distributing signals broadly than by land-based equipment alone. Synchronous satellites with atomic-power packages which are predicted to be available by 1975 will make it possible to transmit effectively signals for reception directly to the home or school television or radio receiver. The development of laser beams for directional and narrow-path distribution of messages will also surely be practical before 1980. Finally, holophotography, with the third dimension of perspective, will probably be widely used by 1980.

The telephone-like radio is a neglected sound medium relative to its practical potentials for instruction. Over telephone lines that already exist the voices of distinguished lecturers from any place in the nation or in the world, when immediacy or simultaneity are important to instruction, can be brought into an active learning situation, amplified and heard by individuals, small groups, large classes, or multisection units of courses. The Pennsylvania State University has explored the feasibility of interconnecting closed-circuit television by telephones with experts on subjects being taught. The telephone apparatus that is available now will make it possible to present and/or record discussions among specialists on different subjects, even though they are widely dispersed. The costs of these uses of telephones are becoming reasonable. The demonstrations of possibilities of telelectures are impressive. The long outward reaches of the telephone to secure supplementary instructional materials are another neglected but possible component that can be woven into a possible system of technology of instruction by 1980.

It is generally understood that media and materials are neutral in value. Technologies can be used, however, to construct or to destroy, to advance health or to produce illness, to encourage culture or produce pseudo culture. We are compelled to advocate the view that the functions served by the media of communication, when used in education and instruction, yield values of different kinds and degrees depending on what content or message is mediated, what methods are used, and what people are affected.

For almost a decade we have proposed that a first step in the analysis, understanding, and management of the complex communicative behavior and the interactional processes of teaching-and-learning would be to define clear measures of base-line behavior which needs to be changed and of terminal behavior which learners need to achieve. The terms of reference or task definition can be made by applying operations-analysis procedures to the study of instruction as defined in this paper. This approach to the study of teaching, the media, and learning, when properly conducted, can result in a number of important determinations, analyses, and perhaps answers to questions. The field of teaching-learning operations and transactions can be defined. What is and is not related to learning behavior can be determined. The requirements and conditions that are necessary for teaching-learning activities can be specified. The instructional materials that are needed, the amount of time required, and the distribution of effort are examples of the many other components that affect learning behavior positively or negatively. The environment or the context (the ecology of the learning situation) can be studied analytically, as well, to ascertain what elements are facilitating and what factors are interfering with learning behavior.

Simply stated, what should the teacher do? What uses should be made of mediating apparatus and materials arrangements?

What should the learner do? What overt or covert performances should characterize his behavior?

Advanced modern instructional technology can be so operated as to transfer and transpose many of the teaching functions from where they formerly were performed in the classroom and laboratory to the activities of producing and testing the efficacy of instructional materials or from the teaching situation to instructional-materials production and testing centers.

FUNCTIONS OF THE LEARNING ENVIRONMENT (THE "ECOLEARNING" FACTORS)

The surroundings and the envelopes of spaces in which teaching and learning take place should be so designed and arranged in general as to facilitate strongly the instructional activities and to reduce or eliminate interferences. To these ends interior climate control should be provided at that level of comfort which is not intrusive on the attention of the people who use the spaces for instructional purposes. Temperature, humidity, and air circulation as well as lighting and sound controls are carefully designed and regulated in modern instructional spaces like the Forum Building at The Pennsylvania State University. The study carrels in libraries and language and science laboratories function to provide a small semiclosed space where all necessary materials are available at arm's length for the completion of one unit of study. The carrel functions principally to regulate sound and light conditions and ideally to reduce or eliminate interferences from whatever source they may come. The learner has in the carrel a semiprivate but economical work space. Thus, it can be that the modern technologies used for making environments more suitable for instruction than formerly may become an increasingly important part of a developing technology of instruction by 1980 and varied learning conditions are provided for specific kinds of learning activities.

The Teaching Functions: The kinds of activities engaged in by teachers are well known generally but in higher education systematic and detailed analyses of teachers' performances are rare. There are programs of research and development now being initiated on the college and university level which propose, as first approaches, to make systematic and analytical observations of representative samples of college teaching. The studies will record, when possible, the total field of instructional events in actual situations, especially in relatively large teaching auditoriums, and attempt to develop new techniques and procedures for the objective investigation of teaching behavior. New technologies of observing and recording events will be used.

Teaching functions can be thought of as occurring in different phases and relationships. There is a phase concerned with the selection and formulation of the objectives of instruction and the definition of boundaries for an area of instruction. This phase consists of defining sequences of events which relate to changing initial performances to terminal performances following instructions. Then comes the phase of selecting and ordering or organizing the materials for presentation to learners and for eliciting responses from the learners. The third phase consists of adjusting and arranging for adjustments in the interactions of the learners with instructional materials and of assessing the effects of procedures and materials. An overlapping phase of all steps in the learning sequences is that of evaluation, assessment, and feedback to the learner and to instruction regulators.

The problem from the viewpoint of developing a technology of instruction is to answer the question: *What must and should be done by what person with what competencies in the set of teaching functions?* The next question relates to what functions can be best and most effectively served by communications equipment, systems, and materials following the first and second phases mentioned above, formulation of objectives, and the selection and organizing of instructional materials.

The Mediation of Instruction: The mediation of instruction can be visualized as falling between and coinciding with the set of teaching and the set of learning functions. A wide range of materials and equipment, some of which have been listed previously, serves parts of the instructional-mediation functions. Generally, these are the following: To accept in some form the stimulus material and store it for timed and meaningful presentation to the learner in some mode or modes of communication. The mediation of information transformation and learning functions operates to bring stimulus materials for perception within the range of sensory capacities. The materials are so organized and presented as to increase the probabilities that the student's behavior will change in the direction desired and his responses at the end of the program will fulfill the criteria which the programmer set at the start as his objective. The function of displaying stimulus materials and of reaching out to the learner (the distribution functions) are admirably served by the modern apparatus of communications; by printing and publishing, by photography, and by sound and music recorder-reproducer. Display apparatus may also show how problems are solved or, by simulation, may represent pertinent aspects of the real world. Other aspects of modern media reach out over distances for information and bring it within the sensory and motor limits of learners. Furthermore, modern media and apparatus may serve to transform, enlarge, or condense impressions of the world and make available phenomena not otherwise available for observation and study. The media can serve the functions and be the means of helping to organize and put into useful sequences the information that shapes and determines the quality and extent of learning.

The Learning Functions: Approaches and strategy considerations for a technology of instruction emphasize the learner or student, the learning cues, stimulus materials, and information with which he interacts. All theories of learning, the learning-task-analysis approach as well as techniques of programmed instruction, put the learner and instructional materials in positions of central importance. The learning environment, teachers and teaching, and the mediating materials and apparatus are, in brief, all means of creating conditions which are favorable for learning by the individual. The probability of a desired pattern of behavior occurring is increased by arranging favorable conditions for learning. When a unit of subject matter is selected, organized and designed, recorded in several media of communication for presentation, it is all done to create a stimulus situation in which the expenditure of effort and energy by the student may yield the greatest learning gains; the increase in information, the improvement in skills, and the perfection of sensory-motor and intellectual performances.

A technology of instruction, to be effective, must assume that the student is motivated, that he will be active and not passive, and that he will strive to perceive and seek to know. Without this "learning set" of attitudes and motivation, and regardless of how perfectly the rest of the technology has been developed, learning objectives cannot be achieved. Since motivation for learning is often a function that derives from the influence of the peer group, a technology of instruction needs to take social factors into account as a condition both favoring and limiting learning. Language laboratories can be instrumented for live conversation and interesting dialogues, and classrooms can be instrumented for group interactions, efforts, and socially reinforced learning.

The concept of the autonomous learner, the person who activates and regulates his own learning behavior, should be considered as one of the results of a properly designed and developed technology of instruction. Gradually, in the period during the secondary school and early college years, it should be possible to reduce the students' dependence on personal teaching functions and to transpose these functions into the *set* of learning functions. More and more, therefore, the library, study materials, and media programs of whatever type should be designed for and made readily accessible to students for their use, not only by individuals but by groups as well. The broad strategy involved in this conception is the progressive adaptation of educational technologies to different levels of maturity of the growing student, the incisive elimination of instructional procedures which are appropriate only for the earlier, immature stages, and the provision of instructional lead-time for academic and professional development. The autonomous learner should require progressively less effort and reduced regulation by teachers and very different access to and assistance from technologies. The general idea for the student is the same as it is for the teacher: to master and control the technology and use it for his own purposes.

◄ ALLAN M. CARTTER

Graduate Education and Research in the Decades Ahead

In SPECULATING about the future development of higher learning in the United States, what can we say about the graduate
education of tomorrow? In what ways are the character and scope
of graduate education likely to change in future decades? What
are likely to be the most pressing problems? What lessons can we
learn from the past?

Anyone closely concerned with higher education today can
safely make one prediction for the future: The changes will be
vast. The past few decades have seen a marked alteration in the
nature of the university on the American scene. Only 30 years
have passed since Abraham Flexner rather bitterly noted that
"American universities look like bedlam," describing them to an
international audience in terms reminiscent of Thorstein Veblen's
description of higher learning in America:

> All of them possess colleges, which are secondary schools, in-
> ferior in solidity to the secondary schools of England and the
> Continent. Many of them possess teacher training departments, in
> which an absurdly artificial technique is communicated to an in-
> ferior student body—this being one of several reasons for the poor
> quality of the American high school and elementary school; even
> more common are business departments, schools of journalism,
> schools of practical arts, and even a department of hotel manage-
> ment. Not satisfied with the miscellaneous aggregation thus

254

brought together to reside in the university, correspondence and home study courses are organized, which endeavor to give by mail the equivalent of resident study. Most of this, of course, is not education; it is not even "service," the catch-word by which it is usually designated.[1]

The representative university of the 1930s was an essentially insular establishment, not deeply involved in the affairs of government or industry, and only sluggishly responsive to the evolving needs of contemporary society. The unparalleled demands made by World War II in the areas of science and technology heralded a new phase in the life of the university. No longer isolated from mundane society, called upon to staff greatly expanded industrial and governmental activities in a variety of areas, and encouraged to probe systematically the frontiers of both knowledge and practice in a host of fields, the contemporary university is far different from its predecessor of a generation ago. The difference is most marked in the graduate education and research functions of the university.

Graduate education, once considered an expensive luxury by many university administrations and boards of control, is today the heart of the institutions that have achieved full university status. The prestige of these institutions in academic circles, their ability to attract outstanding students at both the undergraduate and graduate levels, their support through grants from private foundations and government agencies, come primarily from the strength of their graduate schools. This trend is not without its problems and is viewed as a not unmixed blessing by many, but graduate education is truly the signature of the university today.

ENROLLMENT PROJECTIONS

In recent years graduate education has been one of the most rapidly expanding sectors of higher education. The number of doctorates awarded has doubled in nearly every decade since the

[1] Thorstein Veblen, "American Universities as Institutions of Learning," in W. M. Kotschning and E. Prys, eds., *The University in a Changing World* (London: Oxford University Press, 1932).

turn of the century, and graduate enrollment increased nearly 80 percent during the 1950s while the number of baccalaureates at the end of the decade only barely regained its 1950–51 level.

Projections of the future are always hazardous, and one cannot but be mindful of Sir Thomas Browne's warning:

> Amuse not thyself about the Riddles of future things. Study Prophecies when they are become Histories and past hovering in their causes. Eye well things past and present, and let conjectural sagacity suffise for things to come.

Nevertheless, some tentative projections may provide a measure of the likely magnitude of change in the decade or two ahead.

Undergraduate enrollment is important both because the source of graduate students is the undergraduate student body of a previous year and because it is a rough indicator of the demand for doctorates for the teaching profession. Projections ahead to 1980 are moderately safe in the sense that the college-age population—barring plague, catastrophe, or war—is predictable; its members are already born and approaching elementary school. A major revolution has occurred in the last decade, however, in college-attendance patterns, and how many of the future eighteen–twenty-one-year-olds will enter college is a more dubious guess. Beyond 1980 one must make assumptions about future birthrates, assumptions which are likely to compound the errors.

Most enrollment projections made in past years have turned out to be much too conservative. When the U.S. Office of Education began gazing into its crystal ball in 1959, it projected enrollment patterns for ten years ahead. Its projection of the ratio of college students to the college-age population for 1965 was surpassed by 1961! Current estimates suggest enrollments of approximately ten million to 12 million in 1980, and more than 15 million students in college by the end of the century.

Higher education is not faced with a one-time tidal wave or bulge in enrollment in the late 1960s, but with a continuing expansion of about 1.5 million students in each five-year period (except for the slight breathing space in 1980–85). The supply of potential graduate students, and the demand for doctorates as college faculty, can, therefore, be expected to rise continuously over the foreseeable future.

One can predict reasonably well the impact of expanding undergraduate enrollment on the graduate-student population. Concentrating just on the next 12 years, one can make moderately good guesses on the size of the pool from which graduate students are drawn. Baccalaureates and first professional degrees are expected to rise from approximately 395,000 in 1960 to about 1.1 million in 1980, thus approximately tripling the pool from which graduate students are drawn.

Figures on total graduate enrollment are quite untrustworthy, since they include a high and varying proportion of part-time students, and often include nondegree students, auditors, and the usual share of unknown names that turn up on early fall class rolls, and they often exclude those completing dissertations once they have completed their minimum residence requirements. The best available figures are those gathered by the U. S. Office of Education since 1959 on entering full-time students, and some enlightened guesses can be made back to 1950. In 1950 there were about 38,000 entering full-time graduate students, representing about ten percent of that June's baccalaureate-degree holders. By 1965, entering full-time graduate students were well over the 100,000 mark, representing about 20 percent of current baccalaureates. It seems likely that this percentage will stabilize somewhere between 20 percent and 25 percent for the next decade or two.

The number of doctorates awarded in the past years has averaged between a fifth and a quarter of the number of entering graduate students five years before. Combining what appear to be a number of relatively conservative assumptions gives a nearly fivefold projected increase in doctorates awarded from 1960 to 1980. The number granted in 1960 was 9,800; this had risen to about 18,000 by 1967. Projected numbers are approximately 22,-000 by 1970, 30,000 by 1975, and 45,000–50,000 in 1980.[2] A num-

[2] See the author's "The Supply and Demand of College Teachers," *Journal of Human Resources,* Vol. 1, #1 (Summer 1966), pp. 22–38; and "Future Faculty Needs and Resources," in Calvin Lee, ed., *Improving College Teaching* (American Council on Education, 1966), pp. 99–121.

ber of conclusions are suggested by a review of enrollment and degree projections. The first is that the pool from which graduate students are drawn has been relatively stable over the last few years, and only ten percent larger in 1962 than in 1950, so the recent expansion of graduate enrollment has involved going much deeper into the pool of qualified persons. The marked growth in national fellowship programs (Woodrow Wilson, NSF, NDEA, etc.) may well have meant awards to less well-qualified students, a charge often made by critics of these programs. More important, however, no matter how accurate the actual projections for the next decade or two, the direction and magnitude of change are clearly indicated; the supply of potential graduate students should more than triple during the 1960s and 1970s, and perhaps the increase will be even more marked as undergraduate honors programs expand and student motivations and aspirations continue to improve. The graduate deans, who for decades were pictured as recruiting agents beating the bushes for scarce talents, will soon be sharing the woes of present undergraduate admissions officers in trying to bolster the dikes to keep out waves of students for whom they have insufficient facilities. This pressure will have serious consequences for admissions-policy and screening procedures, which will be noted below.

The most rapidly expanding areas are likely to be in the sciences, led by mathematics, engineering, and a number of the fields that cross traditional disciplinary boundary lines (genetics, biophysics, and the like). In the nonscience areas, education (predominantly Ed.D. rather than Ph.D.) is the most rapidly expanding field. Most other fields are growing absolutely but account for smaller proportions of the larger graduate enrollments.

This expansion in graduate education will raise (or further complicate) many problems concerning admissions, fellowship needs, faculty requirements, and imbalance in support of educational programs, not to mention the physical problems of providing university facilities, equipment, and housing for a graduate-student population three or four times larger two decades hence. In the moments when one's prophetic zeal weakens and the size of the task appears impossibly great, a sobering reminder is that graduate enrollments in the United States have approximately doubled in each decade since 1900 with very little encouragement from government or private foundations. With the active support of both government and foundations today, and the increasing recognition that highly specialized manpower is a critically scarce national resource, it seems likely that the envisioned expansion will in fact be accomplished.[3]

If the author seems optimistic about the continued increase in numbers, he is considerably less optimistic about the implications of this expansion for the quality of graduate education. It is quite clear that the number of "graduate centers of excellence"—to use the fashionable parlance of the day—will be enlarged over the coming decade or two, but it also seems highly likely that the percentage of doctorates awarded by the recognized high-quality graduate schools will continue to decline. Although there is no general agreement about what constitutes "optimum" size of a graduate program (and the optimum size obviously differs for various disciplines), few would doubt that there are real disadvantages of scale in qualitative terms as a program expands beyond some moderate size. The general expansion of graduate enrollments will enhance the quality of graduate programs at some institutions that are presently too small to utilize fully their faculty, library, and plant facilities, but it will tend to lessen the effectiveness of programs at many more, already sizable universities. Somewhere between Mark Hopkins' log and a department with 1,000 graduate students and senior professors serving concurrently on dissertation committees of 40 students— somewhere there lies a happier median. Holding to this median position, once found, has been a difficult—if not impossible— choice for some private and many public universities. The choice is more difficult in an age when external funds are available primarily for "new and expanding" programs, rather than for the improvement and strengthening of existing ones.

[3] A recent National Science Foundation study, *Comparisons of Earned Degrees Awarded 1901–62—With Projections to 2000* (Washington: The National Science Foundation, 1964), projects the following totals for doctorates (excluding medicine): 21,000 in 1970, 56,000 in 1980, 87,000 in 1990, and 123,000 in A.D. 2000 (computed from Table 36, p. 54 of the study).

ADMISSIONS PROBLEMS

The swelling of graduate enrollments has begun to create an admissions problem of major proportion. The number of applications received by each graduate school is rapidly rising, partly because of increased numbers of potential students, but also because of multiple applications. The fellowship-selection process is becoming more burdensome to departments, and most institutions will no longer give "admission without award" to more than a small fraction of the moderately well-qualified applicants because of faculty and space limitations. As noted by one director of graduate studies in a department with adequate fellowship funds: "We are in the anomalous position of saying that if we can't pay them to come, we won't admit them." Just as many younger students (or, more important, their parents) feel that it is their "right" to gain admission to a public undergraduate college if they have met the minimum qualifications of high-school graduation, an increasing number of bachelors are claiming this "right" of entrance to graduate school. Most public institutions are considerably more selective in graduate admissions than in undergraduate, but, as advanced study becomes the accepted pattern, this problem will become more acute.

No general data are available to document the admissions problem, although deans and admissions committees are familiar enough with their own experience. There is a general impression that a decade ago most applicants for graduate study completed two or three applications to schools they would like to attend. Currently, the typical student appears to be submitting four or five applications in the quest for admission and fellowship support. In all likelihood the average will rise to seven or eight a decade hence. If these impressionistic figures are approximately correct, this probably means a total national volume of about 100,000 completed applications in 1950, approximately 500,000 today, and an expectation of 1,000,000 or more by 1970. Since the number of doctorate-awarding institutions will, it appears, barely double in the two decades from 1950 to 1970, this projection suggests that most graduate schools will have a five- to tenfold increase in volume of applications, and perhaps much greater if the number of master's candidates increases more rapidly than that of doctoral students.

The Council of Graduate Schools or the Association of Graduate Schools may wish to study this problem seriously in the near future. Recommendations have been made in the past for a possible centralized admissions service, and serious consideration of such a proposal may be timely. Under such a central program, a student could fill in one complete set of applications and indicate the schools to which he would like to apply. Copies could quickly be reproduced (for example, by Xerox or, conceivably, through some microfilm or microcard process) and forwarded to the indicated institutions. A standard charge of perhaps 20 dollars could be levied on the applicant, with an additional ten-dollar charge for each institution over three to which the dossier would be sent. This central file could also be used by all the national fellowship programs, and thus considerably reduce the volume of requests for transcripts, letters of recommendations, Graduate Record Examination scores, and so on. Conceivably, the system might proceed to the point, somewhat akin to the centralized procedures used by the medical schools in distributing interns, where the student would list his order of preference, and the central office would match these with institutional responses. Although this procedure may appear at first to be rather dehumanizing, it might make more sense than some of the present chaotic selection procedures. It could also simplify the present fellowship-award process, which takes weeks or months of offers, declinations, and alternate offers, and which produces in even the most prestigious institutions in the country fellowship declination rates of nearly 50 percent.

A centralized admissions procedure (without centralized awards decisions) could be begun by a small number of institutions on a voluntary-participation basis, provided only that some of the more prestigious institutions take the lead. When one remembers that the projected one million applications of 1970 will mean three million or more letters of recommendation written by perhaps not more than one hundred thousand faculty members, this burden alone may make the effort worth serious consideration.

The recently introduced standard centralized language examinations being conducted by the Educational Testing Service in cooperation with leading graduate schools is a somewhat analogous attempt to bring order and meaning out of a similarly confusing situation.

FACULTY DEMAND AND SUPPLY

As the economists long ago learned—although still occasionally forget—the problems of any one institution may be solved by money, but the problems of all institutions may be insoluble simultaneously, even with adequate finances. This has long been clear in recruiting outstanding graduate students: attractive awards may entice students to Melrose U., but merely have the effect of redistributing a given number of students. Similarly in the case of faculty, higher salaries in the long run may make an academic career more attractive than some alternative career, but in the short run one institution can rapidly progress only by drawing faculty away from other similar positions. So, too, in the case of rapidly expanding graduate programs, the supply of future doctorates can be expanded by diverting more of the present stream of doctorates back into teaching; therefore, specialized skills in short supply may have to become temporarily scarcer before they can become more abundant.

A similar problem exists in several other critical fields, and the rapid rise in faculty salaries over the last five years is largely accounted for by the increasing competition from industry and government for such highly educated personnel. This is a familiar enough problem in wartime and can easily be met for periods up to five or ten years by what might be called "manpower cannibalism," that is, temporarily swelling present government and industry ranks by reducing higher education's supply of needed faculty. But just as a business firm cannot survive long by living out of its capital, similarly a nation cannot easily provide for an increasing supply of engineering doctorates *and* reach the moon in two or three years—although it may be able to achieve both over a longer period of time.

Awareness of the impact of expanding federal programs on the demand for scarce personnel in science and technology is evidenced in the current work of the U.S. Office of Science and Technology and the President's Science Advisory Committee. Serious consideration is being given to improved means of estimating present and future manpower needs and to the inauguration of a manpower-budgeting process parallel to traditional fiscal-budgeting procedures. In many areas of government concern, financial constraints are less imposing than limitations in the supply of highly educated personnel, and the overlooking of this facet of the resource problem may endanger the major functions of the universities by drawing away their teaching and research faculties.

The problem is more complicated than it might at first appear, for more than three-quarters of the scientists and engineers employed from government funds are not in government service *per se*, but working in industry or universities. Thus a million dollars spent on one type of hardware (for example, a rocket booster) may involve the employment by a government contractor of 20 or 30 scientists, whereas an equivalent amount spent on another type of hardware (say, Jeep carburetors) may involve only workers on an established production line. Neither the Congress nor the executive branch can make rational decisions on federal budgets without much better information than now exists.

The expansion of graduate education over the next decade or two will bring about a wider dispersion of graduate facilities. This is a desirable move from many viewpoints, but it is likely to create a greater demand for outstanding graduate faculty than would a comparable expansion of present institutions. In older institutions, graduate enrollments can be expanded by adding junior staff as instructors. In new graduate programs, an equivalent number of graduate students requires the addition of many experienced senior professors who can direct student programs and supervise dissertations. Institutions such as Duke in the 1930s, UCLA in the

1940s, and Michigan State during the last decade illustrate the peak demand for new faculty of experience and stature in graduate education as a young institution moves to full university status. The added demand for senior faculty over and above what would have been needed to expand existing large graduate schools is a temporary phenomenon, and in the long run such dispersion of graduate facilities is both needed and desirable. The extra burden is nonetheless real and must be met if the quality of graduate education is not to suffer.

On the brighter side of the faculty-supply picture is the fact that the percentage of college teachers holding a doctorate has increased over the last decade, rising from a little over 40 percent to 51 percent in 1953–62. This situation evidently has occurred as the result of a much lower attrition rate owing to deaths and retirements, a more rapid increase in the number of persons earning the doctorate, and the greater attraction of college and university teaching in bidding people away from industry and government, than was projected in the well-publicized earlier studies by the National Education Association, the Fund for the Advancement of Education, and the U.S. Office of Education.[4] Berelson's estimates in 1960 have turned out to be more accurate than those of his more pessimistic critics, and his conclusion that there is a problem but not a crisis in the supply of college faculty appears justified.[5]

More recent studies suggest that there will continue to be significant shortages of qualified faculty though until the early 1970's, but that by the late 1970's, partly as a result of the increased number of advanced degrees awarded and partly as a result of a slowing down in the rate of expansion of undergraduate enrollments (and, therefore, the demand for new teachers), there will be a reversal in the balance of the market. It seems likely that

[4] See the biennial reports of the National Education Association, *Teacher Supply and Demand in Universities, Colleges, and Junior Colleges* (Washington: The Association); *Teachers for Tomorrow* (New York: Fund for the Advancement of Education, 1955); and occasional papers by the Higher Education Personnel Section of the U. S. Office of Education.
[5] Bernard Berelson, *Graduate Education in the United States* (New York: McGraw-Hill Book Co., 1960), pp. 69–80.

the continued upward cost pressure on colleges and universities of rising academic salaries, reflecting shortage conditions, will not be moderated until the mid-1970s.[6]

IMBALANCE IN GRADUATE EDUCATION

"Imbalance" has become a popular term in recent years, although it may refer to a multitude of sins. Imbalance may be felt to exist between the relative emphasis placed on graduate and undergraduate education in an institution. It may refer to the relative value society places on pragmatic, utilitarian disciplines (characteristic of what Veblen called the "barbarian university") as against truly scientific and scholarly pursuits. It frequently refers to the decline of traditional humanistic studies coincident with the emergence of the natural sciences. Most commonly, in reference to the situation of the modern university in America, it is used to describe what many feel to be an undesirable pattern of external financial support in recent decades.

Some few voices will argue that there is absolutely too much support for research studies in some disciplines and that such support actually harms the university through the diversion of its own resources into matching grants and into covering unreimbursed indirect costs. Recently, and as yet *sotto voce,* some university presidents have raised the question whether they have become too involved in research—whether so large a proportion of the time and energies of their best faculty members is diverted from the educational tasks of the university that teaching quality has deteriorated. More commonly, however, it is argued that new outside support programs are needed to redress the imbalance in fields less directly concerned with the immediate research and national-security needs of the federal government.

Approximately 95 percent of all federal funds going to colleges and universities in support of educational and research activities are for "science," for example, the physical and life sciences (including medicine) and engineering. For the institutions fully re-

[6] See Cartter, "Future Faculty Needs and Resources," *op. cit.*

porting in the recent Carnegie study of "Twenty-six Campuses and the Federal Government," [7] federal funds for research were equal to approximately 25 percent of their total educational and general expenditures (the University of California at San Diego, California Institute of Technology, Stanford, M.I.T., and Princeton indicated more than 40 percent, exclusive of the governmentally sponsored national research laboratories). For the same group of institutions, however, only about 40 percent of federal funds were for research in the arts and sciences, the remaining 60 percent being divided almost evenly between their medical and engineering schools.

Closer to the heart of graduate education is the distribution of funds to support predoctoral students. It is not surprising that information in the federal government is poor on the extent of federal support of graduate students, as few graduate deans have complete information on federally financed fellowships, traineeships, and research assistantships even for their own institutions. Perhaps the most ambitious attempt to categorize such student support is found in the 1963 report of the House Committee on Education and Labor.[8] For the fiscal year 1962 it is estimated that 182,911 students received support from federal monies totaling 256,562,000 dollars. (For fiscal year 1967, the Bureau of the Budget has estimated that 323 million dollars was authorized for graduate-student support.) Of this number approximately 40,400 were full-time predoctoral students, distributed as shown in Table 1.

Approximately 70 percent of the students were supported either on research grants and contracts or through traineeships administered by departments—awards which do not regularly come under the control or scrutiny of the graduate-school office. Only about 8,000 of these students received outright fellowship awards

[7] See *Educational Record*, April 1963, pp. 95–136. Twenty-six institutions participated, but some did not report comparable figures. The 26 institutions, ranging from Harvard and California to Lawrence College and Arkansas State Teachers College, accounted for 28 percent of federal funds for research in educational institutions in 1959–60.

[8] *The Federal Government and Education* (report by Edith Green, chairman of Special Subcommittee on Education), Committee on Education and Labor, House of Representatives, 88th Congress, 1st Sess., June 1963.

TABLE 1

Federal Support of Full-time Predoctoral Students, 1962[9]

Support Source	No. of Stud.	Amount (ooo's)
Atomic Energy Commission	261	$ 1,325
Department of the Interior	17	200
National Aeronautics and Space Administration	100	1,866
National Institutes of Health		
Fellowships	995	3,753
Traineeships	6,900	24,150
National Science Foundation	2,749	10,871
U. S. Office of Education		
Teachers of deaf	151	453
Mental retardation	168	933
NDEA Title IV fellowships	4,041	21,371
Foreign language fellowships	1,006	3,918
Office of Vocational Rehabilitation		
Fellowships	20	68
Traineeships	1,921	3,896
Public Health Service		
Fellowships	31	133
Training grants	170	601
Traineeships	2,534	7,925
Research assistants on research contracts and grants (estimate)	19,350	48,375
	40,414	$129,838

[9] *Ibid.*, p. 33. Two adjustments have been made in the figures as originally published. Late information supplied by the National Institute of Health on traineeships has been substituted, and the value of research assistantships on research grants and contracts has been estimated at an average of 2,500 dollars.

administered through the graduate office and/or a national fellowship program. Of the approximately 40,000 supported, roughly four percent were in institutions not directly connected with a college or university (separate teaching hospitals, research institutes, etc.), 27 percent were in professional fields normally outside the province of the graduate school of arts and sciences (medicine, nursing, public health, social work, etc.), 56 percent were in the mathematics, sciences, and engineering area, and 13 percent were in the humanities and social sciences. Of the latter, nonscience category, about one third were in humanities, chiefly the NDEA Title IV and Title VI (language and area studies) fellowship programs.[10]

Thus, although only about 1,600 of the 40,000 predoctoral students receiving federal support were in the humanities, this is a much larger share of the total than is to be found in the support of faculty research in the humanities. There is some concern in Congress over the issue of imbalance, particularly in the House, and one senses a growing understanding of the needs and responsibilities in the broad field of scholarship. Even within the major science-grant agencies—NSF and NIH—there is now a movement to make broad "general research support" or "institutional" grants to supplement the large amounts now spent on specific-project support. The Higher Education Facilities Act authorized approximately 150 million dollars in general-support funds for centers of quality graduate education. In addition, Congress has moved toward the creation of counterparts to the National Science Foundation for the nonscience fields, having recently created a National Foundation for the Humanities and now considering proposals for a similar foundation for the social sciences.

Although the coming decade will undoubtedly see some shift in this balance of support, it is likely—and probably desirable—that there will continue to be a marked asymmetry in federal programs. The social sciences and humanities do not lend themselves

[10] One reader has raised the question of how some 40,000 predoctoral students supported on federal funds can be reconciled with only about 11,000 doctorates awarded in 1962. As the above paragraph indicates, probably less than 30,000 of the students were in fields in which the Ph.D. is the highest degree. In addition, the average student enrolled in graduate school in 1962 who completed the doctorate successfully was probably in the class of 1965, when total doctorates awarded (excluding medicine) were about 15,000. Thus, the ratio is closer to 2 : 1 than the apparent 4 : 1. Full-time work toward the doctorate normally requires at least four years, so the 15,000 expected degrees implies at least 60,000 students now in the "pipeline" who will be successful in obtaining the degree, plus perhaps another 75,000–100,000 who will not complete degree requirements. Predoctoral support of graduate students should be compared with this larger universe of full-time students in doctoral programs. It would appear that about 20 percent of such students now receive some federal support, the proportion approaching 50 percent in the physical and biological sciences.

to the same kind of aid which the sciences have received. The critical needs of government and private industry in scientific research and technology are unlikely to be matched in classics, philosophy, or anthropology. And while the humanist may echo Blake's prayer on occasion:

> May God us keep
> From single vision and Newton's sleep,

his needs are not fully competitive with those of his colleagues in science and engineering. As President Goheen of Princeton stated the case several years ago:

> Personally I do not judge wide-ranging federal support, comparable to the government's investment in the sciences and engineering, to be a desirable solution for the substantial needs of America's colleges and universities in the fields of the humanities or in many of the socio-scientific fields. . . . A federal investment in the humanities and social sciences of any scope comparable to that in the sciences seems to me not only hard to justify but potentially dangerous. For one thing, potential research results in these nonquantitative fields of learning are harder to identify and measure concretely; thus they make a poor basis for contractual relationships. Second, and more fundamentally, I believe that federal interference and other sorts of adverse political pressures are much more likely to follow entrance of the government into these fields.[11]

The burden of balance rests in large part upon the institution itself, for it is within the province of the administration of a university to make decisions that will help to compensate for the imbalance of external support. Attempts to legislate balance within universities by diminishing federal support will be no more successful than attempts to legislate "purity" by banishing Henry Miller and D. H. Lawrence from the public library. Perhaps it would be fair to conclude, however, that the opportunistic university administration which has a Pavlovian sensitivity to the scent of federal funds may be less led astray (or only randomly) if funds are more available across a broad spectrum of fields.[12]

[11] Robert F. Goheen, "Federal Financing and Princeton University," in *Educational Record*, April 1963, p. 176.
[12] This argument is more applicable to the private institution, which has

EVALUATION AND ACCREDITATION

In the decades ahead there is likely to be growing pressure for improved evaluation, and perhaps for formal accreditation, of graduate programs. In an informal sense universities are in fact continuously being evaluated—by students seeking admission, by faculty deciding on academic positions, by foundations in program support, by state legislatures, by review panels and visiting teams of major federal agencies, and so on. The quest for excellence presupposes the means of measurement, although for too long we have tended to judge by purely quantitative standards—enrollments, number of Nobel prizewinners and Ph.D.'s granted, amount of government and foundation grants received, and the like. The Association of Graduate Schools for years has wrestled with this problem, and despite occasional interest on the part of their presidents in the American Association of Universities, formal evaluation or accreditation proposals have never seriously been entertained. A special committee of the AAU recommended in 1960 that "a recognized list of institutions offering acceptable education at the graduate level" be compiled, but the report was filed without action.[13]

Growing pressures from the regional accrediting associations and a number of professional associations, particularly the National Council for the Accreditation of Teacher Education

---

greater freedom in reallocating private funds at its disposal, than it may be to many public institutions. It is also not an argument in support of some voices in government who maintain that Congress has no responsibility for aiding the balanced growth of higher education. (On this point, see the very excellent case William G. Bowen has made in *The Federal Government and Princeton University: A Report on the Effects of Princeton's Involvements with the Federal Government on the Operations of the University* [Privately printed; Princeton University, 1962].) The anguished cries of some Princeton alumni in recent years over the disclosure that approximately 45 percent of Princeton's annual income comes from federal grants and contracts will, one may presume, strengthen the university's future fund raising for nonscience programs. In New Haven the shoe has been rather on the other foot, and recent fund raising has helped to redress the imbalance in favor of the "underprivileged" sciences.

[13] "Report of the Special Committee to Study Growing Pressures in Graduate Work," Sept. 15, 1960.

(NCATE) and the American Society for Engineering Education (ASEE), were called to the attention of the newly organized Council of Graduate Schools by the National Commission on Accrediting in 1962. The CGS in December of that year issued a policy statement: "That it is the conviction of the Council that no group should undertake to evaluate or accredit institutions with respect to their programs of graduate education unless it is responsible primarily to an organization of the institutions themselves." A special committee of the Council was created to review current practices and to study "the characteristics of graduate education of high quality."

Both graduate associations (CGS and AGS) can be expected to maintain their firm stand that, *if* there is to be anything akin to accreditation in the field of graduate education, it should not be done by an outside group which is not ultimately responsible to the graduate schools or their parent universities. The opposition of some college and university presidents and many graduate deans to NCATE in accrediting teacher preparation programs has arisen because it was felt that NCATE did not adequately represent the institutions themselves and the subject disciplines under review.

At present the six major regional accrediting associations in the United States do accredit institutions with graduate schools, and, in the case of at least two of these associations (Southern Association of Colleges and Schools and Northwest Association of Secondary and Higher Schools), guidelines are laid down for the review of graduate education. None of the associations, however, accredits graduate schools as such, in the way that the American Bar Association, the AMA Council on Medical Education and Hospitals, and the Engineers' Council for Professional Development accredit schools in their respective professional fields.

Perhaps accreditation has seemed less necessary in graduate education in the arts and sciences partly because the public welfare is not so critically dependent upon the qualifications of scholarly practitioners as it is upon physicians and lawyers, and partly because Gresham's law is not likely to prevail in the field of scholarship. The academic man is continuously under review by his peers, and the low-quality or "diploma mill" doctorate has been notably unsuccessful. The high cost of graduate education has also helped to deter marginal institutions from inaugurating doctoral programs.

Historically, accreditation of undergraduate colleges has performed a useful service in bringing the institution of dubious quality up to some mutually agreed upon minimum standard. Even with accreditation, however, there is perhaps greater variation in the quality of baccalaureates awarded by approximately 1,200 accredited four-year institutions than there is in the quality of doctorates awarded by the approximately 200 universities awarding this highest degree.[14] The existence of major state universities, until recently, has tended to act as a check upon state legislatures in approving funds for graduate programs in weaker public institutions, thus providing a kind of informal review and evaluation medium for state-supported institutions, and the cost factor has deterred the less well-endowed private institutions from dubious ventures. Over the last several years, however, as central state governing or coordinating agencies have become the major policy-making loci for public higher education, university status has quickly been accorded to an increasing number of former state teachers colleges. When these newer universities are under a different governing board from the older and better-established universities (e.g., as in Illinois, Michigan and North Carolina, but not the case in California), the problem of standards may become much more critical.

Accreditation in a formal sense is unlikely to be established in

[14] This is a personal judgment, although a casual sampling of the views of a number of colleagues tends to support it. Oliver Carmichael, however, in his recent *Graduate Education: A Critique and a Program* (New York: Harper & Row, 1961), concluded the reverse and my respect for his judgment has made me add a qualifying "perhaps." Although there are no "facts" on which a firm conclusion can be based, I would cite one piece of evidence, for which I am indebted to Harold Orlans' stimulating paper, "Federal Programs and the Quality of Higher Education" (given at the University of Illinois Graduate College on March 21, 1963). One-quarter of the four-year colleges in the United States did not have a single graduate who went on to obtain the doctorate in the 1936–56 period; one-half did not have a graduate who obtained a doctorate in the natural sciences. I doubt if there is a single graduate school which cannot boast of at least a few graduates who have received scholarly honors in their later careers.

graduate education in the foreseeable future. The regional accrediting associations, however, are likely to pay increasing attention to graduate programs in assessing the overall strength of universities. To be truly effective, accreditation would have to be quite explicit and restrictive in standards; and the more restrictive it was, the greater would be the opposition by the better institutions, which would view this as unwarranted limitation on their freedom. An excellent institution with outstanding faculty and good students need not obey any rules to be a highly successful educational enterprise; Harvard fellows are perhaps the most outstanding example.

There may be good reasons, however, for periodic *evaluation* of graduate programs. The fact that it is being done already—haphazardly by individual faculty and students, and in piecemeal, if more systematic, fashion by foundations and review panels of government agencies—may be sufficient reason to try to improve existing means of evaluation. As David Reisman has pointed out:

> Data are publicly available for only a limited number of institutions, and even then they are often out of date. Moreover, the question of what is "quality" remains elusive: it refers to a complex of variables and . . . no single scale suffices. . . . While autos carry their advertising, so to speak, on their body shells, which speak as loudly as print or TV commercials, colleges can change inside their shells with hardly anyone's noticing. And the result can be tragic, not only for misled students, but for imaginative faculty and administrators who may not live long enough to be rewarded by the appearance of good students attracted by those changes.[15]

Periodic attempts have been made to evaluate the quality of graduate programs, although the climate of opinion has not always been favorable. R. M. Hughes's studies in 1925 and 1934 attempting to rank AAU institutions in various fields of study were the subject of considerable debate in their day.[16] Hayward Keniston's study published in 1959 was accepted as an interesting,

[15] David Riesman, *Constraint and Variety in American Education* (Garden City, N.Y.: Doubleday & Co., 1958), pp. 3–5.
[16] See R. M. Hughes, *A Study of the Graduate Schools of America* (Oxford, Ohio: Miami University, 1925); and *Report of the Committee on Graduate Instruction* (Washington: American Council on Education, 1934).

but not necessarily conclusive, subjective ranking of institutions.[17] Keniston queried department chairmen in 25 "leading" institutions, asking them to rate graduate departments according to their prestige. Some critics doubted that department chairmen were necessarily the best judges and questioned the basis of inclusion or exclusion, but apart from many reactions that one's own institution did not come out in the "right" place on the scale, the study was taken as a rough measure of relative quality. Bernard Berelson added to the Keniston ratings and extended the categories to include 49 universities in three major groups.[18] The most recent assessment was made under the auspices of the American Council on Education, sampling the views of a broader spectrum of the educational community and seeking to measure factors in addition to the research prestige of graduate faculty.[19]

The climate for evaluation studies has perceptibly changed in recent years. Perhaps this in part owes to the fact that the AAU is no longer a group including *all* the better universities; many non-AAU members have larger graduate enrollments than some members, and quite a few of the newer universities would compare favorably in quality with the member group. Perhaps a stronger reason for the changing climate is that the trend in federal aid to education (and, to a lesser extent, in aid from private foundations) is to seek out and support the promising "second-rank" universities. It is becoming a matter of public policy to expand the number of "centers of excellence," to provide a broader geographic distribution of graduate schools of high quality. It may, therefore, be a mark of favor to be ranked thirty-fifth rather than tenth, since the trend in federal support is toward altering the imbalance in its research and general support to a small number of long-recognized universities.

Traditionally, educators have done less questioning about themselves and the processes of which they are an integral part

[17] Hayward Keniston, *Graduate Study and Research in the Arts and Sciences at the University of Pennsylvania* (Philadelphia: University of Pennslyvania Press, 1959).
[18] B. Berelson, *op. cit.*, especially pp. 124–28.
[19] A. M. Cartter, *An Assessment of Quality in Graduate Education* (American Council on Education, 1966).

than they have about the world outside the university. A few among the historians have analyzed the evolution of our educational structure over the last century or more, but only in the last few years have the social scientists occasionally turned their analytic skills to their own institutional environment. There has been almost a professional code that encouraged free inquiry and public discussion of issues and institutions outside academia, whereas self-analysis and informative debate within have been minimal. In an age when it is increasingly recognized that the quality of our educational system may be a critically determining factor in the future well-being of the nation and when a rapidly rising proportion of financial support is coming from public monies, the claim of society on higher education for improved information and guidance becomes greater.

The graduate schools may be able to avoid the adoption of formal accreditation procedures as long as the Ph.D. degree does not suffer serious devaluation as the number of granting institutions rises over the coming decades. They will do so, however, only if there are commonly recognized standards and informal processes of sanctions imposed on the self-satisfied inferior institution. Public exposure is probably the best safeguard, and institutional vanity, the best guarantee of corrective measures. Few would doubt that on balance the publication of faculty salary ratings by the Association of American University Professors has had a favorable effect on both the level and structure of faculty salaries. Perhaps occasional evaluation studies of graduate education would have a similarly beneficial effect on universities.

FINANCING GRADUATE EDUCATION [20]

One of the major problems of the future is the adequate financing of graduate education. By its nature, graduate education at

[20] Seymour Harris, *Higher Education: Resources and Finance* (New York: McGraw-Hill Book Co., 1962); John D. Long and J. B. Black, Jr., *Needed Expansion of Facilities for Higher Education, 1958–70* (Washington: American Council on Education, 1958); Dexter M. Keezer, ed., *Financing Higher Education, 1960–70* (New York: McGraw-Hill Book Co., 1959); Selma J.

the master's and doctor's level is several times as costly as undergraduate education. This is true because of the necessarily closer working relationship between master and apprentice scholar, the high cost of library and laboratory facilities, and the relatively limited contribution which advanced students can be expected to make to their training. In the major state universities in 1967, the average educational cost per student was in the neighborhood of 3,000 dollars per year, and if one uses a fairly typical budget-formula rule of thumb (such as that of the University of California) that the ratio of costs for lower-division, upper-division, master's and doctoral education is as 1 : 1½ : 2½ : 3½, the cost to the institution of supporting one full-time student in a typical doctoral program is estimated to be in the neighborhood of 7,500 dollars per year.

Prior to World War II, graduate education was concentrated in a relatively small number of well-endowed private institutions and a similar handful of public universities in relatively wealthy states. (The largest 15 universities accounted for two-thirds of the doctorates awarded in the inter-war period.) With the great expansion of higher education over the last 15 years, and the partial funding of programs, fellowships and facilities by various federal agencies, both old and new institutions have vastly increased their commitment of resources to graduate and advanced professional study. Nearly 250 universities now grant the doctorate, and about ten newcomers are added to the roster annually.

Federal and private-foundation grants have substantially supported the strongest university programs, and most institutions have therefore felt it urgent to seek the costly evidences of distinction. Such major support programs as the Ford Foundation's 300-million-dollar capital-grants program, and the National Science Foundation's science-development program, both providing incentive funds which must be matched on an approximate three-to-one basis (three dollars of new funds provided by university

---

Mushkin, ed., *Economics of Higher Education* (Washington: Government Printing Office, 1962), especially Part III; and John D. Millett, *Financing Higher Education in the United States* (New York: Columbia University Press, 1952).

efforts to match initial grants), have provided a great qualitative boost to institutional programs and aspirations, but have also driven many institutions into escalating the commitment of their limited resources.

The last five to ten years has seen a gradual separation of private universities into several distinct categories. On the one hand are those universities whose accomplishments and aspirations are quite limited and which have not experienced the infusion of new funds referred to above. An increasing number of these have been unable to survive as private universities and have been absorbed into state systems. Thus, the Universities of Houston, Wichita, Kansas City, Youngstown, Louisville, Cincinnati, Temple, and Buffalo have become state universities (or, in the case of several, "state-related" with substantial support from tax funds). At the other extreme are those which have successfully broken through (or give great promise of doing so) to greater accomplishments, such as Stanford, Brandeis, Duke and Vanderbilt. In between are a large number of aspiring universities whose ultimate fates may be determined within the next ten to 20 years by whether or not more significant support is forthcoming from public funds, either federal or state. In several cases, such as the University of Pittsburgh and Brooklyn Polytechnic Institute, the very commitment to seeking excellence has exhausted their limited private means and forced them to seek the status of semipublic institutions. Thus, many of those private universities which have tried too hard, or too little, have been unable to survive as independent universities. Unless the pattern of financial support changes substantially in the near future, the toll of private universities is likely to continue to rise.

In many of the less affluent states, there are similar difficulties in adequately funding expensive graduate programs of quality in the state universities. Pressures are growing, therefore, for increased program support from the federal government. Many educators feel that the support of graduate and advanced professional education is properly a responsibility of the federal government, for the benefits accruing from the flow of highly trained manpower into the most skilled occupations and professions are national assets, not limited to the boundaries of any particular state. It would not be too surprising, in the writer's judgment, to find ten or 15 years from now that all advanced graduate students were federally supported and that all universities were receiving general aid for costly advanced degree programs. What was earlier a problem only in selected fields (e.g., the sciences, medical education), and only for a minority of universities, is today becoming an acute financial crisis for all major institutions.

The major problems in the decades ahead will be complicated by the entrance of many new institutions into graudate education. The first 15 universities in quality as classified by Berelson,[21] awarded 76 percent of all doctorates in 1925, 59 percent in 1934, 49 percent in 1950, and only 41 percent by 1960. If, between 1960 and 1980, these first 15 institutions only double in the number of doctorates awarded (and they had increased only 15 percent from 1950 to 1960), they will account for less than 20 percent of all doctorates by the end of this period. The ten private universities among these 15 awarded 32 percent of the total in 1950, 24 percent in 1960, and will probably award less than ten percent of all doctorates by 1980. In earlier periods, when a handful of prestige institutions dominated the scene not only in quality but also in numbers, it was a simpler matter for them to set standards which the smaller and younger institutions could emulate. As the center of gravity shifts to the non-AAU institutions, and from private to public universities, standards of high quality may be more difficult to maintain merely by emulation and self-interest. A large responsibility devolves on the Council of Graduate Schools to help its member schools meet the problems of the coming decades in a manner which will maintain the quality of graduate programs. The older and more restricted membership of the Association of Graduate Schools may find its continuing role as the guardian of standards in graduate education.

[21] Berelson, *op. cit.*, p. 97.

◀ HAROLD B. GORES

The American Campus–1980

THE SCENE

A COLLEGE is at least three things: a faculty, a student body, and a curriculum. Excepting only correspondence schools and learn-where-you-are television colleges, a college is also a place. This chapter deals with the latter—the places, the solids of education as distinguished from its fluids.

The solids of higher education, the parts you can with impunity kick with your foot, make up the campuses. And they are many-splendored things—multiversity networks blanketing whole states; high-rise towers dictated by the economics of land use and raising their students high in expensive defiance of gravity; leaf-strewn retreats in antiseptic towns where undergraduates are prepared to be graduate students; rehabilitated hotels in which students and faculty huddle together under the threat of looming bankruptcy; a mailbox in which the isolated but avid scholar drops his examination paper.

Obviously, there is no such thing as *the* American campus: there are only campuses; and they are as plural as the American society is plural. But there are nevertheless some predominant forms, and it is about these we presume to predict.

It is held in certain quarters that, because teachers are more important than bricks, bricks are not important. Many pundits of higher education ignore or are ignorant of the influence of environment; the rest are careful where they step as they pick their way around the field. Their distaste for education's physical surroundings bedevils those who believe that environment is more than nuts and bolts and who work to elevate the physical setting, the buildings, the equipment, the tools of education.

Yet there is progress and it is showing up in a number of ways:

1. Master planning is increasing. As recently as 1962, an EFL study of planning at 124 small liberal-arts colleges revealed that only 11 of them had physical-plant projections; today nearly every college and university has a plan on paper. Admittedly the plans range in sophistication from Duke's and Purdue's computer-assisted projections to primitive sketches of future growth as suggested by do-it-yourself space-utilization studies. But they are plans.

2. The planning includes the neighbors. A decade ago, Illinois Institute of Technology and the University of Chicago were among the rare exceptions which planned beyond their boundaries. Today, such planning is commonplace. Southern Illinois University at Edwardsville refused to locate on a newly proffered site until local government established buffer zoning to protect approaching highways from becoming miles of neon honky-tonk. Mills College in the West involves in its planning anyone in town who cares; while Mills College of Education in the East literally built an actual bridge five stories above street-level to join its original building to the commercial building it had bought across the street. Everywhere the old moats are being bridged and, in some cases, even drained.

3. The planning includes the government. The confrontation of town and gown is breaking down and so is the defensive attitude toward city hall, the state capital, and Washington. Just as ten years ago Harvard dispatched a full-time emissary to the Cambridge City Council (prompted by a councilman's motion to force the university to secede from the city), almost every college, public or private, is today in personal contact with every layer of government. The reason is as clear as was Willie Sutton's "I hold up banks because that is where the money is."

And the buildings built with government aid have proved to many a doubter that government and imagination can be found in the same place, that the presence of public money does not preclude creativity, the soaring leap of insight, the light touch.

4. There is a growing sense of trusteeship. Fewer colleges today view their task as simply to polish a jewel whose facets were cut a century ago. More colleges realize that they are less the custodians and protectors of their first image than the inventors of their next. Alert colleges are budgeting for ten years, planning to the year 2000, and thinking about themselves a century hence.

Accordingly, we see more land acquisitions pitched a generation ahead of need; more buildings placed now where they later will be needed; more interiors designed as Protean rather than Procrustean space, the better to fit whatever one's successors may have in mind.

At the turn of the decade, John Kenneth Galbraith, one of our culture's sharpest private eyes, observed that public and quasi-public architecture seldom lets itself go. "Only in our airports, and occasionally in our schools," he said, "do we show signs of doing something that flatters the public eye and nourishes the community pride." He now could add the American college campus to his list.

The American campus takes off from a position of strength. As institutions go, its recent record of responsiveness to change is good. And it will continue to respond and be shaped by powerful external forces, not the least of which is economics.

There are those who hold that higher education stands astride the nation's next important economic thrust. If and when the nation's defense requirements diminish, and if and when our expenditures on the exploration of outer space diminish, education in its broadest sense will become the nation's first business. By 1980, when the child in today's Head Start class will be eighteen years of age, it will be the national expectation that all teachable persons to age twenty-one will have a "college" to go to. When the nation is not busy defending itself, education is what it wants. And what it wants it gets.

Expect, therefore, that in 1980 "everyone" will be involved in some kind of higher education, and Gresham's law will have reduced the bachelor's degree to the prestige of today's high-school-equivalency diploma.

What will happen is already apparent: even now—in wartime

—community colleges are being established at the rate of one a week, with over 200 known to be on the planning boards at the moment. Though the community college isn't yet sure what it is—an upward extension of the American high school or a downward extension of the American college—it has already seized the territory, and by 1980 it will command the education of most nineteen- and twenty-year-olds.

While the community college will be the fastest-growing sector, the four-year colleges and the universities will grow apace and together will be spending far more for construction than this year's 2.4 billion dollars.

There will, of course, be private colleges rich enough to go it alone, but already—and gladly—they are connecting with each other to expand their purchasing power, divide the labor, and increase their "critical mass." When such well-heeled institutions as Harvard, Yale, and Columbia find, as they have, that the sharing of library resources is a necessary condition of maximum service, the lesson is clear for all. The rising cost of land alone will speed the day when most colleges will be elements in a consortium.

Just as there are economic forces shaping the campus, so there are forces arising from advancing technology.

The buildings on today's campus are assembled for the most part from the bits and pieces found on the industrial shelf, developed for purposes other than education. By 1980, the systems approach to design and construction will have dragged the building industry, kicking and screaming, into the twentieth century. Buildings, like ships, will have become industrialized, that is, made up of modular components designed to fit each other and thereby reduce on-site cutting and fitting. No longer will buildings have to be designed so they can be built by whatever contractor wins the bid. Instead, systems-oriented corporations will contract in advance for the development of the design concept as well as for its execution. The new names in college building may be Boeing, Lockheed, Litton, General Precision, General Electric, et al.; indeed, some of the new names may sound like COMSAT. In the central cities, the building of schools and colleges may well be subcontracts in a larger contract for the building of whole new towns within old cities. As the scale of urban renewal enlarges, the island college becomes an anachronism.

Despite this thrust toward change, many campuses—and especially those able to limit their rate and range of growth—will be to all outward appearances much the same in 1980 as they are today. Most students, however, will not be on these campuses. Some 80 percent of them will be attending publicly supported colleges and universities whose changing physical forms will reflect, in various ways, their mandate to educate large numbers of students as efficiently as possible, with a minimum of the impersonality that led in the 1960s to undergraduates carrying signs reading, "I am a human being. Please do not fold, spindle or mutilate me."

There will be no monolithic approach to campus development. But in these burgeoning institutions, physical planning will be informed by a growing commonality of attitude and understanding. They will, for example, view the campus as the complex community it in fact is, though there may be wide variations in the scale on which the community is conceived and in the relationships between its parts. And they will see the complexities and the overlap which characterize their environments more as opportunities than as obstacles.

We have come to the beginning of the end of that time-hallowed approach to campus planning which dictates, through a series of tidy zones, that the student works "downtown" in the academic core and lives in a dormitory "suburb," with something vaguely labeled "activities" taking place in the interstices. Instead, colleges will organize campus functions and facilities in ways that are architecturally and administratively less tidy but socially and educationally more functional—more responsive to the ways people do in fact operate as opposed to the ways planners think they should. Much the same principle will govern overall planning as now governs the placement of walks: first see where the people want to walk as evidenced by the paths they tread through the greensward; then pour the concrete.

Colleges will continue to experiment with new types of internal organization and new ways of expressing them physically. On some campuses, facilities for related subject areas and disciplines will be grouped in learning centers with the centers connected to form a continuous teaching environment. Others will do the converse, grouping facilities by function—lecture halls with lecture halls, laboratories with laboratories, faculty offices with faculty offices—instead of by discipline. And elsewhere we will see the proliferation of semiautonomous administrative units within the university, each of which, given appropriate physical form, will meet most of the educational and social needs of the population it serves.

As for the sum of these parts, some campuses will be organized like a blossom, each function and facility located on a separate petal. Others will more closely resemble a bouquet, a harmonious blend of variegated components. And especially in the city the campus will take the shape of a leafy branch, with its several subdivisions connected to a single circulatory stem.

Whatever their overall form, though, as colleges become more urban over the next 15-odd years, they will make more intensive use of the land they occupy. Many will become microcosms of the city—and some will become so much a part of the city macrocosm that town-gown differentiations are scarcely detectable. Or they may have no campus at all, as we use the term today. A subunit within a university—a college, for example—need not be on the same chunk of land as other subunits, but may be separated (or joined) by whole sectors of city. The critical requirement is easy access to the resources of the university—special courses, special teachers, special facilities—and access and adjacency are not synonymous. Nor need such resources be limited to one institution. Often they will be shared and supported by several institutions, and by the community as well.

For we shall see increasing attention to the expanded campus, the natural junctures between college and community. We shall see colleges exercising far more control than they now do over their total surroundings, especially in housing—including public housing—and the many services a knowledge industry requires in its immediate vicinity. Indeed, for many parts of the central cities, the colleges may have become by 1980 the principal agencies through which viable neighborhoods are created and restored. The construction and management of neighborhoods will be a new and possibly unwelcome role for most colleges. But it will be a necessary one, for more people are more likely to entrust the rearrangement of their lives to an educational institution than to any other agency, public or private.

THE LIBRARY—1980

By 1980, colleges and universities will be well on their way to becoming mostly libraries—an honest word that should not be displaced by such ephemeral and brassy nomenclature as "communications center," "instructional-materials center," or even "learning center."

Already, recognition of the critical role of the academic library is at a peak. Top priority is being given the construction of buildings to house them—buildings distinguished by operational efficiency and physical amenities far beyond that of their predecessors. With federal assistance extending beyond the construction of facilities to the acquisition of materials for research, teaching, and student use, library holdings, too, will reach a new high. Those which now fail to meet accepted American Library Association or accrediting-agency standards—70 percent of the collections in four-year institutions and over 90 percent of the collections in two-year institutions—will be helped to overcome their deficiencies. With similar support available for the training of librarians and for research and demonstration projects in the information sciences, there will be a corresponding improvement in services.

But while libraries are getting bigger and better than ever, they are less able to satisfy present needs than were the libraries of 20 years ago, and heroic measures will be needed if the situation is not to go from bad to worst by 1980. For as one college president summed up the problem: "Our library is so filled with books there is no room for students."

The national goal of assuring a college degree to any citizen capable of earning it implies numbers beyond the present ability of libraries to handle them. Longer learning periods and more graduate and professional studies will mean an exponential increase in the demand for readily accessible information. And the problem will be aggravated by the accelerating rate of output of printed information, which is even now beginning to be unmanageable.

It may be that James Baldwin is wrong and Anatole France, right: perhaps the next deluge *will* be in ink. If one considers that the large university library already contains almost two million volumes, that it takes one square foot of floor space to shelve 15 volumes, and that college and university libraries double the size of their collections every 16 years, then, in the words of mathematician J. G. Kemeny, "the cost of building, of purchasing volumes, of cataloging, and of servicing these gigantic libraries could eventually ruin our richest universities."

Clearly, the solution will not be more buildings, more books, and more librarians, but a change in the concept of what a library is. The library will cease to be a depository of books and become a source of information, multiplying the usability of every information unit and extending the geographic and physical limitations of the library building.

Implementation of this concept on a broad scale is far from a reality as yet, but work in the infant field of information science already points to a radical departure from the way libraries have traditionally operated.

By 1980, individual university libraries will have automated the cumbersome clerical procedures now used for acquisitions, serials control, and circulation. Smaller colleges will band together in statewide systems for centralized ordering and processing, converting the library space now usurped for these purposes for use by new technical departments engaged in the production of materials by xerography and other copying means, in the preparation of book catalogs and the like.

As systems grow more interdependent, cooperative efforts among neighboring and regional libraries will be extended to reduce multiplication of their holdings and to place little-used materials in storage centers, thus increasing the total capacity of each one. Greatly expanded inventories in microform will further increase library capacities: it is already possible to get more information per square inch in microform reduction than on the storage discs of a computer, and progress is being made in the development of reading instruments capable of the necessary magnification without distorting the print beyond readability.

Computer sharing will be another fertile area. At MIT, a computer linked to terminals in 52 New England colleges enables students and faculty at distant points to get quick calculations and quick answers to queries at the same time, without waiting. Use is presently limited mostly to the fields of mathematics and engineering. But in the future, by feeding an entire card catalog into such a computer, bibliographic information will be made available long distance to anyone having a console. With such a system, the card catalogs of several institutions might be replaced by a single cooperative catalog, thus joining their libraries as one. But more important is the rapidity and completeness of retrieving information by this means, as compared to the laborious, manual, card-by-card search: a search that might normally take three-quarters of an hour will be reduced to a minute.

Libraries will also see computer uses similar to those of the current Medlars Project of the National Library of Medicine, which is responsible for producing the *Index Medicus*, the comprehensive catalog of medical literature. The Library now uses computers both to organize the flow of current literature from which abstract information is compiled, and to print in book form abstracts and bibliographic citations which are regularly distributed to other libraries and subscribers. (The techniques used to produce the *Index* also make it possible for the Library to offer rapid information searches on request, via the tapes employed in the indexing.)

And beyond this will lie the exploitation of the possibilities of facsimile transmission, through which a document can be reproduced by xerography in one library and the facsimile transmitted over telephone lines to be received in another. The potential of this technique is illustrated by the network set up this year which links 12 libraries covering most of New York State: an upstate student will be able, through his local library, to enjoy access to the vast holdings of the New York Public Library in New York City while the New York City scholar will be able to draw on the special collections of libraries elsewhere in the system.

As such networks expand and multiply, the small or middle-sized college will be able to tie in with great national libraries, through regional subcenters tied together by a transmission system that would include mail, radio, telephone, teletype, and instant transmission by television with print-out facilities at the receiving end.

Eventually, we may see an international link by communications satellite between, say, the British Museum Library, France's Bibliothèque Nationale, and America's Library of Congress.

Yet for all this, in the immediate future—1980—some of the most significant features in the new look of libraries will be the result of forces outside the library field rather than advances within it.

Changes in modes of instruction will displace the classroom as the center of learning. The library will occupy its place. With huge enrollments encompassing a broad range of ability, classroom instruction geared to the "average" will become less tenable. Independent study, largely confined thus far to the superior student, will become the rule for all students regardless of their abilities, enabling each to move at his own pace. Whole new colleges will develop based on the "library-college" concept and new programs with a similar accent will sprout and bloom in older institutions.

These changes will be reflected physically on the campus by a reduction in the total quantity of classroom space and an increase in the total quantity of library space. Within the library, they will be reflected by arrangements designed for the individual user. As much as 80 percent of the space, and probably more, will be in the form of single seating and, of this, 60 percent and probably more in the form of study carrels. Large reading rooms, if they continue to exist, will be a vestigial remnant of a bygone era. In some commuter institutions, especially perhaps community colleges, the library carrel will become office and home base for each student, with coat closets, lockable storage for books and notes, personal bulletin boards, and the like. Learning equipment within the carrel will vary from the simple to the sophisticated. Some will contain no more than earphones and jacks for hooking up portable TV receivers, 8mm movie projectors, tape recorders, filmstrip viewers. (Even now, Oakland Community College in Bloomfield Hills, Michigan, with a student body of 4,000, has such a carrel and one piece of almost every type of such portable equipment for roughly every five students.)

Other carrels will be mechanized with dial-access systems in which students dial a number or push a button to order programs of their choice, transmitted to them via built-in TV receivers or audio outlets. At the last count, there were fewer than 100 such systems installed in colleges and universities, but the number is sure to grow. One of the largest installations, using both a dial-access system for taped programs and portable audiovisual equipment that can be checked out and used in the carrel, is at Oklahoma Christian College. The library there is a three-story building with carrels on the top two floors. There is one permanently assigned carrel for each of the 720 students, with expansion possibilities for more than 1,000. Students can select at will from as many as 136 taped programs, actively participating by using an instructor-prepared workbook keyed to the particular program. Offices for faculty and the dean of instruction are also housed in the building to facilitate guidance of students and discussion with them. The single facility, then, joins together under one roof the library, faculty offices, classrooms, and study centers.

Another version of an entire institution organized around a systems approach to the use of instructional media in the library is Florida Atlantic University. There the carrels are equipped with TV screens and tie-ins to teaching machines, film, radio, and television. The catalog, produced in book format, is scattered around the campus. Students are expected to spend 40 percent of their time learning from these nonprint as well as print sources in the library.

Another vein in the same mine leads to a closer working relationship between teaching staff and library. A present practice in a few places—Bard College, Sarah Lawrence, University of Denver, Washington and Lee, and one or two others—is to require that a portion of faculty office-hour time be spent in the library. At Stephens College, to make the library the natural center of the instructional program, each teacher is part of the library staff, and the librarian and dean of instruction are combined in the same person. "More and more," they say at Stephens, "we are finding that our librarians are becoming teachers and our teachers are becoming librarians." Look, then, to the incorporation on a broad scale of faculty offices within library buildings.

And expect that the library will no longer be buried physically in the heart of the campus simply because symbolically information is at the heart of the enterprise. More likely, especially in commuting institutions, the library will be located on the perimeter of the campus, there to provide maximum access at all hours and at all times. Expect, also, that the library will be located near, or indeed joined to, classroom and instructional space, the better to absorb it some day. And on many a campus, expect the student-union building to be closer physically to the library than to the gymnasium.

THE DORMITORY—1980

It has been argued that the first function of a college is to create a student body, and the second, to create an environment in which it can flourish. If this is so, the importance of student living arrangements is obvious. A number of students living at home is not a student body: it is only a number of students living at home, tied to family hearth (or television set), lacking opportunity for the social encounters which flesh out the dry bones of curriculum into a full-bodied, humane education.

But neither can a flourishing student body be created by simply prying students from the parental home and packing them into boxes labeled "dormitory" or "residence hall."

In the future, then, when we talk of college housing, we will no longer be referring only to those boxes traditionally set up on campus for the housing of students. Rather the residential component of the college environment will be understood to take in the whole complex of services and facilities, on campus or off, which support the extra-academic life of the academic community.

Students have to eat and sleep and play somewhere. When they cannot do so within the formal boundaries of the college, the college boundaries are, in effect, enlarged to take in the areas where students *do* live.

The recognition of this, and the consequent admission to the college purview of areas of student life long considered peripheral to the institutional housing program, will in itself contribute much to that diversity of living patterns which will be the key characteristic of student housing in 1980 and after.

But diversity will not be merely the chance by-product of an expanded vision of what constitutes the college residential environment. It will also, and more importantly, be the conscious goal of institutional policy, the planned product of a more thoughtful response to the demands implied by diverse student bodies and diverse institutions. By 1980, colleges will long since have abandoned the notion that prison design is a valid prototype for dormitory design. The typical dormitory of an earlier day, with its ranks of identical cells marching in double file down a long corridor, will not disappear. Fifteen-year-old buildings with 40-year mortgages cannot be wished away—nor will colleges wish to do so, since these buildings will still provide adequate quarters for at least some students some of the time. But the old pattern will seldom be followed in building anew.

Neither will there be slavish adherence to the pattern which enjoyed such vogue in the 1960s: the house-that-Jack-built structures in which rather elaborate efforts were made to give the student an explicit hierarchy of social units, starting with his own room and working up through suites, wings, floors, houses, and similar devices to the total residence-hall group, usually defined by the size of the kitchen-dining complex.

Variations on this theme, too, will persist through 1980 to the extent that they will continue to provide desirable accommodations for a great many students. But neither this nor any other approach to single-student housing will recommend itself for universal adoption. Indeed, colleges will no longer quest after some ideal housing system which is always just around the corner. Rather, they will seek to develop a balanced mix of housing types, providing students maximum variety and freedom of choice in where and how they live.

The very real individuality of individual students will be recognized in practice as well as in catalog prose. For the college of 1980 to offer all its students the same style of campus living will be as unthinkable as offering them all the same course of study, with no electives and no progression in subject matter from the time they enroll to the time they graduate.

Moreover, while the principal emphasis will be on offering a range of accommodations from which students can choose freely, colleges will be aided in planning new housing by an expanded body of cultural and environmental research which will make it possible to predict with greater accuracy which students will flourish best in which kinds of residential settings.

One result will be the proliferation of kinds of residential settings which are rare or nonexistent in the 1960s. Apartments will no longer be the exclusive preserve of married students, but will also be available to mature single students (undergraduates as well as graduate students) who want the privacy and independence—and can handle the responsibility—of the self-sufficient "householder." The modified apartment plan long predominant in Scandinavia, Germany, and, to a lesser extent, England—that is, a group of single study-bedrooms clustered around a farmhouse kitchen—will be widely adopted.

Students themselves will have a greater—or at least louder—

voice in planning and, often, in administering their own housing. At the very least, this will include the right to "advise and consent" on questions of housing policy. But to an increasing degree, it will also entail student ownership and management of residence halls, in new variations on the traditional co-op.

Another outcome of a more enlightened view of student housing needs and wants, and more active participation by students in formulating housing policy, will be a general improvement in the level of amenity provided in residence halls of whatever provenance.

By manipulating such physical features as circulation routes, patterns of adjacency, sizes of room clusters, and the like, residence halls will be organized to give students varying degrees of autonomy and sociability so that loners will no longer be forced into total togetherness or the gregarious, into splendid solitude. A sense of community will not be imposed but will be permitted to develop.

There will be a distinct shift from public to private in the allocation of common space. The main lounge which graced the residence hall of the 1960s will be broken up into smaller, more specialized areas for dating, meeting, studying, or just sitting. And pieces of it will be scattered throughout the building in the form of floor lounges, study rooms, and similar "private" public places where students can go without taking out their curlers or putting on their shoes.

Planners will pay more attention, too, to the design of the student's own room and the spatial demands of the multifaceted life he lives there. By 1980, his room may contain a desk at which he can study, a chair in which he can sit, storage space in which his belongings will fit. He may even be able to move the furniture as the spirit moves him and hang his own pictures on the wall.

Single rooms will no longer be considered a concession to the physically or socially handicapped, but will have become the rule. But double rooms will still be available for those who want them, and rooms will often be grouped in various suite arrangements, providing companionship as well as privacy.

Hand in hand with this greater respect for the student as a human being will come greater consideration for the student as a student. On the most basic level, this will mean simply making it easier for him to study at home—seeing that he has privacy when the work requires it, delivering him from noise and other distractions, giving him a comfortable, efficient "office."

But well-founded worry over the waste of college-built buildings which serve no educational purpose will continue to spawn attempts to build dormitories where learning can take place.

If a student is to view a televised lecture or demonstration, there is no particular reason that he should do so in a classroom when he could watch the same "program" in a dormitory lounge or, via a multimedia console, in his own room. Nor, if he is to pursue a course of independent study, meeting only occasionally with a tutor-adviser, is there any reason that the teacher-pupil confrontation need take place in a space called "seminar room" or "faculty office" instead of in the student's living room.

Some kinds of classes will be taught in the residence halls, and a variety of instructional devices—television, teaching machines, and even language labs and computers—will be installed there. The teacher will frequently be invited into the student residence —sometimes as resident as in present-day "house plans," but more often as guest. And informal learning will be encouraged through the inclusion of such special facilities as residence-hall libraries or, more simply and more usually, through the unself-conscious introduction of such outward symbols of "the good life" as art, literature, music, and even occasionally architecture.

And the residential colleges which began springing up in the 1960s will continue to proliferate over the next 15 years, not only as a device for blurring the distinctions between living and learning but in response to the fact that, as the multiversity continues to swell, the student's residence may be the only remaining facet of it small enough to give him any sense of identity.

But another school of thought, likely to develop in parallel, holds that—particularly on campuses which do not house a high proportion of their students—such attempts to "integrate living and learning" are merely specious and out of keeping with the realities of mass higher education; that personal associations among students, and between students and faculty, are more properly based on common interests than on common residence; and that it is no more valid to expect a student's academic life to be centered in his residence hall than to expect a man to conduct his business within his home. The argument is strengthened by the fact that many residence-hall "educational and cultural programs" are poorly conceived and ineptly administered, and that they therefore add a great deal to the student's total educational costs (which must include his living expenses) without adding much to his education.

Schools which take this position will not be advocating a return to the old *laissez faire* approach to student life which held that what the student learned might be the college's affair but where and how he lived was not. Rather, they will be attempting to differentiate between the many activities which make up student life and whose frequent incompatibility is responsible for many of the failures of present-day dormitories. They will continue to assume a responsibility for making available convenient, inexpensive housing, but housing of the hostel type. The student's bedroom will be his bedroom, not a bedroom *cum* study room *cum* living room. He may study there and he may entertain his friends there, but other spaces will be provided specifically for these activities. For example, each student, whether or not he lives in campus housing, will be given an office, which may be in a residence hall but may also be in the library, in a complex of faculty and student offices, or in close proximity to whatever facilities house his major department. There will be a recognition here that the type of work space provided should have some kind of functional relationship to the type of work to be done: obviously, the out-of-class work of a classicist is different from that of a chemist and that of a chemist, from that of an architect.

Similarly, recreational and social space need not be tied directly to the place of residence. Special purpose spaces for various leisure-time activities can be sprinkled about the campus—and thereby made available to all students, not just those who live in a particular residential complex. Commuters, then, need not be "integrated" with residents, but all students with the institution.

The hostel and the house (in the Harvard sense), then, represent two widely divergent approaches to the proper role of housing in the university community. But both are viable, and American education has room for both. And both will be developed—in many instances, on the same campus.

Land already acquired and buildings already built will still dominate the American campus in 1980 if only because, in many instances, they will still be unpaid for. Spanking new campuses will not be in the majority; the old ones, renewed, will be. But new or old, the campus will have responded in varying degrees to rearrangements, innovations, and inventions:

1. Buildings—indeed whole institutions—will first be "flown" on a computer ("flown" in the same sense that a missile is "flown" on a computer before it is constructed), then designed by an architect from the computer's print-out response to what the educator told the machine the institution would be. Lest this alarm the architect who rightfully believes that there is nothing wrong with the American culture that less architecture will fix, let it be said that the architect, once freed of the drudgery of drafting detail, may now focus his creativity on form, feeling, and function—three matters requiring talents no machine and no system can usurp or make obsolete. Within the imposed discipline of the systems approach, creative architecture will flourish and recapture its once princely status; architects without talent who do only what a machine can do will be replaced by it.

2. For purposes of planning, space will be regarded as being of two sorts: people space and thing space.

No matter how education may change through the years, it is safe to assume that people will continue to talk with people. Traditionally, we have provided classrooms for this purpose, and traditionally they are standard boxes connected like railway coaches, their interiors consisting of indestructible and reverberative materials selected to please the Department of Buildings and Grounds.

The linear arrangement of ceramic boxes will give way to meeting places more suggestive of a living room's amenity than of the kitchen's. And the spaces will be clustered to enable the quick assembly of larger spaces as needs change from hour to hour. They will still be classrooms, and they will still satisfy a professor's need to possess a territory. But being part of a larger zone of loft space, the rooms will consent to other shapes and sizes.

Spaces where people deal with people, where teacher and students hammer out the values implicit in a matter, are easier to design than are the facilities in which students work with things. For we don't know now what tomorrow's things will be. What, for example, will be the effect of communication by laser on building design? What kinds of energy will have to be piped to what machines not yet invented? About all one can say for sure is that education can't be sure. It therefore should plan all its buildings to be rearrangeable, with wall, floor, or ceiling providing a vascular system for present-day utilities and the space through which new lines of energy may someday be run.

This is nowhere more true than in science. As the various disciplines continue to hyphenate and eventually blur into a single discipline, so will the laboratories dissolve into generalized space, made special only by whatever equipment happens to be required at any moment in time. Colleges can afford to write off equipment but not buildings, for space is the ultimate luxury.

3. The campus will fling new silhouettes against the sky: great flowing curves of shells and domes unlike today's Cartesian boxes whipped out by T-square. Leading the way will be the new field houses—successors to the gymnasiums—great scoops of the sky sheltering interior vastnesses uninterrupted by posts supporting the roof. Colleges will have learned again that the arch never sleeps, that, as every crustacean knows, the cheapest way to fight gravity is with geometry.

Institutions running out of land for playfields will, despite pangs of cultural guilt, have accepted artificial fields in place of nature's own grass. The historic notion that that physical activity is best which takes place in the great out-of-doors will have given way to the practical fact that physical education and sports programs conducted in the mud, the rain, the smog, or the snow are primitive. By 1980, intramural athletics—lacrosse, soccer, field hockey, baseball, and possibly football—will have come indoors, there to be pursued without regard to the vicissitudes of climate at all hours of the day and such hours of the night as parietal rules and the neighbors permit. As at Brown University, most academically rigorous institutions will employ indoor artificial fields which never have to be rested, to adjust to the interests of students who resent having to "play" in the mud at 3:00 P.M. when they would prefer to be in the laboratory or library, but who, at 9:00 P.M., would enjoy colliding with an opponent under the rules of some game fair to all.

IN SUM

The physical campus will respond by becoming mostly library and living room. To be sure, there will be other facilities accommodating the students' creature needs to exercise, socialize, fraternize, specialize, and eat and shop. But the dominating facilities will be library—where the information is—and the living rooms— where the meaning of the information is determined.

The library (and its tentacles) will house the facts—and fancies. The living rooms, née classrooms, will provide the arena where the student, fortified with relevant information and in the company of his fellows and faculty, hammers out the values, the meaning of it all. In this arrangement, where faculties deal less with the dispensing of information than with the imbuing of values, the teacher can return to his ancient trade—philosophy.

If this be true, it behooves every institution to be imprecise in its physical planning, to stay loose, to build no wall or roof or fence which cannot, another day, serve another purpose.

◀ CLARK KERR

Conservatism, Dynamism, and the Changing University

THERE ARE TWO great clichés about the university. One pictures it as a radical institution, when in fact it is most conservative in its institutional conduct. The other pictures it as autonomous, a cloister, when the historical fact is that it has always responded, but seldom so quickly as today, to the desires and demands of external groups—sometimes for love, sometimes for gain, increasingly willingly, and, in some cases, too eagerly. The external view is that the university is radical; the internal reality is that it is conservative. The internal illusion is that it is a law unto itself; the external reality is that it is governed by history.

The university's gate of Janus leads inward as well as outward, and inside the gate the social landscape changes remarkably. When one looks inward toward the "ivory tower," he sees a different "looking-glass land." Here, to get somewhere, you must run twice as slowly. This is as it must be. The university, as an institution, needs to create an environment that gives to its faculty members:

1. a sense of stability—they should not fear constant change that distracts them from their work;

2. a sense of security—they should not need to worry about the attacks against them from outside the gate;

299

3. a sense of continuity—they should not be concerned that their work and the structure of their lives will be greatly disrupted;

4. a sense of equity—they should not be suspicious that others are being treated better than they are.

Inventiveness should be left to the individual faculty member within the protection and solidity of the surrounding institutional structure. Galileo within the conservative institution of Padua in his day, Erasmus at Oxford and Freiburg, Newton at Cambridge helped start the enormous metamorphosis from which the modern world emerged. But their institutions, as institutions, were stolidly changeless.

THE FACULTY GUILD

"Nothing should ever be done for the first time" was the wry conclusion of F. M. Cornford from his vantage point as a classicist at Cambridge University at the turn of the century when Cambridge was stirring with responses to the modern world. He added that "nothing is ever done until every one is convinced that it ought to be done, and has been convinced for so long that it is now time to do something else." [1] John Stuart Mill had looked upon the British universities of his day as largely unrelated to the progress of national life. Harold Laski, a century after Mill, felt that Oxford and Cambridge operated under a form of "syndicalism," which he considered the antithesis of the social usefulness he sought, and that they were only partly saved by being shaken up by royal commissions every 30 or 40 years. Flexner referred to universities generally as "institutions usually regarded as conservative, frequently even as strongholds of reaction," and added that "institutions as such tend for quite obvious reasons to lag behind the life which they express and further." [2]

[1] F. M. Cornford, *Microcosmographia Academica; Being a Guide for the Young Academic Politician* (Cambridge, England: Dunster House, 1923), p. 32.
[2] Harold Laski, "The American College President," in *Harper's Monthly Magazine*, February 1932, p. 319; Abraham Flexner, *Universities: American, English, German* (New York: Oxford University Press, 1930), p. 5.

With reference to the American scene, Frederick Rudolph in his recent authoritative study of American colleges and universities concluded that "resistance to fundamental reform was ingrained in the American collegiate and university tradition, as over three hundred years of history demonstrated. . . . Except on rare occasions, the historic policy of the American college and university [was]: drift, reluctant accommodation, belated recognition that while no one was looking, change had in fact taken place." [3] Nevitt Sanford, after a study of more contemporary focus, observed that there have been few innovations at all and even fewer "initiated by college or university faculties"; when a movement for reform has come, "it is the collective faculty who usually seem to be dragging their feet." [4]

There is a kind of "guild mentality" in the academic profession, as in many others. The guild was isolationist toward society, devoted to producer as against consumer sovereignty, and committed more to guild rules than to quick adaptation to popular demand. The guild was egalitarian, full of senatorial courtesy, selective of its own members. It was also a "sort of club" as Snow has characterized the colleges of Cambridge and Oxford,[5] and an "oligarchy of senior professors" as Ashby has noted about these same institutions.[6] In Germany, the faculty was more a class structure than a guild—a class structure intimately tied into the class structure of the surrounding society, hierarchical rather than fraternal.

The self-contained guild idea is still an attractive ideal. One recent call to faculty members is to "close our gates," become "masters within our walls," assume a "posture of offence" against the surrounding society.[7] Yet, except in a few situations, the faculty

[3] Frederick Rudolph, *The American College and University: A History* (New York: Alfred A. Knopf, 1962), p. 491.
[4] Nevitt Sanford, "Higher Education as a Social Problem," in Sanford, ed., *The American College: A Psychological and Social Interpretation of the Higher Learning* (New York: John Wiley & Sons, 1962), p. 19.
[5] C. P. Snow, *The Masters* (New York: Macmillan, 1951), Appendix, p. 382.
[6] Eric Ashby, "Self-Government in Modern British Universities," in *Science and Freedom*, December 1956, p. 10.
[7] Frank Pinner, "The Crisis of the State Universities: Analysis and Remedies," in Sanford, ed., *op. cit.*, p. 91.

guild has never been a fully self-governing guild in reality, and
almost never a company of "free agents," [8] much as it might like
to believe itself one. However, the guild idea, the "Republic of
Scholars," is often and understandably the faculty member's vision of "pie-in-the-sky."

Some of history has swirled past the "guild"; some has disrupted
it; some has transformed it; some has swept it entirely away.
Much of the Renaissance occurred completely outside the university. The university was generally allied against the Reformation,
although bitter fights were fought within many universities, and
in some the reformers emerged triumphant. The industrial, democratic, and scientific revolutions have gradually moved in on the
universities and changed them almost beyond recognition. Some
revolutions, like the French and Russian, place the "guild" fully
under state control, although it has regained some of its ancient
rights in France. In all of these intellectual and social revolutions,
the university, as an institution, was initially more a "stronghold
of reaction" than a revolutionary force, although the ideas of its
individual members have often been a stimulus to change.

Eric Ashby has said that policy should "seep gradually upward"
within the guild.[9] Sometimes it has. In Oxford and Cambridge,
research of extraordinary quality developed when the guild was
still in control and still devoted to the classics. But, generally,
change, when it has come, has been initiated or at least assisted
from outside the gates, as the case of England today so decisively
demonstrates. The educational revolution now going on there
comes from the outside and above, and finds its greatest proponents in the Labor party.

The individual faculty member, and particularly the political
liberal on the faculty, is often torn between the "guild" and the
"socialist" views of the university. The guild view stands for self-
determination, and for resistance against the administration and
the trustees; the socialist view, for service to society which the
administration and the trustees often represent. The guild view is

[8] Logan Wilson, *Academic Man* (London: Oxford University Press, 1942),
p. 71.
[9] Ashby, *op. cit.*, p. 5.

elitist toward the external environment, conservative toward internal change, conformist in relation to the opinion of colleagues. The socialist view is democratic toward society, radical toward change, and nonconformist. And the political liberal is drawn toward both views. Here is a paradox. Few institutions are so conservative as the universities about their own affairs while their members are so liberal about the affairs of others; and sometimes the most liberal faculty member in one context is the most conservative in another. The natural radical, within the context of the guild, is radically conservative. The faculty member who gets arrested as a "freedom rider" in the South is a flaming supporter of unanimous prior faculty consent to any change whatsoever on his campus in the North. The door to the faculty club leads both out and in.

Change is a traumatic experience for an academic community, as for others. The Yale faculty in 1828 rejected in theory, while proving in practice, that colleges "by being immovably moored to the same station . . . serve only to measure the rapid current of improvement which is passing by them." [10] In a very real sense, the faculty is the university—its most productive element, its source of distinction. And faculty members are properly partners in the enterprise with areas reserved for their exclusive control. Yet when change comes it is rarely at the instigation of this group of partners as a collective body. The group is more likely to accept or reject or comment, than to devise and propose. The group serves a purpose as a balance wheel—resisting some things that should be resisted, insisting on more thorough discussion of some things that should be more thoroughly discussed, delaying some developments where delay gives time to adjust more gracefully to the inevitable. All this yields a greater sense of order and stability.

Institutional changes are coming, however, in areas under faculty control or influence. Some of the needed revisions will be troublesome. In many places, curricula and calendars will need to be restudied; undergraduate teaching renovated; faculty concepts

[10] *Reports of the Course of Instruction in Yale College by a Committee of the Corporation and the Academical Faculty* (New Haven, Conn.: Hezekiah Howe, 1828), in *American Journal of Science and Arts*, Vol. 15 (January 1829), p. 298.

of equality of treatment revised; mechanization of some elements of instruction installed; some fields of study (like biology) revolutionized. These changes will come in the face of much faculty hesitation and even some resistance. At least two changes, however, will have faculty support. One will be directed toward overcoming the fractionalization of the intellectual world, and the other will call for procedures devised to make administration more personal, including faculty administration.

The faculty world seems to sense a loss of unity—intellectual and communal unity. In large measure this can be attributed to "the overwhelming predominance of things that are new over things that are old" and to what Robert Oppenheimer calls "a thinning of common knowledge," [11] Knowledge is now in so many bits and pieces and administration so distant that faculty members are increasingly figures in a "lonely crowd," intellectually and institutionally. It is a sad commentary on the "community of masters" when its elements come together in interchange only when they coalesce feverishly over a grievance about some episode related to a change of the calendar or a parking fee.

Quite fortunately, however, there is a kind of senatorial courtesy within the collective faculty about changes desired by a single member, or a few. Changes initiated from the outside, as in the development of the federal-grant university, which also have their internal supporters, are especially easy to accomplish. The individual faculty member seeking something new has, in turn, often found his greatest encouragement and leverage coming from the outside; the individual scholar is the inventor, the outside agency, the force for innovation. The inventing faculty member almost instinctively knows that internal change will come more easily if he obtains the external support of a foundation or a federal agency. These outside-to-inside and inside-to-outside alliances have been great sources of progress.

Much change also takes place largely outside collective faculty purview, outside the "veto groups" of the academic community—

[11] J. Robert Oppenheimer, "Science and the Human Community," in Charles Frankel, ed., *Issues in University Education* (New York: Harper, 1959), pp. 56, 58.

in the new department or institute, the new project, the new campus. The institute, in particular, has been as much the vehicle of innovation in recent years as the department has been the vault of tradition. Change comes more through spawning the new than reforming the old.

When change does come, it may be by the slow process of persuasion, or by subversion as through the inside-outside alliance, or by evasion as in the new enterprise, or by external decision. The academic community, regardless of the particular process involved, is more changed than changing; change is more unplanned than planned.

"REMEMBRANCE OF THINGS PAST"

If the collective faculties represent the present, the collective alumni represent the past—as much the best of the past as the faculty the best of the present. The alumni are oriented toward their own undergraduate days. There seems to be a rising sense of alumni concern as the rate of change rises. Generally it is over the preservation of an emphasis on teaching as against research; of the beauty of the old campus as against the asphalt and concrete and glass of the recent "improvements"; of the quality of remembered undergraduate life in its totality; of the old admission requirements which let the old grads get in; of athletic teams that never lost a game; of the spirit of the "halls of ivy" as against the technological materialism of the federal-grant university; of the integrity of the old alma mater against the blandishments from Washington. The older and the smaller and the more private and the more distinguished the university, the greater the intensity of these concerns.

If the alumni are concerned, the undergraduate students are restless. Recent changes in the American university have done them little good—lower teaching loads for the faculty, larger classes, the use of substitute teachers for the regular faculty, the choice of faculty members based on research accomplishments rather than instructional capacity, the fragmentation of knowledge into endless subdivisions. There is an incipient revolt of undergraduate students against the faculty; the revolt that used to be against the faculty *in loco parentis* is now against the faculty *in absentia*. The students find themselves under a blanket of impersonal rules for admissions, for scholarships, for examinations, for degrees. It is interesting to watch how a faculty intent on few rules for itself can fashion such a plethora of them for the students. The students also want to be treated as distinct individuals.

If the faculty looks on itself as a guild, the undergraduate students are coming to look upon themselves more as a "class"; some may even feel like a "lumpen proletariat." Lack of faculty concern for teaching, endless rules and requirements, and impersonality are the inciting causes. A few of the "nonconformists" have another kind of revolt in mind. They seek, instead, to turn the university, on the Latin-American or Japanese models, into a fortress from which they can sally forth with impunity to make their attacks on society.

If federal grants for research brought a major revolution, then the resultant student sense of neglect may bring a minor counter-revolt, although the target of the revolt is a most elusive one.

The big state universities are most vulnerable to charges of neglect of students. The private universities, tied more to tradition, to student tuition, to alumni support, to smaller size, have generally far better preserved their devotion to undergraduate life.

In interuniversity competition, the distribution of the ablest students, as shown by the statistics on scholarship winners, is a telling point. A university's share of the ablest students is an important element in its ranking: how attractive is its educational program to the students most entitled to make a choice?

Student pressures for better undergraduate instruction may be supplemented by the complaints of parents, who think their children are being sacrificed on the altar of research. Also, the public at large, whose attention has been riveted on the elementary and secondary schools as the "population bulge" has affected them, may now turn its attention increasingly to the university level when the "bulge" reaches there. Generally the public is more interested in quality of instruction than in quantity of research. The spotlight which the universities have helped turn on the teaching of others at lower levels may now be turned on their own.

EXTERNAL IMPERATIVES

The truly major changes in university life have been initiated from the outside, by such forces as Napoleon in France, ministers of education in Germany, royal commissions and the University Grants Committee in Great Britain, the Communist party in Russia, the emperor at the time of the Restoration in Japan, the lay university governing boards and the federal Congress in the United States—and also, in the United States, by the foundations. The foundations, quickly responsive to needs and possibilities, have been the main instruments, for example, in the reform of medical education, the introduction of interdisciplinary studies, the involvement of universities in world affairs. As catalysts, their influence has been enormous. The new developments might have been undertaken within the universities themselves, but they were not.

Prospective changes can be identified, in part, by the interests of the external initiators—trustees, state governments, foundations, industry, the federal government. What are the current concerns? There are:

1. problems related to costs, identified particularly by Beardsley Ruml—faculty-student ratios, fuller utilization of the calendar, excessive numbers of courses, mechanization of instruction;[12]

2. problems related to accommodation of the vast numbers of young people already knocking on the doors;

3. problems related to public service—cultural programs, urban extension, advice to state and federal legislators and agencies;

4. problems related to the supply of trained personnel for in-

---

[12] Beardsley Ruml, *Memo to a College Trustee: A Report on Financial and Structural Problems of the Liberal College* (New York: McGraw-Hill, 1959).

dustry and the public, particularly engineers, scientists, and doctors;

5. questions about the quality and availability of research, particularly the establishment of additional university research centers;

6. problems related to the exploitation of new discoveries, particularly in the biological sciences and spreading out into the health sciences and agriculture.

Additionally there is a general public concern with "morality" on the campus; with the so-called beatniks, with the young radicals, with cheating, and with sex. There is also a deep concern about how far, and how fast, research discoveries may change the lives of everyone. These "moral" concerns fill the incoming mailbox of the administrator.

The external origin of most changes raises very grave problems: how to identify the "good" and the "bad," and how to embrace the good and resist the bad. There is also a problem of timing—how to adjust not too rapidly and not too slowly. And there are the problems of how to change the content of the university without changing its essential forms; of how to reconcile the conservatism of the collective faculty with the radical function of the total institution as carried out primarily by the individual faculty members. These obligations to select the good and reject the bad, to pace the rate of change, and to discover the methods of change that will do least damage to traditional processes fall primarily on the reluctant shoulders of the administrator. And as Cornford remarked: "You think (do you not?) that you have only to state a reasonable case, and people must listen to reason and act upon it at once. It is just this conviction that makes you so unpleasant." [13]

Today, changes are occurring quite rapidly and spontaneously. In addition, interuniversity rivalry has become so intense that the rate of acceptance of change has been accelerated. The current problem is not so much that the university does not fully control the direction of its own development—it seldom has—but rather that it must make what are judged to be essential adjustments so

[13] Cornford, *op. cit.*, p. 4.

often and so quickly, like an amoeba in an unfriendly environment. This has added to the strains placed on the internal structure of the institution. At the same time, however, the current rate of growth in numbers helps to relieve these strains, for a period of growth necessarily involves considerable flexibility. Still, the major test of the modern American university is how wisely and how quickly it adjusts to the important new possibilities. The great universities of the future will be those which have adjusted rapidly and effectively.

THE NEW FACES OF CHANGE

The universities are currently facing three great areas of related adjustments: growth, shifting academic emphases, and involvement in the life of society. The direction of adjustment in each of these areas is reasonably clear; the detailed arrangements and the timing are not.

1. *Growth.* The number of university and college students in the United States will almost double during the 1960s. This addition of three million will duplicate in one decade the growth of the three centuries since Harvard was founded. The proportion of graduate students will rise considerably, and there are already 25,000 postdoctoral students.

Existing campuses are being enlarged and many new ones founded. This will be the greatest period of campus renovation and establishment in American history. A particularly large number of junior colleges will be formed as the junior-college movement becomes nationwide.

New centers of graduate strength are emerging, and a network of alliances is being formed among the old and the new centers in the competition to offer the greatest total combination of resources.

To accommodate the great increase in enrollments, many calendars are being rearranged, particularly in state-supported institutions, to permit more nearly year-round use of physical facilities. Students will be able to accelerate their work if they wish, and generally students will come and go with less reference to their "class"; more of them will drop in and drop out as suits their particular schedules and needs.

There will be some further mechanization of instruction (television, language laboratories, programmed learning) to improve quality and to save faculty time for other endeavors, including more individual work with students. The sciences will almost eagerly embrace these aids to learning. The foreign-language departments will be rather reluctant, because these devices can threaten their structure of faculty employment and the recruitment and utilization of graduate students.

Because of the competition for faculty members, salaries will continue to rise; fringe benefits of all sorts will be devised to tie professors to a particular campus. In addition to competition among universities, there is also intensified competition with industry and government. This competition has obvious advantages in raising faculty income but it has its negative aspects. As the market becomes more active, internal equity will be injured, for some disciplines are much more in demand in the market than others. Teaching loads will be competitively reduced, sometimes to zero, although more teachers are needed and students are complaining about lack of attention. The identification of the professor with his university will be generally loosened—he will become more a member of a free-floating profession. The rules regarding how much time a professor can spend away from his university assignments and those affecting the sources of his income within the university will continue to be in great flux.

This current phenomenon of rising salaries and benefits, however, may be of relatively short duration, lasting, perhaps, for the remainder of this decade. Faculty salaries have been catching up with incomes in other professions after an historical lag. By 1970, also, the personnel deficit of today may be turning into the surplus of tomorrow as all the new Ph.D.'s roll into the market. A new plateau of compensation may be reached in the 1970s. But in the long run, it is common labor more than uncommon talent that is rising in its comparative monetary evaluation, as the educational process uncovers more talent and depletes the ranks of those willing to do common labor.

2. *Shifting academic emphases.* Knowledge is exploding along with population. There is also an explosion in the need for certain skills. The university is responding to all these explosions.

The vastly increased needs for engineers, scientists, and doctors will draw great resources to these areas of the university. Also, some new professions are being born. Others are becoming more formally professional, for example, business administration and social work. The university becomes the chief port of entry for these professions. In fact, a profession gains its identity by *making* the university the port of entry. This creates new roles for education; but it is also part of the process of freezing the structure of the occupational pyramid and assuring that the well-behaved do advance, even if the geniuses do not. The university is used as an egg-candling device; and it is, perhaps, a better one than any other that can be devised, but the process takes some of the adventure out of occupational survival, and does for some professions what the closed shop has done for some unions. The life of the universities for a thousand years has been tied into the recognized professions in the surrounding society, and the universities will continue to respond as new professions arise.

The fastest-growing intellectual field today is biology. Here there is a veritable revolution where the doctrine of evolution once reigned supreme. To the classifying efforts of the past are being added the new analytical methods of the present, often drawn from chemistry and physics. There are levels of complexity to be explored in all living structures. The "code of life" can now be read; soon it will be understood, and soon after that, used. It is an intellectual discovery of unique and staggering proportions. The secrets of the atom, much as they have changed and are changing human activity on this planet, may hold no greater significance than the secrets still hidden in the genetic code. If the first half of the twentieth century may be said to have belonged to the physical sciences, the second half may well belong to the biological. Resources within the universities will be poured into the new biology and into the resulting new medicine and agriculture, well supported though medicine and agriculture already are.

Another field ready to bloom is that of the creative arts, hitherto the ugly ducklings or Cinderellas of the academic world. America is bursting with creativity in painting, music, literature, the theater with a vigor equaled in few other parts of the world today. Italy, France, Spain, Germany, Russia, England, the Low Countries have had great periods of cultural flowering. America is having one now. In the arts the universities have been more hospitable to the historian and the critic than to the creator; he has found his havens elsewhere. Yet it is the creativity of science that has given science its prestige in the university. Perhaps creativity will do the same again for the humanities, though there may be less new to create than has recently been true in science and the tests of value are far less precise. A very important role remains for the historian of past ages of creativity and for the critic of the current productions. But the universities need to find ways also to accommodate pure creative effort if they are to have places on stage as well as in the wings and in the audience in the great drama of cultural growth now playing on the American stage.

These possibilities for expansion—in the training of engineers, scientists, doctors, and the newer professionals, in biology, and in the creative arts, among various others—raise again the problem of balance. As James Bryant Conant has noted, the Western world has had for a thousand years a continuing problem of "keeping a balance between the advancement of knowledge, professional education, general education, and the demands of student life." [14]

But the balance is always changing; this is the unbalancing reality. The balance is not equal treatment, the provision of equal time in some mechanical and eternal way between teaching and research, or between the humanities and science. The dynamics of balance did not give equal treatment to the available scientist in Padua in 1300 when Giotto was painting his chapel, or to the available artist in Padua in 1600 when Galileo was lecturing from his crude platform. Balance cannot be determined on the scales by blind justice, field *versus* field and activity *versus* activity.

The essence of balance is to match support with the intellectual

[14] James Bryant Conant, *Education in a Divided World* (Cambridge, Mass.: Harvard University Press, 1949), pp. 158, 171.

creativity of subject fields; with the need for skills of the highest level; with the kinds of expert service that society currently most requires. None of these measures is constant. Balance requires, therefore, a shifting set of judgments which relates facilities and attention to the possibilities inherent in each field, each skill, each activity at that moment of time in that environment, yet preserves for all fields their essential integrity. To know balance is to know the potential creativity, the potential productivity, the potential contribution of each competing activity in an unfolding pattern of time and an evolving landscape of environment. To know balance is to know more than anyone can ever know in advance. But decisions must nevertheless be made and time will tell how well. The only certainly wrong decision is that the balance of today must be preserved for tomorrow. Where will the world's work and the university's work best be done? The answer to that question is the true definition of balance.

3. *Involvement in the life of society.* Knowledge is now central to society. It is wanted, even demanded, by more people and more institutions than ever before. The university as producer, wholesaler and retailer of knowledge cannot escape service. Knowledge, today, is for everybody's sake.

The campus and society are undergoing a somewhat reluctant and cautious merger, already well advanced. MIT is at least as much related to industry and government as Iowa State ever was to agriculture. Extension work is really becoming "lifelong learning." Harvard today has four postgraduate doctors in its medical school for every one still working for his degree; so also for many other skills, including business. Television makes it possible for extension to reach into literally every home; the boundaries of the university are stretched to embrace all of society. The student becomes alumnus and the alumnus continues as student; the graduate enters the outside world and the public enters the classroom and the laboratory. Knowledge has the terrifying potential of becoming popular, opening a Pandora's box.

The campus becomes a center for cultural life; it has a ready-made audience in its students and faculty and it has the physical facilities. Persons attracted by the performing and visual arts and the lectures come to live around the campus—also assorted crack-pots. As the downtown area in some cities decays, the campus takes its place as the cultural center of the community. A new dimension has been added to the land grant idea of service.

The New Deal took professors to Washington from many cam-puses, the New Frontier from more than just one. In Wisconsin before World War I, the campus and the state house in Madison were exceptionally close. Today the campus is being drawn to the city hall and the state capitol as never before. The politicians need new ideas to meet the new problems; the agencies need expert advice on how to handle the old. The professor can supply both. Keynes concluded his *General Theory* as follows:

> The ideas of economists and political philosophers, both when they are right and when they are wrong, are more powerful than is commonly understood. Indeed the world is ruled by little else. Practical men, who believe themselves to be quite exempt from any intellectual influences, are usually the slaves of some defunct economist. Madmen in authority, who hear voices in the air, are distilling their frenzy from some academic scribbler of a few years back. I am sure that the power of vested interests is vastly exag-gerated compared with the gradual encroachment of ideas.[15]

As, for example, the ideas of Keynes.

The university must range itself on the side of intelligent solu-tions to sometimes unintelligent questions. These questions more and more arise from abroad as well as at home; and the quality of the answers has been made all the more crucial in a world swept by Communist and nationalist revolutions.

There are those who fear the further involvement of the univer-sity in the life of society. They fear that the university will lose its objectivity and its freedom. But society is more desirous of objec-tivity and more tolerant of freedom than it used to be. The uni-versity can be further ahead of the times and further behind the times, further to the left of the public and further to the right of the public—and still keep its equilibrium—than was ever the case before, although problems in this regard are not yet entirely

[15] John Maynard Keynes, *The General Theory* (New York: Harcourt, Brace, 1936), p. 383.

unknown. There are those who fear that the university will be drawn too far from basic to applied research and from applied research to application itself. But the lines dividing these never have been entirely clear and much new knowledge has been generated at the borders of basic and applied research, and even of applied knowledge and its application.

Growth and shifting emphases and involvement in society all take money; and which universities get it in the largest quantities will help determine which of them excel a decade or two hence. Will federal support be spent according to merit or according to political power? Will private donors continue to do as well as they recently have for those universities which have done well already? Will the states find new sources of revenue or will their expenditures be held under a lid of no new taxes? The answers to these questions will help predict the standings on the next rating scale of universities.

However this turns out, the scene of American higher education will continue to be marked by great variety, and this is one of its great strengths. The large and the small, the private and the public, the general and the specialized all add their share to overall excellence. The total system is extraordinarily flexible, decentralized, competitive—and productive. The new can be tried, the old, tested with considerable skill and alacrity. Pluralism in higher education matches the pluralistic American society. The multiversity, in particular, is the child of middle-class pluralism; it relates to so much of the variety of the surrounding society and is thus so varied internally.

The general test of higher education is not how much is done poorly, and some is; rather, it is how much is done superbly, and a great deal is, to the nation's great benefit. Although it has been said that the best universities in America have been caught in a "stalemate of success," [16] there is no stalemate; there is some success.

[16] David Riesman, *Constraint and Variety in American Education* (Garden City, N.Y.: Doubleday, 1958), p. 33.

CHANGES STILL TO COME

There has been some success, but there are some problems still to be fully faced; and they are problems of consequence.

One is the improvement of undergraduate instruction in the university. It will require the solution of many subproblems: how to give adequate recognition to the teaching skill as well as to the research performance of the faculty; how to create a curriculum that serves the needs of the student as well as the research interests of the teacher; how to prepare the generalist as well as the specialist in an age of specialization looking for better generalizations; how to treat the individual student as a unique human being in the mass student body; how to make the university seem smaller even as it grows larger; how to establish a range of contact between faculty and students broader than the one-way route across the lectern or through the television screen; how to raise educational policy again to the forefront of faculty concerns. Increasingly, also, the better institutions will need to keep in mind that many of their undergraduate students will be going on to graduate school, and therefore that they need individual attention as pregraduate students.

Another major task is to create a more unified intellectual world. We need to make contact between the two, the three, the many cultures; to open channels of intelligent conversation across the disciplines and divisions; to close the gap between C. P. Snow's "Luddites" and scientists;[17] to answer fragmentation with general theories and sensitivities. Even philosophy, which once was the hub of the intellectual universe, is now itself fragmented into such diverse specialties as mathematics and semantics. However, the physical sciences are drawing together as new discoveries create more basic general theories; the biological sciences may be pulled together in the process now going on; the social sciences might be unified around the study of organizations and the relations of individuals to and within them. Chemistry and social

[17] C. P. Snow, *The Two Cultures and the Scientific Revolution* (New York: Cambridge University Press, 1959).

psychology may come to be central focalizing fields. As knowledge is drawn together, if in fact it is, a faculty may again become a community of masters; but "a sense of the unity . . . of all knowledge" [18] is still a very long way off.

A third problem is to relate administration more directly to individual faculty and students in the massive institution. We need to decentralize below the campus level to the operating agencies; to make the collective faculty a more vital, dynamic, progressive force as it now is only at the departmental level; to bridge the growing chasm between the department that does the teaching and the institute that does the research, with the faculty member torn between; to make the old departments and divisions more compatible with the new divisions of knowledge; to make it possible for an institution to see itself in totality rather than just piecemeal and in the sweep of history rather than just at a moment of time; to bring an understanding of both internal and external realities to all those intimately related to the process, so that there may be greater understanding; to see to it that administration serves and stimulates rather than rules the institution, that it be expendable when necessary and flexible all the time; to assure that the university can do better what it does best: to solve the whole range of governmental problems within the university.

Additionally, there is the urgent issue of how to preserve a margin for excellence in a populist society, when more and more of the money is being spent on behalf of all of the people. The great university is of necessity elitist—the elite of merit—but it operates in an environment dedicated to an egalitarian philosophy. How may the contribution of the elite be made clear to the egalitarians, and how may an aristocracy of intellect justify itself to a democracy of all men? It was equality of opportunity, not equality *per se,* that animated the founding fathers and the progress of the American system; but the forces of populist equality have never been silent, the battle between Jeffersonianism and Jacksonianism never finally settled.

If there are to be new departures, they are most likely to come

18 Karl Jaspers, *The Idea of the University,* translated by H. A. T. Reiche and H. F. Vanderschmidt (Boston: Beacon Press, 1959), p. 46.

on the campuses of those old, private universities which have prided themselves on control of their own destiny, and on the totally new campuses of the state universities in America and the new public universities in Britain. The university for the twenty-first century is more likely to emerge from these environments than from any others. Out of the pride of the old and the vacuum of the new may come the means to make undergraduate life more exciting, intellectual discourse more meaningful, administration more human. And perhaps there will arise a more dynamic demonstration of how excellence makes democracy more vital and its survival more assured. Then the universities may rise to "the heights of the times" and overcome "their inspirational poverty." [19]

George Beadle, former president of the University of Chicago, once implied that the very large American university (but not his own) might be like the dinosaur which "became extinct because he grew larger and larger and then sacrificed the evolutionary flexibility he needed to meet changing conditions";[20] its body became too large for its brain. David Riesman has spoken of the leading American universities as "directionless . . . as far as major innovations are concerned";[21] they have run out of foreign models to imitate; they have lost their "ferment." The fact is that they are not directionless; they have been moving in clear directions and with considerable speed; there has been no "stalemate." But these directions have not been set as much by the university's visions of its destiny as by the external environment, including the federal government, the foundations, the surrounding and sometimes engulfing industry.

The university has been embraced and led down the garden path by its environmental suitors; it has been so attractive and so accommodating; who could resist it and why would it, in turn, want to resist?

But the really new problems of today and tomorrow may lend themselves less to solutions by external authority; they may be

[19] Sir Walter Moberly, *The Crisis in the University* (London: SCM Press, 1949), p. 20.
[20] George W. Beadle, "The University of X," in *Context,* Fall 1961.
[21] Riesman, *op. cit.,* p. 64.

inherently problems for internal resolution. The university may now again need to find out whether it has a brain as well as a body.

THE CITIES OF INTELLECT

We have been speaking of the City of Intellect as a university city with its satellite suburbs. The City of Intellect, a university city with its satellites, may be viewed in a broader context, encompassing all the intellectual resources of a society, and the even broader perspective of the force of intellect as the central force of a society—its soul. Will it be the salvation of our society?

The organized intellect is a great machine that has gained extraordinary momentum since the Greeks got it going 2,500 years ago. It turns out its countless new pieces of knowledge but with little thought for their consequences—their impact on the environment—like a new insecticide. Its attention to problems quite naturally does not always relate primarily to their importance but often, instead, to the possibility of their solution. Thus the problems of rising population and rising levels of destructive capacity move along without study commensurate with their inherent significance. Does this machine have within it the "seeds of its own destruction"? Or can it develop an overall rationality? As Lee DuBridge of Cal Tech has said:

> Scientists and engineers do worry about the consequences of their works. But neither they nor anyone else has discovered how to avoid or even to predict these consequences.[22]

The process cannot be stopped. The results cannot be foreseen. It remains to adapt. And here the social sciences and humanities may find their particular roles in helping to define the good as well as the true and to add wisdom to truth. It may not be the conflict of cultures that is so crucial but rather the rate at which each culture moves forward. Can the intellect come to handle all the problems it creates in the course of solving other problems? Can the university help solve the growing war between the future

[22] Lee DuBridge, "The Shape of the Future," in *Engineering and Science,* California Institute of Technology, February 1962, p. 13.

and the past? Can the span of intellectual comprehension be widened spatially and temporally?

Intellect has also become an instrument of national purpose, a component part of the "military-industrial complex." Our Western City of Intellect finds its counterpart or counterparts in the East. In the war of the ideological worlds, a great deal depends on the use of this instrument. Knowledge is durable. It is also transferable. Knowledge costs a great deal to produce, less to reproduce. Thus it only pays to produce knowledge if through production it can be put into use better and faster. The Communist City of Intellect has been a planned community. It grows only in certain directions and in certain ways. This allows concentration of effort but limits growth and recognition except in restricted segments of the intellectual world. This City flourishes in science and in military might but lags in the humanities and the social sciences. Whole areas that would be covered by a really modern City of Intellect are largely unpopulated.

The two Cities of Intellect are not only sources of weapons—they also form a potential bridge between their two societies. Knowledge is universal. Its creators generally prefer freedom. To the extent the Eastern City of Intellect grows and makes contact with the Western, it almost inevitably changes its own society. Here a certain type of society really may carry the "seeds of its own destruction." It either competes and changes, or it loses some of its overall power of competition.

Marx saw technology as the major force in history; but intellect creates technology and the logic of intellect's development may be quite different from the unraveling of the "mode of production" as Marx visualized it. History has seldom, if ever, proved a theorist to be so incorrect and at the same time so influential as Marx. The wave of the future may more nearly be middle-class democracy,[23] with all its freedoms, through its better use of intellect in all intellect's many dimensions, than the "dictatorship of the proletariat" (which, in fact, is the dictatorship of the single party). But it has

[23] Clark Kerr, John T. Dunlop, Frederick H. Harbison, and Charles A. Myers, *Industrialism and Industrial Man* (Cambridge, Mass.: Harvard University Press, 1960).

not yet been proved conclusively whether intellect can preserve and even create the culture of freedom, in which it best flourishes, more effectively than technology, under Communist leadership, can be used to bolster dictatorship.

The intellect, and the university as its most happy home, can have great potential roles to play in the reconciliation of the war between the future and the past, and the solution—one way or the other—of the war between the ideological giants who now rend the world with their struggles. Certain it is, however, that the reconciliation of the future and the past can only be made more elusive in the context of an ideological struggle where survival is almost the sole essence of rational behavior. The two problems compound each other's effects.

It seems appropriate to conclude with Alfred North Whitehead's prophetic words in 1916 on the place of intellect:

> In the conditions of modern life, the rule is absolute: the race which does not value trained intelligence is doomed. Not all your heroism, not all your social charm, not all your wit, not all your victories on land or sea, can move back the finger of fate. Today we maintain ourselves. Tomorrow science will have moved forward yet one more step, and there will be no appeal from the judgment which will be pronounced on the uneducated.[24]

These are the uses of the university.

[24] A. N. Whitehead, *The Aims of Education and Other Essays* (New York: Macmillan, 1929), pp. 22–23.

Notes on the Contributors

WILLIAM ARROWSMITH is Professor of Classics and University Professor in Arts and Letters, University of Texas. He has published a number of translations from the classical writers, as well as criticism, stories, poems, reviews, and articles in many magazines. He was a founding editor of *The Hudson Review*.

WILLIAM BIRENBAUM is president of the Education Affiliate of the Bedford-Stuyvesant D and S Corporation in New York City; he is developing an experimental college in that community. He was formerly Provost of The Brooklyn Center of Long Island University and, prior to that, Dean of the New School for Social Research.

C. R. CARPENTER is Research Professor of Psychology and Anthropology at The Pennsylvania State University. During his years at Penn State, Professor Carpenter has held the following positions: Head, Department of Psychology; Director, Division of Academic Research and Services; Executive Director, Survey Committee; and Assistant to the President, Milton S. Hershey Medical Center. He is a past president of the American Association of Higher Education and served as Ford Foundation Visiting Professor of Behavioral Sciences at the University of North Carolina.

323

ALLAN M. CARTTER, Chancellor of New York University, was formerly graduate dean at Duke University, and vice-president of the American Council on Education. He is the author of the latest authoritative work on evaluating advanced studies, *The Assessment of Quality in Graduate Education* (American Council on Education, 1966).

JOSEPH P. COSAND is President of The Junior College District of St. Louis, St. Louis County, Missouri, and since 1965 has been a member of the Executive Committee of the American Association for Higher Education. Dr. Cosand is also a member of the Carnegie Commission for Study of Structure and Finance of Higher Education, and of the Higher Education Advisory Committee to the Education Commission of the States. He is a past president of The California Junior College Association and has served on the board of directors of the American Association of Junior Colleges.

ALVIN C. EURICH is President of the Academy for Educational Development, a nonprofit organization specializing in the field of educational planning, and Chairman of the Educational Research and Development Division of Famous Artist Schools. Formerly he was a president of the Aspen Institute for Humanistic Studies, a vice-president and director of the Fund for the Advancement of Education, Executive Director of the Ford Foundation's Education Program, a president of the State University of New York, and a vice-president and acting president of Stanford University.

JOHN W. GARDNER, formerly Secretary of the Department of Health, Education, and Welfare, is now Executive Director of The Urban Coalition. Prior to his post as Secretary he was president of the Carnegie Corporation of New York and of the Carnegie Foundation for the Advancement of Teaching. He was a chairman of the U. S. Advisory Commission on International Education and Cultural Affairs (1962–1964), of President Johnson's Task Force on Education (1964), and of the White House Conference on Education (1965). He is the author of the books,

Excellence: Can We Be Equal and Excellent, Too? and *Self-Renewal: The Individual and the Innovative Society.*

HAROLD B. GORES is President of Educational Facilities Laboratories, a nonprofit corporation founded and supported by the Ford Foundation to help schools and colleges with their physical problems. Prior to EFL's establishment in 1958, Mr. Gores was Superintendent of Schools in the City of Newton, Massachusetts. In 1959 he served on the President's Science Advisory Committee and in 1964 on the President's Task Force on Education.

CHRISTOPHER JENCKS is on leave from the Institute for Policy Studies in Washington, D. C., and is currently Lecturer and Research Associate at the Harvard Graduate School of Education.

CLARK KERR is Executive Chairman of the Carnegie Commission on the Future of Higher Education. He was formerly President of University of California for nine years. His major work on higher education is *The Uses of the University.*

A. A. LIVERIGHT is Director of the Center for the Study of Liberal Education for Adults at Boston University. Dr. Liveright has served as Director of Labor Education at the University of Chicago. He is currently Secretary of the International Congress of University Adult Education. Dr. Liveright's publications include *University Adult Education—The Center of Experiment in Education and Strategies of Leadership.*

WILLIAM W. MARVEL is President of Education and World Affairs. Prior to his current position, he was Executive Associate of the Carnegie Corporation of New York. In the 1940s Mr. Marvel served for three years as a cultural-relations officer of the U. S. Embassy in Nicaragua. In late 1960 he was a member of President-elect Kennedy's Task Force on International Exchange of Persons and later was special adviser to the chairman of President Johnson's Task Force on International Education.

LEWIS B. MAYHEW is Professor of Higher Education at Stanford University. He has directed or co-directed a number of national and regional studies. His many publications include *American Higher Education, The Smaller Liberal Arts College,* and, with Paul Dressel, *General Education: Explorations in Evaluation.* He is currently President of the American Association for Higher Education.

ELIZABETH PASCHAL is an independent educational consultant, formerly Secretary-Treasurer of the Fund for the Advancement of Education and Associate Program Director of the Ford Foundation's Education Program. Before joining the staffs of the Fund and the Foundation, she had been Chief of the Program Planning Branch, Bureau of Old Age and Survivors Insurance, and, earlier, a professor of economics. She is the author of *Encouraging the Excellent.*

DAVID RIESMAN is Professor of Social Relations at Harvard University. He is best-known for *The Lonely Crowd,* and has also written *Individualism Reconsidered* and *Constraint and Variety in American Education.*

NEVITT SANFORD is Professor of Psychology and Education, as well as founder and Director of the Institute for the Study of Human Problems, at Stanford University. Dr. Sanford has served as the Director of the Mellon Foundation's Study of Vassar College and as co-director of the Berkeley Public Opinion Study. He is a past president of the Society for the Psychological Study of Social Issues. Dr. Sanford was an editor of *The American College.* His latest books are *Self and Society* and *Where Colleges Fail.*

SIDNEY G. TICKTON is Vice-President of the Academy for Educational Development. He has acted as staff director for long-range planning studies of educational systems in a number of states and served formerly as Program Associate in the Ford Foundation Education Program.

LOGAN WILSON has been President of the American Council on Education since 1961. Prior to that, he was President and later Chancellor of the University of Texas. Trained as a sociologist, he is the author of several books and of numerous articles in leading professional magazines. He is the editor of *Emerging Patterns in American Higher Education.*

THIS BOOK WAS SET IN

CALEDONIA AND PERPETUA TYPES,

PRINTED AND BOUND BY

H. WOLFF BOOK MANUFACTURING CO.

DESIGN IS BY BARBARA LIMAN.